Tilting at Mills

Tilting at Mills

Green Dreams, Dirty Dealings,
and the Corporate Squeeze

Lis Harris

For Laura —
With gratitude and
admiration for
a superb editor
and mighty soul.
with affection,

Lis Harris

11 April 03

HOUGHTON MIFFLIN COMPANY

Boston   New York   2003

For information about permission to reproduce selections from
this book, write to Permissions, Houghton Mifflin Company,
215 Park Avenue South, New York, New York 10003.

Visit our Web site: www.houghtonmifflinbooks.com.

Library of Congress Cataloging-in-Publication Data
Harris, Lis, date.
Tilting at mills : green dreams, dirty dealings, and the corporate
    squeeze / Lis Harris.
p.   cm.
ISBN 0-395-98417-3
1. Hershkowitz, Allen. 2. Environmentalists — United States
    — Biography. 3. Waste paper — Recycling — New York
    (State) — New York. 4. Bronx (New York, N.Y.) I. Title.

GE56.H47 H37   2003
363.7'0525'09747275 — DC21   2002032287

Parts of this book first appeared, in slightly different form,
in *The New Yorker.*

Book design by Melissa Lotfy
Typefaces: TimesTen, Frutiger

Printed in the United States of America

VB 10 9 8 7 6 5 4 3 2 1

❀ Printed on recycled paper

To Martin

Acknowledgments

My thanks to the Rockefeller Foundation, the Fund for the City of New York, the J. M. Kaplan Fund, the George Gund Foundation, Rena M. Shulsky, and the German Marshall Fund of the United States for their generous support. My grateful thanks, too, to William Ferretti and the National Recycling Coalition; my agent, Georges Borchardt; my editor, Laura van Dam; and to Sara Lippincott, Virginia McRae, Erica Avery, Elizabeth Armour, Philip and Alice Shabecoff, Gary Clevidence, Constance Bloomfield, and Lisa Reisman. My gratitude, too, to my dear sons, Nick and David, and to Meg, Dylan, Lea, and Connor for the many hours stolen from them, and most of all to my husband, Martin Washburn, for his astuteness and generosity throughout the project.

Contents

Tilting at Mills

1

Rules of the Game

ON A CHILLY LATE DECEMBER day in 1992, Allen Hershkowitz, a senior scientist for the Natural Resources Defense Council, one of the country's preeminent environmental advocacy and legal action groups, left his office in lower Manhattan at around six-thirty in the evening, drove up to the Mott Haven section of the South Bronx, and inched his green Subaru uncertainly along Prospect Avenue near 161st Street. He had an eight o'clock appointment with a community development group named Banana Kelly and, though he arrived early, it was already dark, the street badly lit, and he was having a hard time locating its storefront headquarters. Hershkowitz had grown up in New York, but in Brooklyn, and didn't know the Bronx that well. He had been invited to speak to Banana Kelly's board of directors by the organization's chair and executive director, Yolanda Rivera, about his idea of their joining forces with NRDC and a paper company to build a paper mill in the South Bronx, an ambitious, innovative project that he had been thinking about for nearly a year. It was an idea that some called visionary, others crazy.

An intense, tousle-haired man in his late thirties with thick, black, upward-tending eyebrows that gave him a permanently quizzical look, Hershkowitz drove past the address he had been given several times, but the shutters were down, so he thought he was at the wrong place. Looking for help, he drew alongside a parked car, where he saw someone sitting in the front seat, but, as he would tell one of his colleagues the next day, "when I pulled up to the car to ask where Banana Kelly was, so help me god, the guy in the driver's seat was shooting up. Now I'm not a naive guy," he went on, "and growing up in East Flatbush you're not exactly sheltered, but that was the first time in my life I ever saw anyone shooting up. He was certainly the wrong guy to ask for directions. So I parked the car and walked up to a door that I thought was the right one, but there was no bell. I knocked but nobody answered, so I stood there for maybe an hour in my suit and tie with my briefcase and, quite frankly, I'm the only white guy around." For a while he watched some young children playing in the street, vainly looking for the adult he wished were looking after them. "Finally," as he told it, "Yolanda comes out and sees the scene, and she's being very solicitous, but she's also laughing—because, of course, the board has been sitting there all that time waiting for me."

A long and complicated path had brought him to Banana Kelly's doorstep. Over the past fifteen years, Hershkowitz, who has a Ph.D. in political economics from the City University of New York, where he had specialized in electric utilities technology and the environment, had become one of the country's leading experts on recycling—especially on waste management, municipal waste, medical waste, and sludge. He had trodden the well-established path of environmental advocacy and, in courtrooms and legislative committee rooms in Washington and across the country, his was a familiar face. He had served as an adviser for the Organization of American States, the World Bank, and numerous municipalities, legislative bodies, environmental organizations, and businesses. His publications included three technical books with titles only an enviro wonk could love (*Garbage: Practices, Problems and Remedies, Garbage Management in Japan,* and *Garbage Burning: Lessons from Europe*), and articles he'd written had appeared in the *New York Times,* the *Atlantic Monthly, Newsday, City Limits,* and the *Nation,* among other publications.

Hershkowitz was overjoyed when NRDC, an organization founded in 1970 by progressive young Yale lawyers and well-connected New Yorkers and that had a hand in shaping nearly every major environmental law, tapped him in 1989 for a full-time job and made him director of their National Solid Waste Project. He believed when he took the job that he would be satisfied spending the rest of his life lobbying for good environmental laws in Congress and helping to prevent bad ones from doing further damage. Over the years, however, his experience as an advocate caused him to question what he perceived as some inherent limitations in the work he was doing.

In 1982, he married Margaret Carey, a tall, spirited, fellow graduate student (she worked in energy conservation), and between 1987 and 1990 they had three children, two boys and a girl. When he watched his children playing or asleep in their beds, questions about the healthfulness of the world they were growing up in—questions to which he had all too many discouraging answers—surfaced often in his mind. And the more he thought about it, the more frustrated he felt about how tough it was for him and for his colleagues to get crucial environmental protections past their deep-pocketed industrial opponents.

Throughout the late 1980s and the beginning of the 1990s, NRDC, in a coalition with cities, counties, states, and other environmental groups, tried to get a National Recycling Act passed that would push industries both to take more environmental responsibility for their products and stimulate the market for recycled material. Hershkowitz had joined NRDC, in fact, to lead the effort to draft that statute. The struggle to get the bill passed occupied four years of his life, and he often had to spend long patches of time in Washington, D.C., marooning Meg and the kids in the rather isolated upstate New York house where they then lived.

The federally mandated closing of open landfills and dumps throughout the country during the 1980s raised waste disposal costs so alarmingly that some municipalities suddenly found themselves budgeting more for garbage disposal than they were for schools or police or fire departments. Not knowing what else to do, many of them began building incinerators as an alternative to the dumps, but once it became known that hazardous air emissions were being spewed from the incinerators, huge, politically divisive community battles erupted about where to site them. In 1987, the well-publicized plight of New York City's garbage-laden barge, *Mobro,* which floated around the southern coast of the United States and Central

America for months (its load finally ended up being incinerated in Brooklyn, then buried in the Islip, Long Island, municipal landfill), briefly brought the larger issue of the country's garbage problems to the forefront of public environmental consciousness.

For an equally fleeting moment, so did a growing awareness of medical waste washing up on beaches, along with dioxin-releasing hospital incinerators, and there was a flurry of public debate about toxic materials in consumer products and battles about interstate garbage and toxic waste transport. The need to get a grip on these issues had become important enough for the twentieth anniversary of Earth Day on April 22, 1990, to be dedicated largely to promoting recycling, by then the most widely supported environmental activity in the country. More and more, members of Congress were hearing from their constituents about these problems and were increasingly troubled by the political battles they engendered. (At one meeting he attended that year, when everyone in the room was asked what they did, a representative of the plastics industry pointed to Hershkowitz and said, "My job is to follow him around and respond to him.") The times seemed not only right but propitious for the passage of a progressive National Recycling Act, or so a great many people outside Congress thought.

On June 6, 1992, the culminating moment of NRDC's four-year campaign on behalf of the statute, Hershkowitz, who by then was considered the chief researcher for people seeking recycling information, mounted the granite steps of the Rayburn office building at seven-thirty A.M. and headed toward a House Commerce Committee room for the Recycling Act mark-up (a meeting to which all the members of a congressional committee are called to deliberate on a bill and have an opportunity to amend it before it is voted on and, if approved, sent on to the full House for a vote). The vote was scheduled to begin at ten o'clock. Outside the committee room a House security guard handed him a slip stamped with the number 189, and told him to get in line.

Industry lobbyists routinely pay a per-hour fee to placeholders to arrive at six A.M. and secure a good spot in line for them when they want to be sure to get in to congressional meetings. About ten minutes before the committee room doors are thrown open, the lobbyists show up and claim their spots. Other lobbyists circumvent the process entirely by being escorted into the room by congressmen they have good relationships with—relationships frequently cemented with handsome financial contributions. By nine-thirty that morning there were already about 450 people in the Rayburn Building corridor, waiting in line to get in to the committee room. Only six of those in line represented environmental groups (according to one legislative aide, Coca-Cola alone had forty lobbyists focusing on the bill to make sure it contained no provision mandating bottle deposits or recycled container content).

Knowing that there were only about 150 seats in the House Commerce Committee room, Hershkowitz walked quickly over to the office of Representative Al Swift, a Democrat from Washington State, the chairman of the committee. Swift had worked closely with Hershkowitz on the bill and had also gone along on one of two fact-finding trips—to Europe and to Japan—that NRDC had sponsored. The purpose of the trips had been to observe sophisticated recycling technologies in countries more advanced in waste management than the United States. Swift had gone on the European tour. Hershkowitz found Swift, cigar in hand, just as he was about to leave for the committee room, and asked him if he would walk him in through a back door so he could secure a seat. Swift was happy to accommodate him.

When they got to the room a few minutes before the doors opened, it was already half filled with industry lobbyists, who, like Hershkowitz, had been walked in by their own congressional allies. Only two other enviros managed to squeeze into the room after the doors were officially opened. As the day went on, the reason for the heavy industry presence became clear: many retrograde industry-sponsored amendments were to be jimmied into the bill. The plastics industry managed to get their waste incineration defined as recycling; there was a provision couched in language that made it seem as if the well-being of the nation depended on allowing the federal government to override local zoning ordinances forbidding the siting of incinerators; and the paper industry had succeeded in getting amendments into the bill that allowed virgin timber byproducts to be labeled as waste recycling. At day's end, but before the legislation was voted on, the enviros felt compelled to kill the bill they'd worked flat out on for so long. Threatening to release them to the national media, they issued to committee members and their staff press releases that attacked the legislators for drafting what had now essentially become an antirecycling bill, one that would, if passed, set the progress already made in recycling back twenty years.

In response to the press releases and the fear of committee members that they would be pilloried by their constituents for being antirecycling, the bill was never even reported out of mark-up and never voted on. By two o'clock in the afternoon, it was dead. The industry lobbyists were ecstatic. No directives about recycling municipal waste would become federal law. And none has been issued since then with the exception of Presidential Order 12873, signed by President Clinton in 1993—despite a pitched battle mounted in Congress by the paper industry trying to prevent it—requiring all federal agencies, including the Department of Defense, to buy recycled paper.

It was in January 1992, six months before the National Recycling Act was killed and when hope for its passage was still high, that Hershkowitz had led the fact-finding mission for members of the House and Senate to Europe and spoken with environmental regulators and people who ran profitable, environmentally sound, large-scale industries.

In Belgium, the group discussed with European Union ministers tentative plans to adopt Germany's broad-ranging recycling ordinances (Germany was recycling three times as much as the United States) throughout the EU—plans that were subsequently adopted. With the EU's population of roughly 320 million collaboratively attempting to change long entrenched habits, the standard U.S. industry argument against adopting more progressive standards—that what worked in tiny European countries could never work in a country with as large a population as the United States—fell to shambles. But for Hershkowitz, the most revelatory moment of the trip came when the group visited a paper mill located in a small town near Stuttgart. The mill drew on recycled office paper to make pulp and used neither chlorine bleach nor any other pollutant that would have made its presence a burden on the town, and it employed local people to run it.

Wherever they went, the CEOs, government officials, and regulators they met were unanimous in their view—anathema to most U.S. industries—that those who made a product had a direct responsibility for its disposal in such a way that it could be reused or recycled.

During the German leg of the trip, after looking at the mill near Stuttgart, Hershkowitz began to think seriously about the possibility of initiating a large-scale project in New York—perhaps even a paper mill—based on the European model. He had seen with his own eyes efficient urban recycling programs that were meeting the ever-growing demand for recycled pulp, and new technologies were also supposedly coming along that used low-grade wastepaper to produce a higher grade of finished product. This was an exciting discovery for him, because the pulp and paper industry, which had relied on wood since the 1850s, was the third biggest industrial greenhouse gas emitter (after the chemical and steel industries) in the world and probably contributed more to global and local environmental problems than any other industry. In the United States, it was also one of the most heavily subsidized industries; there were more than 369,000 miles of subsidized roads in the nation's forests, two times the mileage of the nation's interstate highway system. And even though the world is fast running out of fresh water and the demand for it is expected to be greater than the supply by the end of the first quarter of this century, the paper industry's need for it keeps growing. Paper companies are the largest industrial users of water in the world.

NRDC had sued a number of paper companies and at that time had a lawsuit pending against the EPA in an effort to make it enforce the Clean Water Act's directives regarding the permissible level of dioxin, a toxic byproduct of the chlorine bleach most of the companies used in their pulp plants, directives which the paper companies routinely disregarded. (Eventually NRDC won the suit, but got only a watered-down version of what they and other environmental groups were asking for. As of this writing, the paper

companies have mounted a countersuit and the matter is still before the courts.)

Hershkowitz knew that there had been a wood-based mill in the
city at the beginning of the century, and several aborted attempts
had been made to start other mills. But why hadn't anyone successfully found a way of drawing on New York City's vast supply of
paper waste, sometimes referred to as "the urban forest," Hershkowitz wondered as he flew back from Europe, to supply a de-inking
paper mill in New York? Wastepaper—discarded paper from offices, and newspapers, magazines, and junk mail placed at curbside
by residents—was then the city's biggest export, and there was at
least half as much cellulose fiber per acre potentially available as
there was in the Brazilian rain forest. The city was, as he often said
at panel discussions, the Saudi Arabia of wastepaper, and most of
it was being sent to China, India, and Canada, where it was made
into recycled paper, and the waste that wasn't separated was being
dumped in poor communities in the South. Why couldn't you build
a mill using the latest technology he'd learned about in Europe,
one which did not use chlorine bleach, and which could be in the
city and close to the source of the pulp instead of having to truck
or ship it thousands of miles away to pulp mills? It seemed like a
great idea, though how to do it and where you might put it, he had
no idea. Of one thing he was sure, however. The heady experience
that he and other veteran environmentalists had had over the past
years of being in demand for panels and international commissions
that reflected a growing concern about environmental issues was
not being translated into action. Of course, important gains had
been made, but basically enviros, time and again, found themselves
in the role of petitioners hoping for scraps from the industrial table.
Recalling that moment years later, he would tell me: "We were getting called all over the world. Congress wanted us; the Europeans
wanted us; the European agencies wanted us. I was being interviewed by *Fortune* magazine and *Forbes*. I was on *Larry King Live*
and I was doing *Crossfire*. I was in the *New York Times* and *Business Week* and the *Wall Street Journal*. Suddenly it felt like we were
important. It was all talk."

As soon as he got back to his office he asked one of the staff lawyers who worked on forestry programs if she knew of any paper companies with a good environmental record. She mentioned MoDo, a well-established, Swedish-based company with a sales representative named Jim Austin in New York. That afternoon he phoned Austin, whose job it was to market MoDo Pulp and Paper Company's products in North America, and a few days later they met for lunch. Since NRDC and paper company representatives encountered each other mainly in courtrooms or congressional hearing rooms as hostile adversaries, Hershkowitz was "thrilled," as he later told me, "even to be talking to a paper industry guy on a different basis." Moreover, Austin, a blond, athletic-looking former ski instructor, clearly liked what he was hearing from Hershkowitz. They continued to meet over the summer as MoDo's interest in expanding its de-inking operations and in developing a North American mill became more focused.

By early fall, having conferred with his superiors in Sweden, Austin was saying that he thought that if NRDC were to get the permits for a mill and help generate community support for it and help MoDo navigate some of the local politics, there was a good possibility that they would invest in the project, operate the mill, and market the pulp. Toward the end of September it had become clear that MoDo wanted to move to a higher level of discussion, and Austin told Hershkowitz a few weeks later that he thought it would be a good idea for him to meet Per Batelson, who at the time was director of MoDo's corporate development; MoDo had just bought into a pulp-making plant in Alberta, Canada, and in early December Batelson was planning to visit some paper recycling plants in Wisconsin, to look at their de-inking processes and possibly buy some pulp. Austin suggested that Hershkowitz join them.

By then, Hershkowitz's work was becoming entirely oriented toward market development and studying economic analyses of the potential for recycling investments in urban areas. Nationally, he was serving on the market development subcommittee of the EPA's Recycling Advisory Committee. Even before his discussions with Austin began, he met with a number of New York City officials and businessmen who helped him get a better sense of the world he was considering jumping into and he continued doing that all through the spring and summer of 1992. In June he met with Emily Lloyd, the Department of Sanitation's commissioner, who was eager to find markets for the recyclables her department was collecting, and talked to her about the different types and grades of paper the city found and how the availability of city paper might affect a mill, which she was keenly interested in despite the fact that her relationship with NRDC was less than warm. Like the paper companies, she, too, had mainly dealt with the organization as an adversary, and even while these friendly, exploratory discussions were taking place, NRDC had a lawsuit pending against the city for its failure to adequately enforce the local recycling law.

He also met with an official at the New York State Department of Economic Development's Office of Recycling Market Development (DED/ORMD), an agency that seeks to attract recycling businesses to the state, who told him that DED had lending capabilities and could provide funding for investments in recycling. The official said that they could also offer loan guarantees and help reduce the cost of capital acquisitions for a large investment project like a mill—news that gladdened Hershkowitz's heart. He was desperately looking for any information he could use to entice a paper company to a city infamous for its impediments to industrial development.

At about the same time, he had a long conversation with Lenny Formato, the owner of the last iron and metal scrap yard in Manhattan, whom he had known for years. (They'd served on a number of recycling panels together, and as they left every panel discussion, Formato's parting salvo to Hershkowitz was always, "Well, so when are you actually going to do something about all this?") Formato's family business, Central Iron and Metal Co., Inc., had been around since 1927, and he had run his own business, Boulder Resources, Limited, since 1979, and he probably knew the ins and outs of the city's recycling market as well as, if not better than, anyone. Formato, too, liked the idea of the mill and offered to help Hershkowitz figure out how to get the paper.

At NRDC's annual retreat in Split Rock, Pennsylvania, in November, at which, as usual, there was a review of the organization's strategic approach to big issues, the staff had a general discussion about the need to promote economic tools for advancing environmental goals. In that discussion, Hershkowitz said that he thought they could do this in a direct way by stimulating the development of a mill in the city.

Although they listened politely, from the expressions on many of his colleagues' faces Hershkowitz felt as if he had just told them they were all soon going to be assuming the roles of lead dancers in the Bolshoi Ballet. A month later, however, at a meeting with John Adams, one of NRDC's founders and its executive director, and other key people at the organization, there were further discussions about how to go about promoting the environment in relation to economic issues. Right after the November election Adams had met with Vice President Gore, with whom he had worked closely when Gore was in the Senate. Gore indicated a particular interest in environmental projects that would help promote jobs. At the time, the economy was in recession, and job protection and moving the economy out of the tank was at the top of the president's agenda. He had vowed to produce a million new jobs by the end of his first term—a promise he kept. Gore told Adams that the administration's commitment to the environment was strong but that environmental policies linked to producing jobs had to be a guiding principle. When Adams reported that message to his staff, it only confirmed Hershkowitz's sense that the time was propitious for his plan, the outlines of which were beginning to have more focus.

A month before, in mid-October, just after one of his discussions with MoDo's Jim Austin, Hershkowitz flew to Boston to attend a meeting on recycling and economic development sponsored by the Boston Globe Foundation. In the aftermath of the National Recycling Act debacle, community groups, too, had been talking more about recycling economic development that would sidestep reliance on legislation, and there was much discussion about the dearth of small-scale development of community-based manufacturing using secondary materials. The ur-environmentalist Barry Commoner, then in his early seventies, told the conferees that one of the major undealt-with problems in the environmental cosmos was production systems at the manufacturing plant. Hershkowitz sat transfixed as he listened to one of the sanctified elders of his movement give voice to thoughts that had been obsessing him for months. It was the hostile-to-change economic logic of polluting industries that had to be affected by environmental reform, Commoner declared, as Hershkowitz recorded a silent amen.

At that same meeting, there had again been a lot of talk, but only talk, about "environmental justice." Like all environmental groups, NRDC was dismayed by the country's continued overreliance on incinerators and landfills. It had also become increasingly aware that in urban areas many of those polluting landfills and incinerators too often ended up in black or Latino communities. In the early 1990s, small grassroots environmental groups had become vocal about the need to cease using the inner cities, especially the vast brownfields (abandoned industrial sites) that dotted poor neighborhoods, as garbage dumps. And though the subject came up often in conferences, the larger environmental organizations mostly focused on other issues: NRDC (before it established its own environmental justice program) on pressing for the enactment of good environmental laws and working to block bad ones and bringing suits against major polluters; the Environmental Defense Fund on corporate product policies (it was the EDF that succeeded in getting McDonald's to stop using Styrofoam cups and Starbucks to redesign its packaging); the Sierra Club on legislative lobbying and electoral politics; the World Wildlife Fund on saving species; the Nature Conservancy on land-preserve acquisition; the Audubon Society on habitat preservation; and Greenpeace on corporate boycotts and public consciousness raising. Because of their big-picture, long-range goal orientation and their tendency to have chiefly members of the middle class as supporters and the heads of big corporations as board members, and because in order to win some major battles, they sometimes horse-traded on others, many of the big national environmental groups, including NRDC, were regarded with suspicion by many grassroots activists. NRDC actually worked all the time with grassroots organizations and served as their technical advisers and lawyers in scores of battles nationwide. Nonetheless, it was frequently chastised for its links with "powerful" interests — though, in truth, it was often those detested lawyers and CEOs who helped make the organization such a formidable foe.

In the early 1990s NRDC had joined several Harlem grassroots groups, including the West Harlem Environmental Action Group (WE ACT), in suing New York City to force it to correct design and odor problems that originated from its North River Water Pollution Control Plant, at 137th to 145th Street along the Hudson — a suit that ended with the city committing $55 million in capital funds to fix the problems plus an award of $1.1 million to address a wide range of community and public health problems.

Working in the courts was what NRDC did. What it didn't do was independently initiate large industrial projects. But the more Hershkowitz thought about it after he returned from the Boston trip, the more excited he became about the idea of changing the rules of the game. As far as he was concerned, Commoner had all but suggested as much even decades before; in his 1971 book, *The Closing Circle,* he had called for enviros to climb off the hiking trails and join the boards of big industrial corporations. The mill project, as Hershkowitz had begun to describe it, merely took Commoner's injunction to its next logical step and attempted to make tangible some of the rhetoric, especially about urban problems, that environmentalists had been uttering for years. "How much more obvious does it have to get," Hershkowitz was saying to anyone who would listen at the time, "before we realize that relying on government won't get environmentalists where they want to go. If the sustainable economy doesn't exist — and it doesn't — it will have to be built." Traditionally, Hershkowitz and his fellow advocates expected government to mediate their relationship with business through laws, court decisions, rulings, statutes, and so forth. But the antagonism between business — especially big industrial business — and environmentalists appeared to be a war that would never end, since the goals of development and the goals of conservation seemed so cosmically irreconcilable. His experience in Washington had convinced him that in the twenty-first century business, environmental, and community interests that had for more than a decade been engaged in pitched battles would somehow have to stop fighting with each other and start working together.

At the conference in Boston, Hershkowitz had met Tim Martin, a young, red-haired, Greenpeace representative. When he was a foot soldier at Greenpeace, Martin had dressed up as a gorilla and a whale; more recently, he had served as campaign director for a toxic waste protest against the Great Lakes Paper Mill and was his organization's second highest ranking paper industry expert. Hershkowitz hired him on the spot as a consultant and asked him to write a preliminary report on MoDo. The way things worked at NRDC, senior staff people were given nearly total freedom to develop programs that they thought would ultimately serve the organization's goals, but there was always a lot of back-and-forth discussion and consultation about the viability of those programs. Any allocation of funds, of course, had to be approved by NRDC's board. Hershkowitz knew that his current plan and the idea of corporate collaboration in general was going to be a hard sell, especially to the more ideologically oriented staff members—he was, after all, proposing getting into bed with the enemy—but Hershkowitz also knew that if the paper company had the blessing, as it were, of Greenpeace, everyone would be a lot happier.

The preliminary report that Martin sent back gave MoDo high marks. Most important, after checking with his Swedish colleagues, he found that the Swedish company was years ahead of the U.S. paper companies in terms of environmentally clean de-inking.

It was then, according to Eric Goldstein, an energetic NRDC lawyer with close-cropped, curly, salt-and-pepper hair, that Hershkowitz decided that he would become the coordinator of a large-scale industrial development project. The plan Hershkowitz described to Goldstein sounded ambitious but plausible. NRDC would oversee all aspects of the proposed project that businessmen insist are too much of a hassle in New York: obtaining permits, finding a site, raising money, and seeking community support. A paper company would make a lot of money, and he wanted NRDC to work with a community group as a full equity partner in order to set a new standard for how paper mills should be built and to demonstrate that environmentally sound technologies could create long-term jobs. Goldstein, who would eventually coordinate NRDC's urban program, had been one of the leaders of the 1980s campaign to reduce levels of toxic lead in gasoline and was also in the forefront of suing the city on its recycling failures. "He came into my office," Goldstein recalled, "and said, 'We're going to build a paper mill in this city.' I said, 'What? We don't build mills. And where would you put it anyway? Forget it.' But by the end of the conversation, I was convinced that it was a brilliant idea." Goldstein also thought that if anyone could pull it off, it would be Hershkowitz. He had originally met Hershkowitz in the mid-1980s at a congressional hearing on incinerators, and it was clear to him that Hershkowitz knew more about the subject than anyone there. "Allen can match anyone inch per inch on knowledge of environmental technology and still has strong advocacy skills, so I'm always going to listen to anything he proposes. Could he accomplish this? I didn't know, but it was well worth a try."

Hershkowitz was a child of two Holocaust survivors. His father had lived as long as anyone on record in Auschwitz—four years. He stayed alive toward the end by eating dog food, which he found a way to steal while working on an outdoor detail. He lost his parents, his wife, his two children, a sister, and four brothers and their families at the camp; Hershkowitz's mother, who survived Dachau, lost her parents, too, as well as her husband and daughter, a sister, and two brothers. She had also been subjected to medical experiments. Most of this Hershkowitz learned when he was older, but both parents wept a lot when he was young. Some survivors' children are overwhelmed by the dead weight of sorrow they absorb through their parents' pores. Hershkowitz's reaction to the abiding grief that permeated daily life when he and his older sister were growing up was to embrace engagement with the world; for him, the very fact that he had been granted a future implied a responsibility for shaping it.

Professionally, he tended to be an optimist and was known for his command of technical detail and ferocious energy. "Allen has the highest ratio of facts per sentence of anyone I've ever met," a senior NRDC attorney told me. Hershkowitz was uncomfortable with the Luddite "let's all go back to candles" wing of his movement, and his frustration with the legal-advocacy-as-the-only-proven-path point of view probably stemmed from a deep sense that the world as constituted had to change. His discomfort with what he thought of as sentimental environmentalism had more than once irritated some members of his tribe when he challenged certain sacred cows: in 1990 he infuriated many groups when he refused to recommend that NRDC support a ban on Pampers and other disposable diapers. He'd found in researching the environmental effects of cloth and disposable diapers that both had their pros and cons. Disposables obviously created a serious solid waste problem, but many countries that supplied the cotton for cloth diapers still used DDT, which left toxic residues, pediatric dermatologists pointed out. Moreover, disposables pulled moisture away better and, therefore, caused fewer rashes, while more energy was used both for cleaning diapers and in trucking them to people's houses. Hershkowitz concluded that the choice should therefore be left to parents.

In college, at the City University of New York, he deliberately tested himself by choosing the hardest courses and, at town meetings in his still countrified Westchester town of Lewisboro, New York, where he could be counted on to come out charging at any perceived threat to the local environment, he was considered a huge annoyance and thorn in the side of more development-minded gentry. Perhaps it was because of his personal history that his reaction to many of the world's problems was more visceral than most people's. A 1999 study by the nonprofit group Public Agenda found that despite their acknowledgment of the growth of environmental problems, most Americans had begun to lose interest chiefly because they felt discouraged about the difficulty of finding actual environmental solutions. In 1989, 51 percent of Americans said they worried a great deal about global warming; in 1997, the number had dropped to 40 percent and though more people worried about water pollution than about any other environmental issue, that number, too, had declined from 72 to 61 percent. It was not apathy, the study found, that accounted for these dropping numbers, but frustration and a kind of fatalism about trends people had begun to consider irreversible because of the selfishness of polluters and the imperviousness of consumers. It was hard, people said, to sustain concern in the face of the enormity of the problems. Not for Hershkowitz, who often quoted Emerson, the Dalai Lama, and even Machiavelli as backup for his own idiosyncratic brand of practical idealism. But he was convinced that the environmental movement had to shift away from its anti-industrial focus or become irrelevant. He would not infrequently cap a passionate riff on the need for his fellow enviros to be open to change with a quote from Lao Tzu: "Those who serve life adapt to changes as they act. Changes arise from the times. Those who know the times do not behave in fixed ways." Issues that for many of us are often muted by the ongoing hum of global bad news — annihilation of species or the felling of trees by loggers in national forests — pressed on him. If most of us allow a brief, dim news clip of a forest scene into our mental archives when we are told that taxpayers subsidized industrial logging on public land to the tune of $1.2 billion per year, one could sense that in Hershkowitz's imagination there arose a mighty Dolby sound track of the din of diesel engines in the forest, along with a wide-screen version of huge machines that clamp onto trees, saw them at the base, and stack them in towering piles, then feed them into the blades of a giant chipper.

2

First Steps

AT THE BEGINNING OF DECEMBER 1992, Hershkowitz flew to Green Bay, Wisconsin, to meet Per Batelson, Jim Austin, and another MoDo executive who was in charge of production at one of the company's largest mills in Sweden, and accompany them on their tour of the two mills that produced pulp that would be made into what was called "coated free sheet paper"—the glossy kind used by magazines. Tim Martin went along, too, having been sternly forewarned to keep to himself his association with Greenpeace—the paper industry's detested enemy. Batelson and Hershkowitz liked each other on sight. An urbane, bespectacled, widely read man and polyglot, who was about the same age as Hershkowitz, Batelson was like no American businessman he had yet encountered. Batelson's enthusiasm about the fact that the two mills didn't use chlorine bleaching and still got a bright result in their paper actually matched Hershkowitz's, and he seemed to be no less interested in the general environmental impact of his industry. Their first evening the visitors had dinner with a large group of mill executives. Hershkowitz tried hard to make himself agreeable, but he was uncomfortable at the dinner at which nearly every one of the men seemed inclined to talk exclusively about himself. The next morning, driving to the mills in Appleton, about an hour southwest of Green Bay, to Hershkowitz's great relief, Batelson asked him if he found the dinner strange. Apparently he'd had the same reaction to it.

At one of the mills the owner's son was a chemist who spent a lot of time analyzing the paper's absorbency. Hershkowitz had already begun studying the technology of the paper industry as if he were working on a second Ph.D., and although some of the others looked a little bored as the young chemist went on and on about the paper, Hershkowitz couldn't get enough of the data.

Over dinner that night at a local steakhouse, they discussed Hershkowitz's project plan in greater depth, and Batelson told him that he was seriously interested in it. His company was aggressively trying to expand their de-inking fiber capacity and he loved the idea of doing it in New York if the well-known permitting obstacles could be overcome. "We'd like our officials to meet with your city officials and for you to see our mills and other operators soon," Batelson told him as they left the restaurant, and he suggested that Hershkowitz arrange for a group to come to Stockholm in a month.

Back in New York, Hershkowitz spoke with a still somewhat skeptical Eric Goldstein. "Okay," he told Goldstein, "now we're going to Sweden. In a month." As it turned out, it proved impossible to put the trip together by the day he and Batelson had targeted, and it took place at the end of January instead.

Meanwhile, Hershkowitz continued to explore options with other potential paper company investors. These explorations were not encouraging. From the outset, he made it clear that NRDC would not accept any profits made by the mill, but despite this amazing perk most of the companies had encountered NRDC only as an adversary, and few of them could forget that if the petition the organization then had pending before the EPA banning discharges of dioxin were put into effect, it would probably force some of their mills to close. Hershkowitz also found that the idea of working in New York was about as attractive to the senior paper company executives as kissing the backside of a bee (one company representative refused even to venture into Manhattan for his discussions with Hershkowitz, insisting on meeting at a hotel near LaGuardia). When Hershkowitz mentioned that inclusion of a community group as a partner was a component of the plan, the already cool reception that greeted his presentation plummeted to subzero.

From Hershkowitz's point of view, the community participation and community benefits parts of the overall plan were key. The latter, a plan to write into the agreement an allocation of money for health and education projects, was an element that he didn't dare even mention in some of his exploratory talks. So, amid all these disheartening encounters, the player who gave the project its biggest vitamin jolt was Yolanda Rivera, the eloquent, charismatic, forty-year-old head of Banana Kelly. When he first began thinking about his project, Hershkowitz was predisposed to try to site the mill in Brooklyn, where he grew up. The Bronx became focused in his sights after he attended a meeting in the office of Bronx borough president Fernando Ferrer (though Ferrer himself was not there that day), where the desperate need for jobs in that borough was discussed. According to the latest census, the South Bronx was still the poorest part of the city and the unemployment rate for men was almost 20 percent. Rivera's name had first come up a few months before the Wisconsin trip through a young NRDC law intern named Ricardo Soto-Lopez, who at one time had worked for Banana Kelly. "Rick kept coming by and saying, 'You've got to meet Yolanda Rivera. She's an incredible lady, and she's looking for manufacturing for the South Bronx.'" At that point Hershkowitz was planning for NRDC to issue a report on the viability of building a paper mill to the city's fifty-nine community boards to see if there was any interest out there in hosting a mill with the technical support of his organization. But Soto-Lopez had been pressuring him to meet with Rivera, and since Soto-Lopez was soon leaving NRDC to attend law school, Hershkowitz said, "Okay, arrange a meeting."

Though Soto-Lopez had been singing Hershkowitz's praises to Rivera, too, she was more than a little skeptical. She didn't have much enthusiasm for enviros, who seemed never to have been around to stop illegal dumps from coming to her borough. But the meeting, which took place at NRDC shortly before Hershkowitz went to Wisconsin to meet Batelson, went well. Rivera didn't know anything about manufacturing development—her organization's focus had been on housing—or about the environmental science issues that were so important to Hershkowitz. But she very much wanted help in rehabilitating an industrial site in her community, and if NRDC could help with that, she said, she would encourage political support in her community. "Look," she said, "we've got no jobs, we've got a lot of vacant land, and we want manufacturing, but we don't trust manufacturers. Will you help us?" Frances Beinecke, NRDC's deputy executive director, who oversaw all programs at the organization, was at the meeting, too, and she, like Hershkowitz, left feeling optimistic. Both of them were impressed by Rivera and thought he should accept her invitation to meet her board in late December. No one was assigned the task of scrutinizing her organization the way Tim Martin had checked up on MoDo or, indeed, the way due diligence—a legal term for scrupulous examination—would be done on the other firms the project became involved with. Neither at that point nor at any other, after the dramatic evening when he drove up to the South Bronx to speak to Banana Kelly's board, did Hershkowitz make further inquiries into the inner workings or current status of the organization. Banana Kelly's good name and Hershkowitz's assumption that a nonprofit group that existed basically to serve a public need, as his own did, would by definition always have the interest of the community at heart, conferred on it a special kind of laissez-passer for him.

On January 11, 1993, shortly after his night visit to Banana Kelly's headquarters, while he was in the midst of hastily putting together the Swedish trip, Hershkowitz met with the executive director of the SURDNA Foundation, a philanthropic organization, who expressed enthusiasm for the project and agreed to help fund its predevelopment work to the tune of $125,000. While he was there he vetted the idea of working with Banana Kelly with Anita Miller, the well-respected head of the Comprehensive Community Revitalization Program (an institution that was part of SURDNA but later became independent), which helped community groups develop ambitious neighborhood projects. Miller had long experience in the banking, foundation, and community development worlds, and although she had not worked with Rivera personally, she had known and worked with her predecessors for years. According to Hershkowitz, Miller told him: "Banana Kelly would be perfect for this!" It was a moment that, in time, Hershkowitz would play over and over in his mind. The following week he tore around the city, persuading a clutch of city officials, lawyers, and consultants to accompany him on the Swedish trip; somehow, the idea of issuing a report to the fifty-nine community boards fell by the wayside.

The organization Rivera led—officially the Banana Kelly Community Improvement Association—started out in 1977 when a group of residents saved a crescent (or banana) shaped, landlord-abandoned section of Kelly Street in the Hunts Point section of the Bronx from demolition. In the aftermath of the uprooting of thousands of Bronx residents caused by Robert Moses's Cross Bronx Expressway, of the flight of the middle class to the suburbs and Co-op City, and of the decade-long burning of the vast majority of the South Bronx's housing stock, small community development groups made up largely of residents who didn't want to leave the neighborhoods they were used to and remembered in happier days began to turn the tide of the borough's decay. On Kelly Street, instead of moving out when they were told to, a handful of residents applied for a rehab loan for three buildings on their block. While they waited for loan approval (a process that took a year and a half), they cleared the rubble from alleyways, planted a garden, and came up with a slogan, "Don't move, improve," which still serves as the organization's motto.

Over the years, under the leadership of a local youth worker named Harold DeRienzo, who was instrumental in nurturing the group, and of his successor, Getz Obstfeld, a neighborhood organizer, Banana Kelly developed into a thriving, well-respected, well-run organization with strong community support and a reputation for being one of the nation's most successful community development groups. By the time Hershkowitz entered the picture, which was shortly after Rivera became its executive director, Banana Kelly was managing forty-one buildings, had helped thousands of residents buy and rehabilitate apartments, had real estate holdings whose worth was estimated at more than $50 million, and had transformed a substantial patch of the South Bronx from a rubble-strewn no-man's-land into a neighborhood dotted with tidy row houses and well-kept buildings where low- and middle-income families might actually want to live. It also helped build a pediatric health clinic, ran an adult vocational training school, and had worked to revive a neighborhood commercial strip by providing low-interest loans for businesses. Though it depended on city, state, federal, and private foundation funds, Banana Kelly, like many similar groups around the country, was opposed to the kind of bloated government contracts and huge housing projects that had poured into the borough in the late 1970s and enriched legions of outside builders, planners, lawyers, and politicians, but rarely added to the prosperity of local residents.

Rivera, tall, broad-shouldered, attractive, and determined-looking, had been having discussions with her board for months about the need for industrial development in the borough. For that reason the board members liked what they heard when Hershkowitz made his presentation to them in December. They were pleased that the project was going to go far beyond the usual (and oft-evaded) requirements for environmental soundness and that social services for the community would be written into the deal, but some of them wondered about Hershkowitz despite the tie, suit, and polished leather shoes (he usually wore sneakers) he'd gone to some length to scrutinize for appropriateness for the occasion. "Allen is not a board of directors' idea of a developer," Rivera told me. "These are conservative people. They're used to business types who look fairly buttoned up. They didn't know what to make of his longish hair or his enthusiasm. They thought he looked a little flaky. I said, 'Visionaries always appear to be a little flaky.'"

In the end, however, the Banana Kelly board felt that the mill sounded like a risk worth taking, and when Hershkowitz received a letter formally inviting NRDC to be Banana Kelly's technical consultant on the development of a de-inking plant in the South Bronx, he became incredibly excited. The first step had been taken, he felt, toward breaking with the long tradition of excluding community groups from projects that impinged so mightily on their lives. Further, the usual urban formula—industrial venture enters, local groups rally to block it—might actually be avoided by structuring the process in a way that any rational person would have to acknowledge made sense. According to Goldstein, Hershkowitz ran around the office saying, "We got invited! We got invited!" Six weeks later, Rivera, who had never been out of the country, accompanied Hershkowitz and nearly a dozen officials, enviros, and community leaders to Sweden to meet their local counterparts and the people at MoDo and to meet with community groups, the staff of Swedish Greenpeace, and others who lived and worked in the places where MoDo's mills were. Though Hershkowitz scarcely admitted it, even to himself, they seemed at last to be on their way to launching what he hoped would be not only a model for future environmentally sound, money-making, community-based industry but just possibly a radical new industrial ecology movement.

One of the local officials who went along on the Swedish trip did so with considerable reluctance—the Bronx borough president, Fernando (or as most people referred to him, Fred) Ferrer. At a pre-trip meeting in Ferrer's office on January 25, 1993, attended by Hershkowitz, Sanitation Commissioner Emily Lloyd, and Carl Weisbrod, the president of New York City's Economic Development Corporation (both of whom were also going to Sweden and were positive about the idea of the mill), Ferrer's enthusiasm for the project disappeared when he learned that NRDC had decided to work with Banana Kelly. "If you are sole-sourcing it to Banana Kelly," Ferrer told them, "I'm not going on this trip." Hershkowitz was shocked by the vehemence of his reaction, especially because the trip had been set up for weeks, and it was now only three days before he was to leave to help finalize arrangements for the group's January 31 arrival. For a brief moment he wondered wildly if the idea of a trip to the Arctic Circle, where they'd be looking at one of MoDo's mills, had suddenly seemed less attractive to Ferrer than watching the Super Bowl, which was taking place the day they were leaving. He never did learn exactly why Ferrer was so unalterably opposed to NRDC's choice of Banana Kelly as a partner, but he was given to understand that the proper protocol would have been to consult the borough president about whether he considered the project to be a good idea, and let him pick the groups that would participate in a project in his borough.

Hershkowitz did not handle the moment well. Although he had as a sometime adviser Richard Schrader, who was then the city's deputy commissioner of consumer affairs and who had a sophisticated grasp of city politics, Hershkowitz's own lack of knowledge about the way things worked politically in the city, and particularly in the Bronx, where Byzantine turf politics were the rule, blinded him to the breadth of the political obstacles that lay ahead. He interpreted Ferrer's reaction solely as a manifestation of a bruised ego. It was clear that Ferrer felt that his traditional role as arbiter of political spoils was being violated, and when Hershkowitz was told later that Yolanda Rivera had once run against one of Ferrer's protégés for an assembly seat, and that though she lost Ferrer might well still hold a grudge against her, his reading of the situation was only deepened. Hershkowitz could understand how Ferrer might not want Banana Kelly gaining political capital with the union job allocations and economic development that he felt rightly belonged to him, but he couldn't grasp how that kind of grudge would prevent Ferrer from supporting an obviously valuable economic and environmental initiative in his struggling borough. Mirah Becker, who then served as Ferrer's chief environmental adviser, told me that there was a bitter rivalry between the two that went back to the days when they were both working as tenant advocates. Because of its potential for national recognition Ferrer somehow feared, she surmised, that Rivera might be eclipsing him with this new project.

At the moment, however, cooperation was desperately needed. MoDo thought of Ferrer as more or less the equivalent of mayor of the Bronx, and his support of the mill was important to them, so his presence on the trip was crucial. Eventually, he was persuaded by Emily Lloyd to go along, but not before Hershkowitz promised him that Banana Kelly was not going to be the ultimate owner of the mill. No one yet knew who the owner of the mill would be, but clearly it would have to be a big for-profit company, ideally a paper company like MoDo. Community group ownership of the project was never part of the plan, so Hershkowitz made that promise, although ownership of the pre-closing development project was going to be given to Banana Kelly to protect them from having their community and job interests cut out once the pot began to boil and paper companies or other high-powered financial interests entered the scene. Ferrer was told that Banana Kelly would be there rather like a pool reporter for the community and that his presence on the trip to Sweden would not be construed as approval of any future

Banana Kelly involvement in the project. This was, of course, not how Yolanda Rivera interpreted her role. Despite the diplomatic efforts and assurances, Ferrer never once spoke with Rivera or the two Banana Kelly board members who accompanied her on the trip, and several people noticed that he seemed uncomfortable the whole time he was there. Whether that discomfort was related to the project or was just the way Ferrer seemed to act at public gatherings, as several reporters would observe when he ran for mayor some years later, was unclear.

MoDo had reserved rooms for everyone at Stockholm's Grand Hotel overlooking a bright expanse of the city's harbor and, in the distance, the royal palace, the opera house, and the earth-colored, crenellated rooftops of the old city. The last time Hershkowitz had visited Stockholm he had been working for a public interest group and had bunked at a youth hostel. Although on his fact-finding tours with congressmen the hotels they stayed at were up several notches from the hostels and plain-as-pie hotels he was used to, the elegant, well-appointed Grand Hotel was in another league altogether. But Batelson and others at MoDo had suggested to him that in the business world, especially for an enviro, the appearance of enterprise prosperity was all important—and so now nice hotels became part of his globe-trotting life and of his budget at NRDC.

After Hershkowitz's arrival in Stockholm, while they were reviewing the itinerary for the trip, MoDo officials suggested holding a press conference when the full group arrived, announcing their intention to build a mill in New York City. But city officials back in New York thought it was too early for that, so the idea was scotched. The afternoon the group showed up, the president and CEO of MoDo, Roland Martin-Lof, a charming, smartly dressed, good-humored man, made a presentation in the company's headquarters on the Strandvagen, a prosperous commercial and shopping district. There was a discussion about how MoDo had striven to get out of chlorine bleaching and general discussions about the economics of paper-making, about forestry processes, about the company's research and development program for environmental issues and about Sweden's environmental laws, which are, for the most part, far stricter than U.S. laws, especially as they pertain to paper production. Per Batelson talked for a while about MoDo's other mills, and invited everyone to visit their Alizay mill in France. On the conference table were little crossed yellow and blue Swedish and red, white, and blue American flags, a detail that appeared wherever the group went, including the paper mills they visited, where the two flags flapped side by side outside, and at the prime minister's office. In Stockholm MoDo sent stretch Volvos to transport their visitors around the city. (In fact, MoDo made more money from its exports than even Volvo.)

That evening MoDo hosted a sumptuous dinner in a private room of the Operakallaren, a first-class restaurant near the City Opera. At one point during dinner Rivera turned to Hershkowitz in the soft candlelight of the room and said, "I feel like Cinderella."

On February 2, 1993, following several days of more technical discussion at MoDo's office, the group flew to northern Sweden to visit MoDo's Husum mill. Husum, which is just one hundred miles south of the Arctic Circle, was one of the world's largest mills, producing 690,000 tons of paper per year. It is so big that its workers get from one end to the other on scooters. Because it had been built long ago (it opened in 1919), the Husum plant was not yet fully chlorine free (though it was on its way to becoming so) and existed in a purgatorial state known in the industry as "elemental chlorine free." In between further discussions with MoDo came an eye-popping tour of worker amenities—including gyms, saunas, and well-designed houses. Some of the members of the group who were in good shape played a game of field hockey in the workers' gym.

When MoDo bought the local *skog,* or forest, they also acquired a large handsome mansion with an elegant banquet hall that was formerly owned by a Swedish industrialist. Hershkowitz had had a few friendly exchanges with Ferrer that day, but despite the swell of good fellowship and enthusiasm nearly everyone noticed Ferrer's lack of engagement with what was going on. Hershkowitz smiled a great deal at Ferrer, but he felt certain that his efforts at establishing a foundation of bonhomie were falling flat and, worse, that a degree of obeisance was required that he was unable to summon. The mansion was used for special occasions, and that evening a glittering gala dinner was held there. Both Lloyd and Weisbrod came up to Hershkowitz just before the banquet and made remarks about Ferrer's aloofness. Perhaps the Swedes noticed it, too, and took it the wrong way, because amid the flowing wine Roland Martin-Lof toasted the New York officials and said he hoped that the city would not be biased against his company because it was not an American firm. They should know, he went on to say, that he and the rest of his colleagues were really enthusiastic about the project. Hershkowitz looked over at Eric Goldstein, who was there with his wife, and who, though he was receptive to the idea of the mill, had made it clear that he thought it was an exceedingly long shot. "I was in heaven," Hershkowitz told his wife, Meg, on the phone later that night. "We're actually going to get this thing done." Martin-Lof had gone on to say that they were equally enthusiastic about the prospect of working with an environmental group and representatives of the South Bronx community.

The next evening, there was yet another lavish dinner at Stockholm's City Hall, where the group communed with city officials in the same room where the Nobel Prize banquets are held—a soaring gilded space that outshone every other in which they would dine. Over their last few days, the group jumped on and off buses and trains that carried them to paper mills all over Sweden, and they consumed a great deal of salmon. Emily Lloyd met with her counterpart, the Stockholm sanitation commissioner, and they visited a company that converted paper mill sludge into ethanol, which was used as a fuel for cars. There was a bit of a problem with MoDo's Jim Austin, who for some reason seemed unable to refrain, whenever the group settled in on a bus or train car, from telling jokes that embarrassed the women and annoyed several of the men. After a number of complaints were lodged, Austin was removed from the project. Per Batelson, on the other hand, impressed everyone as the very model of the humanistic businessman; and whatever good impression they had of him previously took on a new dimension when, at the end of the farewell dinner at a restaurant called Fem Sma Hus, he amazed them by serenading them with a beautiful Swedish song. Emily Lloyd and Carl Weisbrod had been impressed by the environmental attributes of the industry they had learned about. Rich Schrader believed that Hershkowitz and the city could learn a lot from the Swedish model, and all in all most of those who had gone along thought it had been a good trip and shared a certain measure of euphoria about the future of the enterprise. Hershkowitz wrote in his diary that they'd come back with renewed enthusiasm and "a clearer vision" of how to proceed.

3

Who's Driving This Car?

WHEN HERSHKOWITZ RETURNED to New York, he met again with Lloyd and Weisbrod at the law office of Frederick A. O. Schwarz, Jr., the chairman of the board of NRDC. Hershkowitz looked up to Schwarz, who was called Fritz by all who knew him. A sharp, articulate, well-known public figure in city affairs, Schwarz had worked on the reorganization of the city charter, had a peerlessly sophisticated grasp of advocacy issues, and also served on the board of the NAACP's Legal Defense Fund. Hershkowitz needed his help in figuring out how to proceed with the project in a practical way; confident as he was of his own technical knowledge and vision, he understood full well that he knew hardly anything about being a developer. Schwarz, however, was a major player in the New York legal world, and big-scale development was one-third of the holy trinity—the other two being mergers and acquisitions, and securities—that large New York law firms occupy themselves with. There was no one in Hershkowitz's own office to go to—this project was too far removed from normal NRDC initiatives.

At that point David Dinkins, a Democrat, was New York City's mayor and, with the city's sanitation commissioner (Lloyd), the head of its Economic Development Corporation (Weisbrod), and its deputy commissioner—soon to become commissioner—for consumer affairs (Schrader) on board, Hershkowitz felt he had a good line to the mayor's office. Potentially, he also felt he had a good line to the city's municipal and commercial wastepaper and beyond that to the state level via the Democratic governor, Mario

Cuomo, especially since the borough president was a Democrat. He wasn't too worried about Ferrer, because the staff at Banana Kelly and several assembly people he talked to reassured him that it was they, not the borough president, who truly represented the community, and they could get whatever support was needed. He also hadn't been too worried when Ferrer had bad-mouthed Schwarz on the Swedish trip. Part of the reorganization of the city charter, led by Schwarz, after all, had taken away most of the power of the borough presidents. In time, Hershkowitz would come to see that whatever his politics, Governor Cuomo's style was to enforce his political power by making sure the projects he supported fitted the agendas of his local officials, assemblymen and -women, and borough presidents, and he seemed not to be terribly interested in environmental issues. There were, of course, many extra-environmental aspects of the project Hershkowitz was taking on that he did not understand; on the other hand, it was probably his outright ignorance of industrial financing and the complications of development that allowed him to proceed with the plans for the mill with such undiluted confidence.

Hershkowitz's immediate problem was to figure out a way of transforming what had been until now a series of discussions, statements of principle, and explorations of economic possibilities into a viable business plan. At the meeting at Schwarz's office, which Eric Goldstein also attended, Hershkowitz outlined the progress of the project up to that point and told him that MoDo was eager to come to the city to meet with the mayor, to reconnect with the city officials whom they had met on the trip, and to start exploring potential sites. Weisbrod, also present, said he thought that jobs generated by the project could be successfully used for the city's Welfare-to-Work Program and Lloyd said that she thought the project "could be of tremendous value to us" and promised to give Hershkowitz an analysis of New York City's wastepaper availability. Batelson had asked Hershkowitz to send a sample of New York City paper to Japan, where the company in charge of their de-inking technology, the Nippon Company, was waiting to have a look at the kinds of paper they'd be working with. Toward the end of the meeting, Weisbrod told him that he would provide an inventory of available sites, both public and private. Schwarz, in his off-hand way, said he thought the project sounded promising and that they should try to get it off the ground. He recommended a real estate development lawyer he'd worked with, Marty Gold, as someone who had extensive background in New York City real estate deals involving complicated zoning law. Gold also knew a lot about environmental issues, he added. Not long afterward, Hershkowitz was appointed to Mayor Dinkins's Recycling Market Development Advisory Council. For years, the city had depended on being able to ship its garbage to poor southern counties, and it badly wanted to reduce that dependence. At a meeting in late February at City Hall, discussions focused on ways of encouraging small and big projects that stimulated recycling ventures—all of which further heartened Hershkowitz.

Over the next few weeks he became a demon of activity, assembling an early research and development team whose members—from investment bankers to environmental experts—were characterized by Goldstein as "the undisputed all-stars of their fields." Besides Schwarz, Schrader, and Gold, it included Michael Gerrard, one of the country's most respected environmental lawyers, who had worked pro bono with NRDC on several major battles. Gerrard was the general editor of the seminal, eight-volume *Environmental Law Practice Guide: State and Federal Law* and had been editor since 1989 of a monthly newsletter, *Environmental Law in New York;* the team also included Philip Sears, an environmental planner and vice president of one of the country's most experienced environmental engineering firms; Irving Gotbaum, a specialist in zoning law whom Marty Gold had recommended; Richard Campbell, a soft-spoken investment banker and lawyer who specialized in companies that focused on recycling and environmental issues; and, through him, Bruce Pulver, another investment banker, then working for a U.S. subsidiary of Hambros, a venerable English merchant bank that had a long-standing relationship with MoDo. Pulver, like Campbell, had quite a bit of experience in environmental investments, but, unlike Campbell, he also was experienced in single-asset industrial project financing, the economic development category into which the mill project fell.

Hershkowitz met Pulver, a full-chested, fit-looking man with sharply defined features who looks rather like a smart cavalry officer in some small, benign principality, at Rick Campbell's office at 45th Street and Park Avenue. Pulver listened for a while to Hershkowitz's description of the project, then asked, not unkindly, "Who's driving this car?"—a question to which Hershkowitz frankly acknowledged he didn't have an answer. The truth was that at that point he was still assembling the car. But it was also the first time that he understood the limitations of his collaborative vision for the project. In the business world, there had to be a "driver." Obviously, the next thing to do was to put together a management structure. The only certainties at that point were that NRDC was going to help with the permitting, Banana Kelly was going to help with the local politics, and MoDo was going to finance the project and hoped eventually to take it over and handle all its technical aspects.

The project looked promising to Pulver. Whatever the unconventional aspects of the plan were, the magic name that held the whole thing together was MoDo, and MoDo was apparently also talking about bringing in S.D. Warren, a subsidiary of Scott Paper Company and then one of the largest suppliers of glossy paper in North America. At that point there were three or four de-inking pulp projects at various stages of development, but the problem potential investors had with them was that they didn't have enough industry participation. In the single-asset project finance business, financing was based solely on the difference between what the paper was expected to sell for and what it cost to make it. It was hard to make these kinds of projects succeed without having some contracts on the output side and without someone, early on, agreeing to buy the paper at a certain price. Most of the other de-inking projects went ahead without those contracts or with no firm contracts and in time virtually all of them failed. But the Bronx project looked like it was going to have a paper company or paper companies willing to put in money or at least agree to take output at some kind of fair pricing. On the other hand, Pulver was quick to point out, the pulp market was volatile. Prices were high then, he told Hershkowitz, but if they tanked everything would look different.

Also, besides the economic risk, there was a technological one. The technology that MoDo was proposing was new—not brand-new, as it was being tried at a couple of other plants, but it was fairly new, and those plants weren't producing magazine-quality pulp. There wasn't a long history of using wastepaper to make magazine paper, as was now the plan—usually wastepaper was used for making tissue and other inferior grades of paper. But all this would soon be researched and analyzed, and Pulver knew that with a paper company as a co-developer assuming the responsibility for evaluating the paper, Wall Street would have a lot more confidence in its viability.

In Hershkowitz's last conversation with Batelson, the Swedish executive had asked that a financial pro forma be provided spanning the project's first five years, as well as a time and responsibilities chart with the goal of being on line by the end of 1996. There also needed to be further clarification, he said, of how NRDC and Banana Kelly would help reduce his company's entry risks in the city. Toward the end of February, Carl Weisbrod had talked again to a resolutely lukewarm Fred Ferrer. Ferrer was still keeping the project at arm's length but mentioned that a site might be available in the Hunts Point section of the borough—his strong political bailiwick. Wherever it ended up, however, it looked like Banana Kelly's role would be problematic. As Hershkowitz noted in his diary at the time, Ferrer had repeated that he did *not* want Banana Kelly to be a financial beneficiary of the project. Weisbrod was concerned about Ferrer's continued hostility toward the community group and about his opposition to its affiliation with the project and any possible credit that might accrue to it in public. Ferrer's opposition made Hershkowitz nervous, too, but he didn't really know how to respond to it. Banana Kelly had invited the project to their community; NRDC did not want to proceed—indeed, would not have proceeded—without being invited in by a respected community group, and Rivera was sure that she could win broad support for it at the local level.

Later, on the same day he'd met with Weisbrod, at an afternoon meeting with Rivera and several other people, he mentioned the borough president's concern that other players needed to be brought into the project and added that NRDC's interest, in general, in the community aspect of the project was to have as wide a coalition of the community as possible involved and working along with the team. Rivera received this news coolly. "Basically," Hershkowitz wrote in his diary that evening, "Banana Kelly said, 'No. We're going to take care of the community projects, that's something that we're going to coordinate.'" Hershkowitz and the two colleagues who were at the meeting with him really didn't know what to say in response or how to press their point. For all their sophistication working the corridors of power in Washington and around the globe, the Bronx was foreign terrain to them and the politics of South Bronx community groups a total unknown. With Anita Miller's words ("Banana Kelly would be perfect for this!") still ringing in his mind, however, and with an unexplored, somewhat fuzzily romantic perception of community groups in general and Banana Kelly in particular (grassroots bottom-up wisdom was surely more important than the blessing of a pol on top), he left that meeting feeling a bit perplexed. Still, he was confident that Banana Kelly could "lead the charge," as he wrote, for building a broader coalition.

In early March, Batelson came to New York with several of his colleagues from MoDo, and he and Hershkowitz went to Emily Lloyd's office downtown. Lloyd, a slim, energetic woman who found herself growing increasingly enthusiastic about the mill, had brought a large team of Department of Sanitation people to the meeting, including her deputy commissioner, John Doherty, and her head of recycling operations. They had collected two or three large rolling canvas bins filled with office wastepaper. Batelson scrutinized the paper, nodded with what Hershkowitz interpreted as approval, and eventually asked Lloyd for a ton of it to be shipped to Japan for analysis.

That same day, March 3, 1993, a large meeting was held at NRDC's offices with people from MoDo, Banana Kelly, and NRDC, in which the importance of forming some kind of official entity was discussed, along with the urgent need to clarify the specifics of the project: its size, the quality of the paper required, the process that would be used, the output to be generated, the kind of wastepaper that would be required for raw material — and, of course, they had to start looking for a site.

MoDo initially estimated that the project would cost about $43 million: $14 million for processing equipment; $11 million for building; $10 million for electrical equipment; $1 million for data equipment; and $2 million for infrastructure and transportation equipment — and if it evolved that they needed to dry the pulp to market it, that would cost an additional $5 million. But at the next meeting company representatives said that realistically they now thought it would cost about $60 million. A few days after that meeting, Hershkowitz, Batelson, Lloyd, Rivera, and Tim Martin boarded a large helicopter procured by the Economic Development Corporation to get an aerial view of possible sites. It was a bright, clear day and the water of New York Harbor glimmered brilliantly below them. From the air the Bronx looked large, and its abandoned industrial sites beckoned invitingly.

O possibility! Since bringing such sites back to healthy life was to Hershkowitz what finding an overland route to the Pacific was to Lewis and Clark, it was a gloriously exciting trip. The helicopter pilot looped around the Empire State Building and the Statue of Liberty for the hell of it, and each potential site they gazed down at as they circled the borough ratcheted up his hopes exponentially. There on the ground his dream could be transferred, as it were, from the realm of speculation, sited chiefly in his brain, to that of the real, on terra firma. The sites they looked at that day included several city properties that were too cumbersome and would take years to acquire, as well as some private ones: a parcel of land at Hunts Point near the city's food market; Oak Point, a site that the *New York Times* had looked at for a printing plant and rejected; the so-called Rodolitz parcel (named after its owner), the site of a warehouse formerly owned by Alexander's Department Stores, one of the largest indoor warehouses in the city; and Barretto Point, in the southeast part of the borough, where the New York Department of Sanitation was thinking of putting in an incinerator. Rivera had assured Hershkowitz when they first met that there were plenty of sites available in the Bronx, and that seemed to be true, but as it turned out she knew very little about problems that any of the sites might present or, indeed, of their viability for a large industrial project, as Hershkowitz, Tim Martin, and Eric Goldstein would find out over the next months. Rivera knew a great deal about housing development, but industrial land parcels were far from her realm of expertise. But on that sunny March day, disembarking from the helicopter, pretty much everyone who had been along on the ride came away feeling excited. Hershkowitz's immediate favorite possibility was the Barretto Point site, because of the Department of Sanitation's incinerator plans for it; how great it would be not only to prevent another incinerator from being built but to build there instead a state-of-the-art, high-grade, clean de-inking mill, a model of modern recycling technology: swords into plowshares.

Over the next year the project acquired an official name—the Bronx Community Paper Company (BCPC)—and, after a twenty-minute conversation with Hershkowitz, Maya Lin, the much admired designer of the National Vietnam Veterans Memorial in Washington, agreed to design the mill. During that year, the development project became a joint venture of Banana Kelly and MoDo and acquired a financing team, a marketing team, a PR team, a political team, a technology and construction team, and a job training and recruitment team. Of the $260 million it was *now* estimated to cost to build and equip the mill, over $6 million was earmarked for projects Banana Kelly had long hoped to finance: a joint learning and family health care center, a dormitory for homeless students from Bronx regional high schools, an off-site daycare center, a college endowment fund for local students, a literacy program, a bookstore, and a revolving loan fund for small businesses and housing. In addition to the jobs these projects would generate, the mill itself was at that point expected to provide nearly six hundred full-time jobs for people in the community and nine hundred construction jobs while it was being built. Rick Campbell and Bruce Pulver figured that the community entitlements had to be factored into the capital costs of the project rather than as a development cost.

Rivera and Hershkowitz, talking with each other almost daily, became a symbiotic team. To explain their plan and get the community's input, they went to housing project basements, met with community groups like We'll Stay/Nos Quedamos and Mott Haven Action Coalition, and spoke with local politicians and community board members. Sometimes they made presentations to community groups where there was a lot of shouting, and Hershkowitz would come out saying, "Oh, god, that was awful," whereupon Rivera would look at him as if he were crazy and say, "No, that was a good meeting." At other meetings, including one at the White House with buttoned-up officials, Rivera came away saying, "That was a disaster, wasn't it?" and Hershkowitz assured her that it had been a great success.

But an encounter took place that troubled him greatly. One evening, as he and Rivera were leaving an event, a community representative approached him. The person was a member of the South Bronx Clean Air Coalition, an organization that had helped shut down a disastrous incinerator at Bronx Lebanon Hospital. The South Bronx Clean Air Coalition represented a number of grassroots organizations, and Hershkowitz was delighted that the emissary was there, because he wanted the permitting process, when the time came for it, to be as transparent as possible. NRDC was committed to meeting, even exceeding, the highest standards for air quality, and he wanted to be sure that people in the Bronx understood that.

The representative smiled brightly at Hershkowitz and told him, "I would like to help you with your problems with the South Bronx Clean Air Coalition."

Hershkowitz stared at the person in some confusion and said, "What do you mean?"

The reply was, "Well, you're going to have problems with the coalition on siting the mill."

"But we haven't even chosen a site. Why would we have problems?" he asked.

The answer was, "I need seventy thousand dollars to take care of your problems with the Clean Air Coalition."

Hershkowitz was stunned. When he asked, "Is that for you personally, or is it for your research or other kinds of resources you need?" the answer was that it was the former.

Hershkowitz remembers looking down at his shoes after that

and mumbling something about the delegate's having to talk to Yolanda. Later that evening Rivera had a heated discussion with the person and said that the project was not going to pay.

The next morning, when Hershkowitz expressed his dismay about what had happened, Rivera told him that if they continued to plan to build the project in the Bronx, he shouldn't be surprised if that sort of thing happened more frequently. In fact, it happened the very next day. Richard Schrader, the New York City consumer affairs deputy commissioner and mill project adviser, was approached by the same person and told that the project was apt to have trouble with community groups. There was going to be well-organized opposition, based on the same objections that had been raised with the medical waste incinerator, Schrader was told.

"But these are two entirely different projects," Schrader said — to which the reply was, "They're organizing and there's nowhere else to go. They're going to use all their organizing to do this. But I think I can make the problem go away."

Schrader said, "Do you mean we have to give them money?"

"Oh, more like jobs and stuff, but yeah, right." Schrader responded that his advice would be not to give them anything and that "we can't be shaken down like that."

Hershkowitz and Schrader did not mention their conversations to each other or anyone else until many months later — and both would regret that. Hershkowitz said nothing because he found the whole thing hugely embarrassing and a sour note, and because he still couldn't believe that what the person had said was true. He trusted the integrity of grassroots groups; for much of his career he had acted on their behalf, and he took their basic virtue as a given. Schrader said nothing at the time because he sensed it was news Hershkowitz would not want to hear.

In the months that followed, the person who had approached Hershkowitz and Schrader became one of the project's leading opponents, along with the other members of the South Bronx Clean Air Coalition. At one point one of these opponents even claimed that the mill was going to kill babies and was a violation of the Universal Declaration of Human Rights and the United Nations Convention on the Elimination of Genocide.

For the moment, however, the more pressing matter obstructing the development project pushed other concerns to the sidelines. Worried that down the line somewhere the people who guided the closings of big industrial projects—the money people—would try to muck around with some of NRDC's social goals, Hershkowitz decided that all decisions had to be made by consensus. He gave Banana Kelly veto power, and the BCPC board, then composed of Campbell, Rivera, Batelson, Lennart Westberg, the chief financial officer of MoDo, and himself, approved of that plan. Later on that year, he would idly speculate in his diary that there probably needed to be a mechanism written into the board's procedures in case it got deadlocked by one person vetoing votes—but he never did anything about it.

At a roundtable discussion on environment and economics at Columbia University on March 26, 1993, Hershkowitz discussed the project with Vincent Tese, the head of the New York State Department of Economic Development under Governor Cuomo. After the discussion, Tese invited him to come to his office to explore ways he might be helpful. Unfortunately, however, Tese developed an extremely serious case of Lyme disease and left his job, and the state official Hershkowitz would deal with next was Lee Webb, the executive vice president at the New York State Urban Development Corporation, a nice man who was polite about the project but seemed less inclined to reach out to help.

Frustratingly, all the sites they had peered down on from the helicopter and hoped to build on turned out to be duds. After the helicopter ride Rivera, Hershkowitz, and several of his colleagues had met with half a dozen Bronx officials over rice and beans in Banana Kelly's basement and asked them about the various sites, but none of them seemed to have strong opinions about them one way or another. Hershkowitz had the impression that for political reasons, they didn't want to express support for any site that might present problems down the line. The Barretto Point site that Hershkowitz favored was too small to accommodate a mill; the owner of the Rodolitz abandoned warehouse site that Maya Lin liked best, because she loved the idea of recycling a building that itself would be used for recycling, had bankruptcy problems; the Oak Point site was too polluted—it would have cost $60 million to clean it up and the current owners weren't offering any indemnification; and the site next to the Hunts Point Market recommended by Rivera turned out to be needed by the Hunts Point food distributors themselves for a refrigeration warehouse. They had been working, in fact, on acquiring that site for years. When Eric Goldstein appeared to make a presentation about the mill project to the Hunts Point neighborhood association, he was met with rage and indignation. It was clear that despite her promise Rivera had not made inquiries to find out about the availability of the site and Goldstein, who considered himself sophisticated politically, felt blindsided and left the meeting shaken. Although she had been doing a good job enlisting support from local community board members and politicians, Rivera's assurances about the many available sites in her borough turned out to be baseless.

There were other problems arising with Banana Kelly that some of the members of the development team had begun to find troubling: sloppiness about paperwork, frequent failure to return phone calls, and a tendency not to show up at important meetings. Bruce Pulver attributed these lapses to Rivera's unfamiliarity with big industrial projects. Although large sums from foundations flowed in and out of Banana Kelly all the time, "handling foundation money and using it to undertake local level activities is different from actually being a board member and shareholder of an industrial development company," he said to me some time later. "Hershkowitz was placing Rivera in a role," he added, "that was totally unusual for a community development group."

Hershkowitz himself was beginning to worry about the screwups of his community partner but tended to make excuses for them. He figured that with all the housing and local problems they were undoubtedly struggling with, and with all the outreach efforts they were making on the project's behalf, some things were just too much for Rivera's already full plate. Not infrequently, when she failed to write a letter that was needed by a certain deadline, he'd write it himself and ask her to sign it; he called four or five times to remind her about meetings; he'd make a point when other members of the team complained about something she didn't do of stressing how important to the acquisition of permits a community partner and the jobs goal of the project were; and, as each letter of support came in from a local pol or community board member, he'd wave it in front of them. At home, however, his wife, Meg, told him there was something about Rivera's attitude toward these lapses—she never said she was sorry and never seemed to be able to adequately address them—that troubled her.

In the summer of 1993, after meeting with the mill manager of MoDo's Alizay plant in Normandy, Hershkowitz settled in for three weeks in Paris for what amounted to a crash course on paper de-inking. Meg and the kids were there, too, in an apartment MoDo owned that was used for its visiting executives, but most of the time, while they went to the park, he stayed at the MoDo office on the Champs-Elysées, poring over all the engineering and operational details and the environmental integrity of the Alizay plant. Chiefly, he was examining its plans for a future de-inking pulp plant that the Bronx mill was to be modeled on.

By the fall of 1993, the project was moving ahead in terms of its internal structure. In general, in the United States, virtually every kind of paper business was booming. While visiting Japan with a group of scientists to celebrate the formation of the Green Cross International headed by Mikhail Gorbachev, Hershkowitz ran into Batelson, who was there to get the North American licensing agreement for the use of the new de-inking technology they were going to use. Hershkowitz introduced Batelson to Gorbachev, as well as to Prince Albert von Liechtenstein (a figure of some renown in the global environmental world, who had expressed interest in the project), which he slyly thought was a bit of a coup. Over the same months Mike Gerrard, leading the effort to organize the environmental permitting, was proceeding with dispatch, even though NRDC had demanded that the environmental standards that needed to be met by the project be more stringent than those required by law. Hershkowitz had met again with MoDo in Stockholm to discuss technical issues about the project. MoDo had raised the possibility of using private carters instead of the Department of Sanitation if the delays involved in the often elaborate Request For Proposal (RFP) process with the city turned out to be too lengthy—and Hershkowitz began to explore the carters' world, which had a dubious reputation.

And MoDo and Banana Kelly signed an agreement. They would eventually sign a more binding document—this was an agreement on an agreement. The project also found, through the National Minority Supplier Development Council, an engineering firm that NRDC thought could handle the project, though the firm was ultimately rejected by MoDo, which felt that they didn't have enough mill-building expertise to handle the job. In that same period, believing that it needed a strong U.S. business partner, MoDo moved more directly to bring in S.D. Warren. Warren would bring its strength in paper marketing and, together, they would own 50 percent of the plant. Also, there was a discussion about using the rejected paper from the wastepaper sorting plant and converting it into ethanol that would be used instead of diesel fuel to power the trucks delivering the wastepaper to the mill.

Despite all the forward motion everyone was so energized by, however, there was still no place for the mill to go. The previous spring, Hershkowitz had received inquiries from other community groups in Chicago and LA about developing similar mills and, by the time the leaves had fallen in late November, he'd begun to wonder if he might have to switch his project to Chicago, since nearly a year of searching had yet to turn up a viable site. He expressed his concern to Rivera, but she told him not to worry, though she had no fresh suggestions. In some way he couldn't exactly put his finger on, her reaction seemed odd. She didn't seem to acknowledge that she had played any part in the past year's futile search. Nor did she acknowledge the emptiness of her earlier reassurances that there were hundreds of acres of brownfields available and suitable for a mill. Another difficulty had emerged—a chronic problem of Banana Kelly's staff turnover. From one week to the next, no one on the development team was sure whom to call about meetings or paperwork. In the summer of 1993, after he'd returned from Paris, Rivera told Hershkowitz that the person who had replaced an earlier one who was supposed to coordinate paper mill matters was himself going to be replaced by someone new named Fermine Garcia. By then, the Comprehensive Community Revitalization

Program (CCRP), Anita Miller's organization, had given a $12,500 grant each to Banana Kelly and NRDC to help with outreach work for the project with a matching amount to be contributed later on.

Banana Kelly was one of six Bronx community groups that had been given support for pet projects and, except for Banana Kelly, every group that had been asked to submit their version of a strategic plan did so. But Rivera did not deliver hers, though CCRP tried many times to find out what the problem was and to offer assistance. When they finally did submit something, it was sloppy and half baked. Miller had worked with Banana Kelly since the 1970s, and when she'd spoken to Hershkowitz about the group so enthusiastically, her recommendation was based on her experience with Rivera's two predecessors, both of whom she had great respect for. Rivera had only recently taken over as the group's head, and she was beginning to seriously worry Miller. From her own past experience, Miller knew that the broadest possible community involvement was necessary so that people wouldn't feel that they were being duped. The outreach money was supposed to be used for a staff person and for an early, aggressive campaign to make it widely known with fact sheets and lots of big community meetings that this was a great project, designed to clean up the environment and provide jobs. Rivera had successfully found support among many elected officials and community groups, but Fermine Garcia, who was the front person for the broader outreach program, was not being given enough direction to disseminate facts about the project, and was not galvanizing the community in a positive way.

If his community partner was causing him worries, Hershkowitz's main business partner, Per Batelson, whom he was getting to know better as they both scuttled back and forth across the Atlantic, was, as he reported to Meg, "changing his life." Before Batelson's mentorship on sophisticated industrial ecology, Hershkowitz had thought, "Okay, we'll build a model"—one that would help the forestry problem and help address solid waste issues and hopefully be replicable at other brownfield sites. But what really excited Hershkowitz about the mill plan was that it could be a more far-reaching good project for the people who lived near it and worked for it and a demonstration of how *business* has the potential to advance the humanistic goals he'd been so interested in since graduate school. Over the next years, various observers, even people close to him, would worry about the emphasis he laid on parts of the project that most businessmen considered economic burdens—the community entitlements, the designs of Maya Lin—what even Carl Weisbrod, his enthusiastic supporter at the Economic Development Corp., called its "bells and whistles." They failed to grasp, however, that for him, no less than the making of pulp or cleaning up of an old polluted site, these *were* the project. Batelson was one of the few members of the team he talked to who was as interested as he was in the challenge of the mill not only to modify a product, but, by bringing together cultures (business, community, environmental) that rarely spoke each other's language, to actually change the way people think about industrial development.

While Hershkowitz was in Paris studying paper technology, he met with Batelson and one of his colleagues at MoDo's office and the two Swedes stressed the importance of finding a site soon and making sure that it was near a wastewater treatment plant, something no one had especially focused on before. They already knew that the mill would need between 3.5 and 5 million gallons of water a day. The MoDo executives wanted to make sure there was a plant nearby to treat the mill's effluent; Hershkowitz also was committed to finding a way to use treated sewage water instead of fresh in the plant process itself. Not long after he returned to New York, MoDo brought eight representatives of Scott Paper and S.D. Warren to NRDC's office to discuss Warren's participation in the project, and by late fall, the plan was for MoDo and S.D. Warren to put up two-thirds of the development money, while it was expected that NRDC would raise the rest. By then, Hershkowitz, John Adams, and Robert Kennedy, Jr., a senior NRDC attorney, had made a trip to Washington to lobby Vice President Gore, Leon Panetta, director of the White House Office of Management and Budget, Alice Rivlin, the deputy director of the same office, and Robert Rubin, the director of the National Economic Council, on behalf of the presidential executive order, for which they had high hopes, requiring federal agencies to increase their use of recycled paper, using the mill proj-

ect as an example of businesses that would benefit from it. Hershkowitz had shuttled back and forth to Washington to lobby heavily
(with help from Vice President Gore) for the order. On October 20,
1993, the newly signed executive order was announced by the vice
president in New York City. In his announcement, which he made
in the City Council chambers at City Hall, he singled out the Bronx
project for praise. The executives at MoDo were suitably impressed
by NRDC's clout in Washington and input on the executive order,
but experienced as they were in the extremely volatile paper commodity world, they were getting more and more nervous about the
time schedule and the failure of their New York friends to identify
a reliable site. At the end of the year, representatives from NRDC,
Banana Kelly, and Hambro met in S.D. Warren's office in Boston.
Besides approving the engineering and paper analysis companies
they had decided to work with, they agreed that a site *had* to be
found by June 1994 at the latest, and that the engineering feasibility study on wastepaper and a financial feasibility report needed to
be finished by September.

Toward the end of December 1993, on one of Hershkowitz's
many trips to Stockholm to work with the people at MoDo, he received devastating news: Batelson, who by now had become a good
friend, was resigning from MoDo. Sweden had recently privatized
its federal employment pension, and the director of the new company persuaded him to become his number two man. MoDo would
remain in the project, Batelson assured Hershkowitz. But Batelson
had been the strategic driver of the New York project at MoDo
and—especially in view of the fact that there was some turmoil at
MoDo, involving a general reshuffling of management and ownership teams—it worried Hershkowitz that he would no longer play
that role. Batelson made his announcement at the same popular
Swedish restaurant, Fem Sma Hus, where he had serenaded the city
officials on their earlier tour, and he promised to continue to help
Hershkowitz in any way he could.

Unfortunately, despite Batelson's good intentions, the truth was
that the company's board even then was thinking of ignoring the
advice of its upper management team, which wanted to expand its
markets to New York and Berlin. They pulled Jim Black, the chief

company representative of S.D. Warren, aside at a meeting when Batelson was out of the room and told him that "Per was much further out" in his idea of commitment to the North American project than others at MoDo were. At that point, they were considering using their investment capital to buy out the French owner of the Alizay mill and building another pulping machine there. Batelson had recently also been wondering if a newsprint mill would make better sense, since there were so many papers to market newsprint paper to in the city. He didn't mention this to Hershkowitz at the time, however, because he thought he had already given Hershkowitz enough to adjust to. Nor did he convey his fear that once he left, the focus on the French plant (for which the economic projections were fairly dismal) and the attempt to make it profitable would become for MoDo an insuperable obstacle to serious development work in the Bronx.

4

The Harlem River Railyard

BY EARLY 1994 there were fifty-six people on the development team. NRDC had committed more than a million dollars of its own money to the project. Hershkowitz, Rivera, and the others were working with fifteen state and city agencies and twenty-six private firms. By the spring of that year they had also received, in addition to the SURDNA money, substantial support from the Pew Charitable Trusts, the Educational Foundation, and the Kaplan Fund, as well as smaller grants from the R.S. Clark Foundation and the Fund for the City of New York, and MoDo and S.D. Warren had each invested a quarter of a million dollars. Hershkowitz also had commitments for grants of $400,000 and $700,000 from the New York State Urban Development Corporation.

But they still didn't have a site. That year, however, an important new recruit joined the effort—Jonathan F. P. Rose, an environmentally aware son of one of the city's most successful real estate development families (his father, Frederick, who died in 1999, was one of the city's major philanthropists—his family name adorns the main reading room at the New York Public Library and both his parents' names are embedded in the façade of the new planetarium of the Museum of Natural History). Rose, whose company was then called Affordable Housing Development Corp., was initially approached as an investor. He declined but said he'd like to join the team and help with its site-search and lease arrangements if they thought his experience would help. A tall, stocky man who favors soft shirts and sweaters over traditional businessman attire, Rose had carved out his own particular version of his family's world; his company, working with public/private partnerships, built low-income housing and other projects for cities and not-for-profits, packages that usually relied on complicated financing. Although he had never worked on an urban recycling mill or, indeed, on any large industrial project, the process of working with community groups in putting together a complex project was familiar to him. Like not a few people approached by Hershkowitz, Rose's only previous experience with NRDC was being on the other side of a legal dispute (they had once helped oppose a project of his in Brooklyn for what he still believed to be insufficiently examined reasons), but he was willing to put that experience behind him. At first he was given the jobs of trying to help Banana Kelly develop its neighborhood projects and of finding a site. Later on he became involved in helping to structure the project's finances as well.

Rose's work with Banana Kelly was from the beginning fraught with tension. Rivera saw herself as a developer and believed there was no reason to include any more developers in that phase of the project, so she resented Rose's role. Rose, in turn, was frustrated by Banana Kelly's apparent inability to focus on their neighborhood projects; eventually he helped them develop the beginnings of a plan for one. The finance team also tended to regard Rose as an amateur in the large industrial project world and didn't like the high-handed tone of some of his e-mails, which came to be referred to as "nasty grams." It was Rose, however, who at last found the mill a site: the Harlem River railyard—ninety-six acres, of which the mill would use seventeen acres of a long-abandoned, polluted former railyard (one of the nation's 650,000 abandoned and contaminated sites) at the southern tip of the Bronx under the Triborough Bridge, which in its glory days in the eighteenth century was the site of the Manor House of General Lewis Morris, the patriot and signer of the Declaration of Independence. The yard was perfect from the point of view of its infrastructure. It was big enough; it had railroad and barge access; it was near the Ward's Island water treatment plant; its sewage pipes had already been permitted, and because it was in a state economic development zone, it was eligible for a 47.5 percent utility-rate discount. Furthermore, the yard's landlord, a successful upstate developer named Francesco Galesi, was willing to charge a reasonable rental rate for an industrial site—$25,000 a month—and would also forgive the rent for a year and a half, after which it was expected that construction would begin. When Rose first telephoned Hershkowitz and said, "We have a site," Hershkowitz's initial reaction of deep relief was immediately clouded by his recollection that there had been some community resistance to the site. The yard had actually come up earlier—one state senator had mentioned it at the meeting after their helicopter ride with local officials, but someone else had told him there was some community opposition to Galesi. "If the grassroots groups have some problem there," he told Rose, "I don't think we can use it." But he didn't really know what the problem was. Rose's call came in early January. The next day, Rivera suggested that they meet with the main group that had voiced opposition to the use of the yard, the South Bronx Clean Air Coalition.

On January 13, 1994, they met, with Hershkowitz more than half expecting to be persuaded that there might be good reasons to avoid the new site. But much to his surprise, the group did not raise any environmental issues; instead they focused on the vexed ownership history of the yard and their frustration with Galesi himself, whom they regarded as a rich white guy who had invaded their community. In the 1980s the New York State Department of Transportation had planned to develop the site entirely as an "intermodal" freight yard—that is, a terminal where piggyback railcars could unload their wares and attach them to truck cabs to be driven to their destinations—in the hope that better freight access would reduce air pollution and traffic congestion in the area. But as market demand for rail freight continued to decrease, the New York State Department of Transportation (DOT) finally decided that the yard would be better off in the hands of a private developer who might be able to bring some manufacturing business to the site in combination with a smaller rail freight terminal. This is where Galesi—whose assets were then reported to be more than $250 million and who had successfully run a similar project in upstate New York—entered the picture. His company, Harlem River Yard Ventures, signed a ninety-nine-year lease for the yard in 1991;

the paper company, if it signed a sublease with him, would be just one of several tenants who would lease space from him. But, in the meantime, some local residents and community groups were angry that the DOT had gone ahead and privatized the yard without sufficiently consulting them.

Throughout the early weeks of 1994 Hershkowitz continued to meet with a small group of members of the South Bronx Clean Air Coalition (including the one with whom he had had such an unpleasant encounter). With each meeting he felt more convinced that the group's objections to the site and to its development by a "capitalist" were misguided and, when weighed against the potential real-world benefits of the mill, even capricious. One of the Coalition members suggested the substitution of a park for the current industrial plans, but when Hershkowitz and others looked into the industrial zoning terms of the lease they found that a park would not be possible. Nonetheless, his long-held feelings of deference toward grassroots groups prevented him from going ahead with the Harlem River site, and they continued to explore other sites. Sometimes the discussions between Hershkowitz and the group took place by phone, and it was during that period that he received a call from someone who worked as a legislative aide to a Bronx state senator. Just as the South Bronx Clean Air Coalition representative had done earlier, the aide indicated that she could take care of the troubles with the Harlem River yard if Banana Kelly were dropped from the project and replaced by what she simply described as "our community group." Although she didn't specify the group, Hershkowitz had the strong impression that she meant the South Bronx Clean Air Coalition. The call so unnerved Hershkowitz that he sent a memo to Eric Goldstein, and Goldstein said that if it happened again, Hershkowitz should let him know about it. At one point in the ongoing discussions, someone from the South Bronx Clean Air Coalition said, whatever happened, a "community advisory group" was needed, and Hershkowitz and a few people from NRDC thought that that was a good idea. Rivera was asked many times to set one up, but it never happened.

Then in April, a trip to Stockholm was arranged so that Hershkowitz and his wife could meet with a member of MoDo's founding family and its director of strategic development, Karl Kempe. Kempe was silver-haired and hardy. His wife, Marguerita, a dignified, straightforward woman, despite her position, still worked at a modest desk job at MoDo's office. The dinner took place in the restaurant at the Grand Hotel. It was an elegant, pleasant dinner. They talked about the evolution of the project, about the ways that NRDC differed from green parties, which, in Europe, sometimes functioned as part of the legislature. As the meal was drawing to a close, Kempe rested his hand on Hershkowitz's arm and said, "You have my interest and support." But while Hershkowitz was happily licking his dessert spoon, Marguerita Kempe said very plainly to him, "Get a site," and something about the look in her eye and the way her husband looked fixedly at his plate left little room for doubt that the injunction needed to be acted on with haste.

Thus it was that on May 6, 1994, an article written by John Holusha appeared on the front page of the business section of the *New York Times* under the headline PIONEERING BRONX PLANT TO RE-CYCLE CITY'S PAPER, announcing the launching of "the first inner city project of its type in the nation," and noting that it was to be built at the old Harlem River yard. The article quoted John Adams as saying, "We get everything we want: jobs, recycling, a process we like, and social equity." He went on, "We save lots of trees and end the waste of putting a valuable resource into landfills." The president of the New York City Department of Economic Development, now working under a new mayor, was quoted as saying that the Giuliani administration supported the plan and that "we will do what we can to help see this vision brought to reality." The article quoted from the City Hall statement made by Vice President Gore when he announced the president's recycling order: "This initiative shows that economic development, job creation, and environmental protection can work together for the benefit of us all."

For all the celebrating, however, it was still all too clear that a lot of the project's financing needed to be put in place and that it remained to be seen whether its numbers crunched, so that the venture would be regarded as potentially profitable by the outside investors who were still needed to take the project to closing. Although recycling plants had proliferated across the country over the past decade, most of them were part of old paper mills and rural sites in the Midwest, where there were few political or bureaucratic obstacles to their development and where land and labor were cheaper. But along with community support—always a concern for developers in urban areas—the project also had at least one unique ace in the hole: its location. "The economics of transportation work in our favor," Hershkowitz told the *Times* reporter. "Most mills are hundreds of miles from cities, so we will have a fifteen-dollar-a-ton cost advantage."

On July 1, 1994, Hershkowitz's mother died. They'd been close and her death affected him powerfully. By all accounts she was a gentle, generous woman, and when he thought about her early life, as he so often had, and its inordinate degree of sorrow, it increased his determination to try to succeed in the task before him.

Over the next months Hershkowitz and the other members of his group continued to meet and talk with the handful of members of the South Bronx Clean Air Coalition who continued to oppose the project. One of the NRDC staff members who ought to have been helpful was Vernice Miller, the director of its environmental justice program, an energetic African-American woman who as a co-founder of the West Harlem Environmental Action Group (WE ACT) had previously worked as a grassroots activist on the successful lawsuit against the city on the North River Sewage Treatment Plant issue. Miller had more than ten years of environmental justice and public policy advocacy experience under her belt when she arrived at NRDC in the summer of 1993. She had worked with some members of the South Bronx Clean Air Coalition and was considered to be a great resource for the BCPC project. NRDC was glad to have someone with her experience on staff and valued her expertise on environmental justice issues, but something very soon went seriously awry in relation to the Bronx project. Miller became convinced that "a community already on the edge," as she expressed it to me, should not be asked to host *any* project that brought more diesel trucks into the neighborhood. Even after seeing data that demonstrated that the mill itself would be benign and the truck traffic's effects truly minimal—data that had been gathered by people who had been among her mentors—she remained unconvinced of its validity. Hershkowitz came to believe that Miller harbored some resentment about the fact that before she arrived on the scene he had independently been spearheading a project that was in her bailiwick—environmental justice. Another problem, he thought, was that he was hindered from bringing her in as a full consultant because there seemed to be some Latino-African-American tension felt in the Bronx and none of the people at or around Banana Kelly were interested in working with her. Miller was viewed as someone who fought for West Harlem—just as, they believed, Harlem's Representative Charles Rangel did; they were convinced that because of their turf loyalties, neither Rangel nor Miller would take the interests of the Bronx particularly to heart. In principle she approved of the project and, at first, told him she thought it was a good idea. But in practice, and much to everyone's dismay, she seemed to try to sabotage it.

At one of Miller's most astonishing public appearances representing NRDC at a transportation planning educational workshop at Banana Kelly's headquarters attended by community activists, city planners, and a representative of the Port Authority of New York, she characterized the mill project as a disaster in the making. Painting the mill's environmental impact in the direst possible terms, Miller, an effective public speaker with a rapid-fire delivery style, reminded her listeners about the high asthma rates in the Bronx, the well-known serious consequences of diesel fumes from trucks for respiratory disease, and the degree to which outsiders had historically neglected to demonstrate concern about the negative health impacts of their projects on local communities. It was impossible not to conclude from Miller's remarks that the current mill project was no different from any of its predecessors and that her purpose in making the presentation was to sound an alarm about it.

By the time of the meeting Miller was aware that the scientific data about the project contradicted her representation. The project's Environmental Impact Statement, painstakingly drafted by the environmental lawyer Mike Gerrard and a team led by the environmental planner Philip Sears—with the help of Hershkowitz,

Tim Martin, and technicians from MoDo and S.D. Warren—had been issued, and NRDC had for the first time in New York State development history actually sent an approved air quality permit back to Albany to be readjusted because they thought the state's standards weren't high enough. (The explanatory cover letter so floored the bureaucrat who received it that he told Hershkowitz he was going to have it framed and mounted on his office wall.) Although they were not required to by law, they took into account hot spots in the vicinity and also modeled cumulative impacts from other sources—even including the dust raised from the streets. Hershkowitz had requested that all ongoing environmental data collected at the mill be continuously monitored and made available to all relevant state and city agencies. Moreover, he asked that the project, to better serve the surrounding community's right to know, set up a Web site reporting on the data and install appropriate computer equipment and software in a local public library so it could be readily scrutinized. Hundreds of thousands of dollars had been spent using validated EPA methods for modeling environmental impact and risk assessment to make sure that the background levels of particulates would not be a public health threat. (By rounding off their findings upward, which they did because they thought no one would believe that they were so low, Gerrard and Sears found that the project would raise the area's background particulate matter from 29.8 parts per million to 29.9, an impact that was considered negligible, especially when the project's contributions—recycling millions of tons of wastepaper, clearing up a brownfield, cleaning up sewage water, and bringing manufacturing jobs to the community—were factored in.)

Admitting that what she said might be considered controversial, and separating herself from the organization she worked for, Miller not only didn't acknowledge NRDC's effort but strongly suggested that no one else involved with the project had the community's interests at heart. "Has anybody," she asked at the transportation planning workshop, "any one person, any group of people, looked at what the potential public health costs are going to be for the South Bronx . . . ?" Painful as it might have been for her to badmouth the organization that she worked for, it seemed, it behooved her as an act of conscience and as a loyal grassroots emissary to bare the facts.

Miller told me that she resented Hershkowitz's interpretation of her inquiries as a deliberate effort to undermine the project. She insisted that though she disagreed with the Environmental Impact Statement's conclusions about the negligible effect of the truck traffic, she was in fact an admirer of the mill model, as long as it was sited somewhere else. Although as far as I could tell when I looked at a video someone made of her presentation at the transportation workshop there was no light showing between her opposition to the truck traffic and her opposition as a whole, she maintains that the two issues were entirely separate in her mind.

Perhaps because she was not present at the earlier meetings, she is convinced that little effort was made to get community input on the project. "You are not *asking* this community, you are assuming the benefits of your project outweigh the broader public health objectives of this community." She added, "They were so gung-ho about its technology and building a new manufacturing facility in New York that they were willing to make this community a sacrifice for that." Miller had worked with both Gerrard and Sears for years, and I asked her if she really believed they would do that. "You can make that EIS say whatever you want it to say," she insisted. In principle, she strongly supported the idea of providing jobs in low-income neighborhoods and cleaning up abandoned industrial sites, but at the same time she couldn't condone the use of even one extra truck. "One truck exhibits x number of particulate matter, ten trucks exhibit ten times that impact." Miller spoke about the high asthma rate of her own neighborhood of West Harlem and the South Bronx. She acknowledged that recent studies had shown that because people spend 90 percent of their time indoors, inside environmental factors are often the cause of asthma and other respiratory problems. But, she agreed, these are exacerbated by particulates from diesel fumes. (The studies have emphasized that inside factors such as cockroach fragments, improperly maintained furnaces and stoves, chemical cleaners and disinfectants, and formaldehyde—which is used in everything from carpet and wallboard to bed linens, plywood, and even paper towels—are a major cause of conditions such as asthma, especially in children. The inside of people's homes, according to EPA research, typically contains levels of pollutants two to five times higher than the air outdoors, and in some cases is one hundred times higher.)

Miller maintained that "the excess mortality rate from asthma in the South Bronx and Harlem" was the main reason that she could not have the same kind of conversation about the project that the others were having. Still, the old, badly maintained, asthma-exacerbating buildings that are so eternally and dangerously a part of inner-city life are surely closely related to lack of jobs and low incomes. And while Miller said that the reclamation of abandoned industrial sites and the bringing in of new industry to create jobs was desirable, in practical terms there seemed to be a contradiction between that wish and her determination to keep industry out because of her conviction that by definition it only does poor neighborhoods harm.

At the same time that NRDC was working on the Bronx project, she pointed out, it was also talking to the Department of Transportation and the Metropolitan Transit Authority about converting their fleets to non-diesel-based fuel—even though there was no public policy that demanded that this happen. (Miller herself testified before Congress in support of more stringent air quality standards.) It was hypocritical of the organization, she felt, at the same time to support a project that in essence would bring more particulate matter and in fact "more death" to a community.

No environmental advocate and few informed citizens remain unconcerned about the serious health impact of diesel fumes; the trouble was, many of her facts were wrong. Despite the Bronx's real problems as a borough with too many highways going through it, the air quality of the South Bronx site and surrounding neighborhood is *not*, as she suggested, far worse than most other places in the city. In fact, though it seems counterintuitive, because of complex air transport patterns the air quality along the gilded corridor of Madison Avenue near the Whitney Museum and around the luxury apartments on East 72nd Street is worse. The South Bronx site, a peninsula on a major water body, is actually in compliance with the Clean Air Act and suffers less from pollutants than the so-called canyon on Madison Avenue; the EIS compilers actually overestimated the particulate impacts, assuming a worst-case scenario—old, poorly maintained trucks—rather than underestimating them. And while it is a proven fact that too many waste transfer stations get dumped in poor neighborhoods, the Bronx among them, there were not, as Miller told her audience, sixty-four of them dotting the borough, but eighteen, according to the Department of Sanitation.

Miller maintains that she could never truly get Hershkowitz's ear; Hershkowitz and other team members—Tim Martin in particular—remark that after a brief rose-petal period, she never approached them in a collegial way or tried to sit down and discuss the issues she felt so passionately about. Martin also remembers that contrary to what Miller told me, Hershkowitz was welcoming toward Miller and seemed to encourage her participation when she first arrived. Perhaps because communication between her and Hershkowitz and the other team members was poor, she appears to have been unaware that they were having ongoing conversations around the city about converting the trucks that would be bringing paper to the yard to natural gas. Before the paper was actually promised to the mill by the city, however, they were still in the position of being supplicants and had no leverage to insist on such a policy change; but they hoped in time that they could.

She was aware, however, that another NRDC staff member, the director of its Dump Dirty Diesels campaign, was also striving to get the EPA to call for the reduction of the sulfur content of diesel fuel, which would *radically* reduce its harmfulness—a campaign that eventually succeeded. But the long-term, incremental, and undramatic struggles that characterized that effort seem not to have much altered Miller's sense that the tweedy, comfortable lawyers, advocates, and engineers who swim in NRDC's waters basically didn't care that much about poor people.

Eventually Miller would leave NRDC, but while she was still there and amid all the highs and lows that attended the mill's development phase, it was a constant source of worry to Hershkowitz that she was working against it. At one point she was told not to have anything to do with the project and not to talk about it, a stricture she believed was instigated by Hershkowitz, though he declares that it wasn't. Miller complied with the gag order, she insists, even though it was difficult for her, considering her feelings, but Hershkowitz complained to a few of the people on the development team that she continued to speak "with a forked tongue" about it—lambasting it in public while telling him, even after that workshop (which he learned about only because someone sent the video to him), what a great project it was. Many people had trouble fathoming the complexities of Miller's stance, and the technical people especially couldn't understand her utter rejection of the quantifiable data. In the long run, Rich Schrader suggested, one component of it might be that the enemies of the project were more important to her as a constituency than its friends.

Despite the loss of Batelson, the project was gathering momentum. The Harlem River yard was being cleaned up, a new rail link (which would substantially reduce the numbers of trucks going to and from the yard) was being connected to it, support was arriving from both public and private sectors, and prices were high for paper. With the upswing in the economy, demand for recycled materials, according to the *Wall Street Journal,* had skyrocketed. The mounds of newspapers and plastic that had once piled up in recycling centers, gathering mold, had "melted away," and demand for materials pushed the price of recycled paper to a record high. In early 1994, there had been a potential disaster when Jim Black, S.D. Warren's vice president in charge of paper production, phoned Hershkowitz to say that Warren's parent company, Scott Paper, would not participate in the project and wanted Warren out of it altogether. But Hershkowitz, Rivera, the lawyer Irving Gotbaum, John Adams, and Robert Denham—an NRDC trustee and the chairman and CEO of Salomon Brothers, which sold Scott's stock—essayed a full-court press by journeying by train two weeks later to Philadelphia to meet with Philip Lippincott, Scott's chairman and CEO, on the third floor of Scott's headquarters, and persuaded him to let Warren stay in.

Rivera, always a compelling speaker, told the Scott executive in passionate terms how important the project was to her community.

Lippincott seemed moved by her remarks but told the assembled group that Scott was leery of the socially progressive aspects of the plan, saying that if the project failed, people would only remember that they didn't succeed. Their good efforts would be forgotten. If that was the way things worked out, Hershkowitz assured him, NRDC would be sure to give them good public credit for trying. More crucially, Lippincott was worried that the production costs using state-of-the-art technology were going to be too high, as well as labor costs, because of what he described as "labor discipline" (he felt the city's building trades' unions were too costly). Hershkowitz, having been helped by Gotbaum's father, Victor, a well-known union leader and city *macher,* had already met and worked with a local union, and the mill was then being listed as one of the AFL-CIO's top projects in New York State, a fact Hershkowitz was proud of, though as he later joked with me, for the ultraconservative paper industry "it was like giving them cancer." Lippincott also didn't think that the equity share between three parties—Warren, MoDo, and Nippon (the technology supplier and licensee that if the deal went through, wanted to receive royalties for its role in the process)—was going to look attractive to the investors. Despite these reservations, by the end of the meeting, Lippincott, whom industry sources describe as an eminently decent man, said he didn't want to be the one to kill the deal. Of course, between the time Black had telephoned Hershkowitz on February 17, and February 25, when the meeting took place in Philadelphia, Hershkowitz had brought out the marines in the form of a massive letter-writing campaign designed to change Lippincott's mind. He persuaded Larry Rockefeller, a strong NRDC supporter and staff member, to write a letter asking Scott not to withdraw. John Dyson, New York's deputy mayor, also weighed in, as did Jonathan Rose, Lee Webb, Fritz Schwarz, and a small army of community representatives from the South Bronx. There was such a deluge of mail importuning Lippincott not to pull out that at one point he turned to Hershkowitz and said with a sardonic smile, "If we stay in, will you stop the letters?" As a result of the meeting, S.D. Warren was back in, along with its $250,000 in development money.

Not long after the Warren scare, there had been a MoDo flurry

as well. On March 15, at six in the morning, Hershkowitz was awakened by the shrill sound of the telephone. It was the secretary of
Torbjorn Nillson, acting president of MoDo, who asked him if it
would be possible for him to meet with her boss for lunch the next
day. Hershkowitz said he'd be glad to: "Is he in town?" No, the secretary said, he wanted to meet him in Stockholm. So much had
happened since their last meeting that Hershkowitz figured Nillson
wanted an update. Maybe this was how things went in the strange
world of international big business, he speculated, as he rolled over
to tell an amazed Meg that he'd be flying to Sweden that evening
for a MoDo lunch the next day. The cool, brilliant winter light of
Stockholm struck him as particularly beautiful the next morning
when he arrived in the city, armed with the latest tidings about
the project's planned press announcement, a copy of the current
financial reports, a summary of the site acquisition process, another
about the political support they were getting, and his take on the
status of S.D. Warren.

Nillson was summoning Hershkowitz to tell him that the strategic approach of the company was shifting and that MoDo, too, had
decided to pull out of the project in order to focus on European
production. He'd called him there because he wanted to tell him in
person. Somehow, however, that conversation never took place. Instead, MoDo, with its $250,000, remained in, Hershkowitz promised
to send MoDo an "options paper" describing how MoDo could
best participate in the project, and after the two put away a good
lunch, they walked to a Leonardo da Vinci exhibition at the museum. As they wandered around the exhibition, Nillson impressed
Hershkowitz with his knowledge of art history. He had noted with
satisfaction over lunch that Nillson was wearing a dapper blue
shirt; throughout his peregrinations with the project, he couldn't
help but be struck by the fact that nearly every American paper industry executive he encountered was "a white guy wearing a white
shirt." Hershkowitz's own wardrobe contained a fair number of
elegant colored shirts—many of which he wore sans jacket to the
office—often draped with a wool scarf of surprising length. It was,
of course, part of his project's mission to find a way for the various
cultures—business and enviro communities, whatever their charac-

teristics—to get past stereotypes. Nonetheless, a little cloud unfailingly passed over his generally optimistic take on the project whenever he thought about the vast army of pale, white-shirted (and often white-haired) operatives that stretched across the American paper industry landscape.

During the rest of the early part of 1994 the project gained momentum, and many of the people associated with it had reason to feel optimistic. Whatever problems may have been posed by the eccentricity of an environmentalist-spearheaded business project, the strong institutional connections enviros had forged over the years by working closely with government bureaucrats proved to be a unique asset. William Ferretti, the director of the New York State Office of Recycling Market Development, helped the project with two grant commitments from the state totaling $1.1 million, to be channeled through the State Urban Development Corporation, which dealt with the sale of state land and the awarding and approving of state loans and grants. Ferretti, with whom Hershkowitz had served on recycling advisory boards since the 1980s, had a long history of helping recycling initiatives. He was an enthusiastic booster of the project and was solidly behind it. But Ferretti was something of an anomaly in the state bureaucracy; Hershkowitz continued to find that the main thing that the current Democratic leadership seemed to care about was making sure that whatever monies or jobs were given out accrued to the greater glory of the current Democratic state leadership. He had no sense that issues per se had any independent life, apart from being a means to enforce party power. In the higher echelons of state leadership the general attitude toward environmental remediation, or social justice, or even business development matters, was neither positive nor negative. The crucial question that always needed answering was: How does our involvement shore up the party's power?

Hershkowitz had already met several times with Lee Webb, a congenial man in his mid-fifties, who was the executive vice president of the State Urban Development Corporation; Hershkowitz had been grateful for his help in keeping Scott in the project. So he wasn't surprised when on May 26, 1994, he was asked to show up for another meeting in Webb's office in mid-Manhattan. But much to his surprise, after exchanging the briefest of pleasantries, Webb directed him to an office down the hall and told him that waiting there were Carmen Arroyo, a Bronx assemblywoman from Banana Kelly's district and a strong backer of the New York mill project, and Kevin Nunn, the president of the Bronx Overall Economic Development Office. "Work it out," he said, smiling, and opened the office door. "I had no idea what he was talking about," Hershkowitz later told me. Nunn didn't say much, but Arroyo made plain what she was there for. "We want the jobs," she told him. "My people should get the jobs." Hershkowitz, who grew up in a union household but nonetheless wanted to give whatever jobs emerged at the mill to local people, didn't know how to respond to this sally. Arroyo was one among many who had spoken to him about the jobs. It was certainly part of the plan to give the mill's permanent jobs to neighborhood people, and in fact whenever they made presentations a sign-up sheet was circulated for those who might be interviewed for future positions. He had already had lengthy conversations with Edward Malloy, the president of the Building and Construction Trades Council of Greater New York, and found him unbendable about giving construction jobs to neighborhood people who weren't in the union. If, like the grandmotherly Arroyo, he were representing an assembly district, he knew he'd be fighting to get jobs for "his people," the people in the community; on the other hand, the fact was that he couldn't promise jobs to anyone. Still, he was the one who nearly everyone connected with the project phoned or faxed or met with to find out what was going on, and he was the one who sent messengers out to deliver letters and contracts after struggling to get Rivera's signature on them—a necessary formality since Banana Kelly had been made the development project's titular owner. But officially he was only the project's coordinator. This was definitely not clear to many people and surely not to Arroyo, who, since the project's inception, had seen Hershkowitz everywhere the mill's business was being conducted. After an awkward pause, he told her, "You're talking to the wrong person. Of course there'll be jobs, but you'll have to talk to the paper companies, and at this point,

I don't even know what kind of jobs they're going to be . . ." For a few seconds his words just hung there. Nunn gave no indication of his reaction to what he'd said. Then Hershkowitz left and said good-bye to Webb, feeling, he later reported, somewhat foolish. He remembers standing in front of the bank of elevators, thinking, "This sucks."

5

Communitas

ON SEPTEMBER 8, 1994, at the Mott Haven Community Center in the auditorium of the Eastside Settlement House at 375 East 143rd Street in the Bronx, the New York State Urban Development Corporation (UDC) held a public meeting about its financial support for the mill project. Two weeks earlier, it had filed a general project plan for the Bronx Community Paper Company and printed a notice in several papers stating that the plan was available for inspection at its office in midtown Manhattan and that copies and digests of it would be made available without charge to anyone who wanted them. Few people had seen the notice and to make matters worse the meeting was scheduled for noon by the UDC's project manager. Not only were most local people at work but the somewhat poor press coverage and poor timing, together with the inconvenient scheduling, charged the ambient paranoia that had evolved over decades of having garbage dumps and other large, unsavory projects ramrodded past neighborhood objections.

Rick Soto-Lopez called up the people at the South Bronx Clean Air Coalition, who told him they felt they were being hoodwinked. Soto-Lopez, like Hershkowitz, tried to explain that both the economics and science were good on the project. But his entreaty fell on deaf ears. Worse, he said, some of them "set out to disrupt the meeting." The meeting turned into a circus—and one with a nasty, violent edge. Hershkowitz couldn't attend (he was in Sweden meeting with people from MoDo), but Rivera was there, as were Tim Martin and Soto-Lopez, who at that point was attending law school at Rutgers and serving as a member of Banana Kelly's board. The meeting, which was attended by a few members of the South Bronx Clean Air Coalition and a scattering of neighborhood activists, ended almost as soon as it began, because when Tim Martin, the Greenpeace radical, began to make his presentation, someone shouted at him, "Shut up, you white motherfucker." Then people started yelling things about pollution, asthma, and greedy interlopers. Looking back on the incident after some time had passed, Martin told me that although he had the feeling that "a lot of the fracas was posturing," he nonetheless considered it a strong possibility that someone was going to smash his head with one of the auditorium's fold-up metal chairs. So he moved to the side of the room.

Shortly thereafter, the meeting's organizers decided to break it up and reconvene at a later date. On the street outside the building, however, a man approached Rivera and put his hands on her face in what Soto-Lopez felt was a threatening way and started to say insulting things to her. When Soto-Lopez stepped forward to put himself between the man and Rivera, he pushed Soto-Lopez fairly hard and things looked like they were about to escalate, but just at that moment some cops (whom someone had called when the meeting began to turn ugly) showed up and escorted Rivera and the rest of the would-be speakers to the subway.

Soto-Lopez, who, though still young, had been working with neighborhood groups since the mid-1980s, recalled how he interpreted what had transpired that evening. "The South Bronx Coalition folks and some of the others had been fighting the ninety-nine-year lease that the Cuomo administration had given Galesi to develop the yard, and they themselves were looking for involvement with urban development. So then comes Banana Kelly with their project and complicates things. I kept pointing out how the thing itself was beneficial for everyone in the Bronx, but these are militant people who are older than me. I'm a city planner. We weren't trained the same way." Soto-Lopez was a teenager living in the South Bronx when that part of the borough started to burn, and his father moved his family to Co-op City, but he can remember when small industries thrived in the borough. His father worked as a foreman for Eastern Rolling Mills, which made industrial sheet metal, and all his uncles worked in industries in the South Bronx. "But his company left. They all left," Soto-Lopez said. Part of the reason he does the work he does is that he hopes there might be a chance to rebuild the blue-collar neighborhoods of the city.

"But even so, the thing was I didn't take even NRDC's word for it that this thing was clean; I sent it to some independent colleagues in Puerto Rico who were beyond reproach and had no stake of any kind in what happened; they said there was nothing wrong with it. But the people protesting had another agenda. Their methods chased people like me, sympathetic people, away. I worked for well over a month to try to set up a local meeting so the South Bronx Clean Air Coalition folks could meet with the scientists from Puerto Rico and discuss their findings. But they boycotted them. They had it already set in their minds that they were going to fight this thing come hell or high water. They wanted a piece of the pie. They just didn't care that this project was about changing the culture, changing the industrial patterns that are essentially choking us to death, utilizing land in a more productive fashion. Getting it done—that is, *really, really* changing things for inner-city communities and getting beyond the BS."

A second meeting convened three weeks later by the Urban Development Corporation at the large Veterans' Memorial Hall of the Bronx County Courthouse provided a fair opportunity to get "beyond the BS." This time it was better publicized and planned. It took place at six-fifteen P.M. and Rivera helped get word out that people who thought the project would benefit their community should show up—and 250 of them did.

Unfortunately, whatever positive feeling may have emerged from that second meeting was nearly entirely eradicated by yet another large public information hearing held three months later on December 9 by the New York State Department of Transportation. It was a so-called public scoping meeting, held to discuss and get the community's input about environmental issues that were being evaluated in the BCPC's Environmental Impact Statement. This meeting was not actually required by law but was held at Hershkowitz's urging, in large part because of a lawsuit that had been brought in August against the project's landlord—the New

York State Department of Transportation—and its lessee, Harlem River Yard Ventures (Galesi), by the South Bronx Clean Air Coalition and a handful of other community groups and individuals who alleged that adverse environmental impacts would result from the development plan then proceeding at the yard—in other words, the mill. But it was also held because Hershkowitz still clung to the conviction that, if he just presented everyone with the scientific facts and made the progressive goals of the project clear enough, if he let Phil Sears, the smart, sophisticated environmental planner whose round face radiated good sense and kindness, and Mike Gerrard, one of the most respected environmental lawyers in the state, who with Sears had worked on the Environmental Impact Statement, explain the benignness of what they were doing, if he just made the whole process transparent enough—everybody would see things in a different light.

But that was not to be. Despite the fact that the meeting itself was unusual and that the information presented during the environmental review process had been translated into Spanish, the principal language of most of the community's residents, and that it had been well publicized and scheduled for a convenient hour, suspiciousness and hostility once again set the tone of the evening. Lurking behind some of the ill feeling now, of course, was the lawsuit, a new group of out-of-borough ideological opponents, and perhaps the full weight of the history of the Harlem River yard. The paper mill ultimately had gotten caught in the crossfire in some of the community residents' fight against the larger powers they felt had once again pushed them aside: Galesi, the DOT, and finally, the state.

This frustrated group was eventually to be represented by a Wall Street lawyer named John McHugh, a tall, rangy, fifty-four-year-old former U.S. Department of Justice attorney with yet another axe to grind. An avid rail advocate known in certain transportation circles as Choo-choo McHugh, he believed that the twenty-eight acres Galesi had set aside for rail use were inadequate, and he was convinced that the yard should be all rail or nothing. Hershkowitz and his colleagues first encountered McHugh in the summer of 1993, at a meeting called to address community concerns about the plans for the yard, and McHugh met with them two more times before the suit was brought. On one of those occasions, he said that he felt "inclined" to challenge Galesi's lease and that he would file the suit under the State Environmental Quality Review Act. This was a piece of legislation that was put on the books by environmentalists to give communities a larger voice in developments that affected them (ironically, the same legislation had been invoked many times by NRDC in their fights against polluting industries). Hershkowitz was now being hoisted with his own petard, in what he viewed bitterly as a perversion of the process.

He regarded McHugh's invoking of environmental principles as pure cynicism, since after McHugh had taken a helicopter ride of his own over the South Bronx, he had remarked to Hershkowitz how ideally suited the area was for an "intermodal railyard" because "nobody really lived there." Rich Schrader, who was at that point working as an adviser for the mill project, asked McHugh at that same meeting if he had a client, and according to Schrader's notes McHugh was vague. First he declined to answer, but then he admitted he was "looking for someone with standing"—although at that point he had already consulted with forces in the South Bronx about filing the suit. He later told me in a phone conversation that if the yard weren't "saved" from what he depicted as a sweetheart deal with the state, the city—indeed, the region—was doomed. McHugh was convinced that the loss of manufacturing in the New York area was due to its poor rail freight delivery system. He envisioned an economic rebirth that would follow the opening of a new full-access freight line in the city. The current plans for the yard were short-sighted projects that would create jobs for the few, whereas a full intermodal yard, he maintained, would create jobs for thousands. The paper mill could just as well be built somewhere else.

McHugh's views on the old yard's importance as a precious resource strike a resonant chord with anyone who loves trains and worries about pollution from trucks. His concern was shared by the Regional Plan Association, which believed that the DOT didn't have a coherent rail freight policy, and by Representative Jerrold Nadler and former comptroller Elizabeth Holtzman, who had issued a report critical of the DOT's privatization of the yard. But lifelong rail transportation planners at the Port Authority, the Cross Harbor Railroad, and Conrail, whom I spoke with at the time the lawsuit was brought, characterized McHugh's ideas as out of touch with the prevailing realities of the freight market in the region. Instead of helping New York's economy, his opposition to the Harlem River yard plan, they maintained, would have the effect of delaying development altogether, leaving the city with an abandoned, debris-strewn yard on its hands. Steven Berger, an investment banker and a former executive director for the Port Authority of New York, remarked that there was "no economic reason to put a full intermodal terminal at the Harlem River yard, and anyone who says there is, is either a romantic or naive. The market simply doesn't support it."

Carl Weisbrod, who by then had left the Economic Development Corporation to become president of a group called the Alliance for Downtown New York, which managed the Downtown Lower Manhattan Business Improvement District and was still keeping tabs on the progress of the mill project, was angered by the suit. Like many people watching what was happening from some distance, Weisbrod never felt the suit had any merit or chance of being won, but he nonetheless felt it was "outrageous" and "just designed to be obstructionist. . . . The suit was designed to preserve the Harlem River yard for the basically . . . misguided notion that it could somehow be the great key to transportation in the Northeast and for New York City. Nadler still believes in this." He went on, "If anything was possibly going to be able to take advantage of the yard as a rail freight site, it was the mill." One of the great ironies of the project, he thought, was that "Allen was trying so hard to make this into the best project from almost every perspective and then along come these people who once again underscore the old adage that the perfect is the enemy of the good. Because in their view, for all the perfection of this project, it wasn't perfect enough, because there was an even higher truth than even all the conceivable truths that Allen thought had to be achieved. There was something even above and beyond them and that sense of purity, as some people saw it—though it was not my vision—was so important, their *sense of higher truth was so important*—that it was worth sacrificing a project which had to have been, from their ideological perspective at the very least, *good.* I think that says a lot about development in the city."

Many of the transportation people shared Weisbrod's view and thought that the Regional Plan Association, McHugh, Nadler, and later on, to NRDC's astonishment, the local Sierra Club chapter, hadn't modeled their position on any contemporary data. Most expressed the hope that the smaller twenty-eight-acre, intermodal yard planned by Galesi would eventually work in conjunction with other intermodal railyards in the city, but hastened to add that more train access alone could not solve the region's ills. Daniel Cleary, a former general manager of the Long Island Railroad Freight Services, noted that Tony Riccio, the vice president of Galesi's Harlem River operation, was "the best advocate for rail freight we've had in New York in the past twenty years." He added, "To portray him as an enemy of economic development is ridiculous."

Riccio was commissioner of Ports and Trade and director of Rail Freight under Mayor Koch. A courtly, cautious, alert man who seems, with his mixture of civic knowledge and shrewd political acumen, to have popped directly off the pages of Lincoln Steffens, he had known McHugh for years, and considered himself a train buff. "But when John argues that we've lost rail and because of that we've lost manufacturing, he's dead wrong," he says. "If rail were the only reason New York lost business, we would have built rail lines all over the place. There are companies that *have* rail access and still leave because of labor issues, because cheaper land is available elsewhere—for all kinds of reasons. Rail doesn't drive business; business drives rail. John really believes in what he says, but we're not rogues out to destroy the system. Did rail freight fail because of some Machiavellian plot or because we're such a fast-paced society and want everything door-to-door? Trains have schedules. By contrast, I call up a trucker, he's there." Our conversation took place at the time of the lawsuit, before which Riccio had been feeling optimistic about the progress of the project. Any lawsuit had a chilling effect on development plans, of course, and the politics of the whole thing was making Riccio feel gloomy.

"What we're trying to do with the Harlem River yard is to bring back rail in an efficient way. If the demand were here for a full rail-yard, do you think this valuable piece of property would have remained fallow for nearly twenty-five years?"

McHugh's clients in the contesting lawsuit were for the most part members of a handful of grassroots Bronx organizations, the most vocal of which was the South Bronx Clean Air Coalition. Its reasons for opposing the mill and the development were in fact far less clear than McHugh's, but I gathered, in speaking to several of them, that their main objection, apart from ongoing concern about potential pollution problems in their neighborhood, was still to "privatization" and to Galesi himself. They had become convinced that if the mill or any other potential tenant brought in by Galesi went away, "the community" would somehow have more jobs and a greater share of whatever prosperity ensued. Beneath the surface of these convictions, however, lay a cauldron of residual rage and suspicion about any outsider coming into the South Bronx to do anything. According to the few published reports that had appeared about him, Galesi was a low-key, smart businessman who apparently only had one mark on his record: one of his subsidiary companies made campaign contributions to Governor Cuomo and other candidates in the 1989 election year that exceeded the $5,000 legal limit by more than $11,000. Riccio characterized the excess as "an unintentional accounting error." The State Board of Elections investigated the matter but found "no evidence that this violation was willful."

By the time the December 9 Department of Transportation public hearing rolled around, the South Bronx Clean Air Coalition now had the righteous indignation of legal petitioners incorporated into their public posture, and despite ongoing efforts on the part of NRDC to meet with them they continued to insist that they were being kept in the dark about what was really going on with the project. One of the coalition's members, Carlos Padilla, complained bitterly that something was being put over once again on the people of the South Bronx, adding that there had been improper notification of the meeting. "This is bullshit, you know, that's what it is," Padilla said. "We weren't properly notified. Everybody from the public that came here got in by luck." Padilla's complaint was echoed by other speakers at the meeting, who characterized the paper mill as "the death penalty for the South Bronx" and wondered why the development issues had not been discussed on TV. Padilla made no mention of the fact that Hershkowitz, who, with Rivera, listened to these accusations in mordant disbelief, had met with the Clean Air Coalition five times. Actually, this time around, notices about the meeting had appeared in *El Diario–La Prensa* on November 20, 21, and 30; in the *Daily News* on November 21 and 22; and in the *Bronx Press Review* on November 24. Rivera, who spoke at the meeting about what she saw as the real hope the mill held out for the community, had also hired a young woman to distribute flyers about the meeting in the local projects.

Padilla reserved his harshest words for Rivera. He acknowledged that Banana Kelly had done a lot for the community but suggested that perhaps its very success had made "some individuals a little bit beyond accounting to the community," and added, "We sometimes get on a level and sometimes we forget who we are."

Another member of the Clean Air Coalition, Amerigo Casiano, echoed the suggestion McHugh had made to me—that Galesi had somehow brought in the paper mill as window dressing. Casiano characterized the project as an example of "environmental racism": "What we oppose of the paper mill also is the manner in which it has been allowed to come into the Harlem River yard to sort of justify a dirty political filthy rich billionaire's plan to make money on the backs of people of color."

Since so much of NRDC's work has historically been based on allying itself with grassroots groups, and since this project itself was so focused on issues of environmental justice, the charge of "environmental racism" leveled against NRDC seemed particularly strange, though in fact it was the one that then came up not infrequently among grassroots groups focusing on environmental justice issues. The largely white movers and shakers who sat on its board were seen as an impediment to real empathy with inner-city problems, for example, and the fact that so many senior staff people at the organization were also white didn't help. NRDC's major successes, such as its efforts in passing the Clean Air Act and the

Endangered Species Act, had been directed toward the welfare of the general population; while this was well known in all environmental circles there was a certain suspicion in the environmental justice world that the Timberland and Patagonia crowd, the trail hikers and tree huggers, simply didn't have that much interest in the environmental problems of poor people, especially poor urban people. Yet another of the ironies of some of the ongoing mistrust of NRDC in the environmental justice movement was that to a certain extent, in its fight against incinerators and sewage treatment plants in poor neighborhoods, NRDC had all but given the movement its public health vocabulary in the context of law.

The NRDC lawyers who oversaw many of its legal actions were painfully aware of the not-so-subtle way racism was reflected in investments that were made in the infrastructure of cities and how poor communities suffered from that. That was why, in the late 1980s and early 1990s, there had been ongoing discussion about how the organization could better address those problems. Nonetheless, when John Adams accepted an invitation to attend the First National People of Color Environmental Leadership Summit on October 24–27, 1991, in Washington, D.C., along with five or six leaders of other national groups, he was "roasted," according to Mike Gerrard, who was there, too. At the time Gerrard was chair of the New York State Bar Association's Environmental Law Section; he would later edit a book published by the American Bar Association called *The Law of Environmental Justice: Theories and Procedures to Address Disproportionate Risks,* and he also founded a New York State Bar Association Minority Fellowship in Environmental Law, which offered summer internships in environmental law to minority law students (Rick Soto-Lopez had been among the first to win one of them—which is how he got to NRDC). Gerrard said that Adams and the others from national groups were severely taken to task for their lack of sensitivity. "They didn't say much," he added, "because it became clear that they were mostly there to be dumped on."

One result of the summit was the adoption of seventeen Principles of Environmental Justice—part call to arms, part blueprint for future political actions (Vernice Miller served as a member of the drafting committee). The principles reflected the determination of the summit's frustrated participants to right historical wrongs. Most of the principles, like Number Three ("environmental justice mandates the right to ethical balance and responsible use of the land and renewable resources in the interest of a sustainable planet for humans and other living things"), seemed drawn from a Universal Environmental Advocates Credo; others, however, like Number Seven ("environmental justice demands the right to participate as equal partners at every level of decision-making including needs-assessment, planning, implementation, enforcement and evaluation"), seemed not only depressingly grandiose and high-pitched but even counterproductive insofar as they reinforced the conservative view that enviros are out of touch with the way business works.

Mike Gerrard, defending the statement, believes that it is imprecise language that gives the statement its grandiosity; he thought it was important to remember that even if the rhetoric might be "overstated," it was meant to be read as "aspirational as opposed to prescriptive." He went on, "If you substitute the word 'stage' for 'level' in the statement, then it makes better sense. It wasn't meant to suggest that community representatives would be there at every boardroom meeting, but that they should be consulted at every stage of the project, and that seems like a good goal. This wasn't a collection of English professors in that room." In any case, after the Washington meeting NRDC eventually launched its environmental justice program with Vernice Miller as its head.

By the time of the DOT meeting, the "Principles" were a powerful and well-established part of the arsenal that community groups brought to their opposition to projects, as was a more recent Executive Order issued by President Clinton on February 11, 1994, which required all federal agencies to collect data about the health and environmental impact of their actions on minority and low-income groups and to develop policies that strive to achieve environmental justice. Along with the order, the president issued an accompanying memorandum that gave it more teeth, by identifying certain provisions of already existing law that agencies could use to promote environmental justice goals. The order, which NRDC staffers were instrumental in shepherding through the White House bureaucracy, not only reflected the growing importance of environmental justice as a social issue but also the clout of the environmental justice movement and its civil rights lobbyists, who had lent the president their support in his 1992 campaign. At long last the traditional development method for siting unwelcome and polluting dumps, incinerators, and other harmful projects in a community—"decide/announce/defend," or, as Gerrard put it in the May 1996 article he wrote for the *New York Environmental Lawyer,* "the developer selects the location, tells the world and hopes to withstand the political and legal arrows loosed by opponents"—was no longer going to work. Nowadays, Gerrard also points out, because "modern environmental law has evolved a series of sequential veto points . . . if enough people are sufficiently unhappy about a project, they can . . . sink it."

In fact, over the last twenty years not a single new hazardous or radioactive waste landfill has opened anywhere in the United States, Gerrard remarked, where there was "sustained opposition consistently backed by local government." The article goes on to offer a kind of procedural blueprint for building environmentally just projects and cites the Bronx mill as one that has striven to follow the principles in an exemplary way. A more enthusiastic champion of environmental justice goals than Gerrard would be hard to imagine and, yet, in the responses he authored for the project's Final Supplemental Environmental Impact Statement, he cited and demolished the project's opponents' claim that the proposed mill in any way violated environmental justice principles. He wrote, "The proposed BCPC project is not a dangerous facility and would not have adverse health impacts. In particular, the proposed . . . project will not cause or exacerbate any violations of health-based air quality standards (section II.1, 'Air Quality'); it would not generate water pollution (section II.N, 'Water Quality'); it would not increase public exposure to hazardous substances (section II.0, 'Hazardous Materials'); and it would not have any other adverse health effects (sections II.P and II.Q, 'End Uses' and 'Public Health')."

Gerrard further observed that "utilization of the site exclusively as an intermodal rail/truck terminal, as some project opponents have urged, would bring far greater amounts of heavy truck traffic into and through the community than would the proposed BCPC project, with consequent adverse impact on public health and safety." And in response to the charge that the development team had not sufficiently educated the community about the project, Gerrard wrote, "The project developers have held scores of meetings with the local community boards, local elected officials and other community and public representatives." A table listing more than two hundred of these meetings is appended to his comment.

From the beginning, Rivera herself had made it plain that she shared many of the general beliefs and misgivings of the people in the environmental justice movement, and for months she and Hershkowitz had been meeting almost weekly with community groups, often in basements of housing projects, to explain their aims and methods. In June 1990, Tony Riccio, two months after he was hired and even before the railyard had been chosen as the mill site, had himself appeared before Community Board 1, in whose territory the yard is situated. By the time of the DOT meeting, he had been back five more times to discuss the evolution of the plans.

Why then did people have a sense of being left out? Had several decades of outsiders disregarding the needs and rights of the community left some of its members permanently unable to differentiate between harmful projects and benign ones? Some people believed that if Galesi went away "the community would run the yard and everyone would be better off," as Gwynn Smalls, another member of the Clear Air Coalition, said to me in a phone conversation. She spoke in a vague way of more desirable options for local businesses at or near the yard. When I pressed her to identify them, she said she'd get back to me, but never did. Vernice Miller and her friend and former colleague at WE ACT, Peggy Shepard, told me that there were many good people working for the South Bronx Clean Air Coalition who had genuine fears about the project, and who simply did not show up for meetings and so didn't get to meet either Hershkowitz or Rivera—but whose fault was that? Padilla explained that he had been told by McHugh that if a full freight yard were to be built on the site, he, Padilla—who had once run a trucking company and then worked at a medical supply company—could be trained to run it. "The people from the mill are coming in saying, 'Take my word for it, the mill's a good project.' Well, it might or might not be, but we just want the facts," Padilla told me. "Hershkowitz said that they had no need to explain themselves, that they know it's safe, and that that should be proof enough."

Occasionally, Hershkowitz's ideas are couched in arcane, acronym-besprinkled eco-speak that can be fairly confounding—as it was on one occasion when he and Mike Gerrard were privately discussing a FONSI on a SNAD (a Finding Of No Significant Impact on a Special Natural Area District). Hershkowitz was acutely aware of this, and he had had many discussions with Rivera about how to address technical issues with her neighbors—how to be *heard*—and he tried whenever he spoke in public to phrase things plainly. Sometimes, faced with looks of incomprehension by his audience, he opted for the say-it-really-slowly approach, with decidedly mixed results. He desperately wanted to share his techie knowledge, and though he knew he wasn't that good at translating what he knew into everyday speech, he hoped his efforts were meeting with success. But according to members of the Clean Air Coalition, and to Miller and Shepard, he came across as "arrogant" and "condescending." The communication problem was compounded by the fact that the language in many of the official documents that were sent out was even knottier. The only official written communication NRDC got from the Clean Air Coalition suggested a level of aggrievement that might have been impossible to remedy: "The language identifying formulas and technologies . . . used . . . are not at community levels," the group wrote, "and therefore not allowing for the full understanding of the scope of the project and the proposed impact it is supposed to analyze." It's hard not to sympathize with a genuine plea for clarity and access, but in this case, especially since the lawsuit became part of the picture, it is fair to say that the group had every opportunity for clarification from a wide range of advisers, had they truly wanted it.

As if the lawsuit with its danger sign to Wall Street weren't enough, two other major unforeseen events dealt body blows to the project.

In late September MoDo, after a series of visits by Hershkowitz to Stockholm and many phone conversations, withdrew with expressions of regret. A few months later, in early January 1995, S.D. Warren followed suit—though Jim Black, Warren's vice president in charge of paper production, had joined the BCPC board as its president and director and would remain on it for several months after his company pulled out. "It was easily the most interesting project I ever worked on," Black, a genial white-haired man with a long, placid face, would later confess. In an early memo to Hershkowitz he had described the Bronx enterprise as "more attractive than any other alternative we have looked at" and warned that the project "will flounder if a strong traditional presence does not soon appear. Warren could be that presence."

At MoDo, a new management team was more concerned with the company's debt and felt a stronger urgency to improve business at its Alizay plant. During the summer there had been a dramatic flurry of excitement when a rumor reached S.D. Warren that MoDo was moving forward on a competing recycling project, the so-called Great Lakes Project in Menominee, Michigan. It turned out upon investigation, however, that though MoDo wasn't involved with the project, a MoDo employee had secretly become one of its development partners; helping to advance a competing project was unacceptable to MoDo and the employee was dismissed. When MoDo pulled out, Hershkowitz received a commitment from them that the company still planned to buy pulp from whoever developed it. But the reality was that MoDo's withdrawal as an equity investor was a serious loss; in a market as volatile as paper, potential investors always wanted—needed—to be assured that serious paper industry owners with long track records were behind a project.

At about the same time the rumors were reaching Hershkowitz about MoDo and the Great Lakes Project, the *Wall Street Journal* reported, "Scott Paper's new chief executive is cleaning house: asset sales, sharp staff cuts are intended—to regain focus in a mature market." Scott's profits had in recent years been in a slump. Phil Lippincott had retired and the new man in town was Alfred S. Dunlap, widely known as "Chainsaw Al" for his draconian methods and ruthlessness in restructuring and revitalizing troubled companies. While Lippincott had planned a restructuring involving the slashing of 8,300 jobs, or 25 percent of Scott's workforce, and the closing of some plants over a three-year period, Dunlap vowed in late June to accomplish the same thing by Christmas, arguing that though the three-year plan might be less painful, it "distracted" employees and "paralyzed" the company. By 2001, Dunlap, who had by then written a best-selling memoir promoting his take-no-prisoners approach, was facing fraud allegations by both a subsequent employer and the Securities and Exchange Commission. By the following year he and other executives had agreed to pay $15 million to settle one of the lawsuits filed against him.

One month after taking over as CEO, Dunlap announced that he planned to get rid of S.D. Warren, which had suffered a $30 million loss the previous year. Five days before Christmas, S.D. Warren sent out a letter from its Boston headquarters to all its associates announcing the completion of Scott Paper Company's sale of S.D. Warren to a South African company called SAPPI, Ltd.—Africa's largest forest products company and, with its acquisition of Warren, the world's leading producer of glossy magazine paper. With lightning dispatch, SAPPI withdrew its support for the Bronx mill. Officially, the new company said that it felt it had to recover its $1.6 billion investment in Warren before committing itself to new projects like the mill. Unofficially, it was fairly well known around the company that SAPPI's new executive chairman, Eugene Van As, had little interest in the Bronx mill's goals and was unwilling to put up with the stresses and costs associated with building it in New York.

Desperately hoping that SAPPI might be persuaded to stay in, Hershkowitz, Pulver, and Jim Black coordinated plans for a last-ditch presentation at the end of December to Van As. Even if SAPPI did not remain in the project in the same role as Warren, they hoped to persuade him to release the $15 million equity earmarked for the project that had somehow survived the sale of S.D. Warren to SAPPI. A couple of weeks before the meeting, which was held in Boston at SAPPI's (formerly S.D. Warren's) headquarters, Black had been cautiously optimistic about convincing SAPPI to release the funds. "I'm going to get this done," he told Hershkowitz. The evening before the meeting, when Black, Hershkowitz, and Pulver ate at a downtown Boston steakhouse, Black still held out hope that the door might yet be open, but by breakfast next morning he seemed considerably less optimistic. Looking miserable, he announced that his boss had told him that Hershkowitz could not be included at the presentation. "They don't want enviros at their meeting," he said, shrugging. Hershkowitz stared at Black in disbelief and muttered, "Fuck it. Again?" because the same thing had happened before — with S.D. Warren. On several occasions, senior company executives held briefings about the project and Pulver was allowed to attend them, but not Hershkowitz. It was no secret to him that there was heavy paper industry animosity toward his sort. From the outset he had encountered paper company representatives, even senior ones, who absolutely refused to enter NRDC's offices. But he was upset that the brush-off had been so absolute and had come this late in the day, when his bona fides as a man who wanted to change the relationship between enviros and businessmen, a man who had written in his diary, "For-profit environmentalism needs to come out of the closet," were so well established. "I was frankly naive about how angry they are with us," he said a few days later.

By then he'd also learned from an S.D. Warren employee that before the presentation a New York City wastepaper broker friendly with Van As, named Michael Koplik, reportedly told the SAPPI owner not to invest in the project. "Of course the project was going to take away a lot of paper from Koplik if it went through, because we were going to get it instead," said Hershkowitz. "But how he put it to Van As, I was told, was 'Don't go into this, you won't get the paper — it's controlled by the Mob and it's being run by enviros.' I was told that he just bad-mouthed the whole thing." He continued, "Anyway, after Bruce and Jim made their presentation in Boston, Bruce said Van As apparently tore them apart and that was that. No $15 million. It was only then that I understood that Jim really didn't have the authority to represent what he was representing; I was quite angry with him for a while."

With his company now out of the picture, Black could no longer be a part of the team, nor could he keep the titles he had been given—director and president of the Bronx Community Paper Company. In his May 9, 1995, letter of resignation, which effectively severed his last formal connection with the project, Black wrote that he "understood and supported" his company's decision, but that he would very much miss his collaboration with the people on the development team. "You are doing a good thing," he wrote. "You are doing it the right way and I've never been part of a group that worked with such intensity and energy." S.D. Warren's departure was a serious setback for the project, and Black knew it. He nonetheless chose to end his letter with an optimistic fortune-cookie flourish. "Eventually," he wrote, "you will be successful."

6

Banana Kelly: Slipping from Grace

WHEN THE LAWSUIT first arose, NRDC consulted lawyers from three top New York law firms, all of whom felt confident that the suit would be dismissed, but it wasn't. A lower court judge looked on it favorably and his ruling, on March 10, 1995, which invalidated their landlord's lease on the basis that the state had granted it without considering alternative options for the site, not only chilled the financial team's effort to raise money but put the mill's very future in question.

The day before the judge's decision was announced, Hershkowitz got a call from a lawyer who represented a company that had hoped to lease to the mill development team the Oak Point site, which had been rejected because it was too contaminated. The lawyer asked him if he was possibly interested "now" in this site. Hershkowitz was perplexed by the question since, as he reminded the lawyer, they already had a site. When the unfavorable decision came down the next day, however, he wondered if the lawyer had some privileged hot line to the court and had called because he knew the Harlem River yard site would soon no longer be a sure thing.

In the spring of 1995, when I first visited Banana Kelly's headquarters at 161st Street and Prospect Avenue the lawsuit had not yet been resolved. Rivera, who has a cool gaze counterbalanced by a warm, easy laugh, talked about the history of her organization and her worries about the lawsuit and the Bronx project opponents. In her office, which was festooned with commendations and photographs of Rivera with New York City politicians, she told me that she was thirteen when the building where her family lived in the Hunts Point section of the Bronx was abandoned by the landlord. The tenants, frightened but unwilling to leave, decided to try to keep it going themselves. Because Yolanda was good at math, she was encouraged to keep the building's books, and when the tenants, who were mostly Spanish-speaking, had to appear in court or consult a lawyer, she went along as translator.

"The inspectors would come around and tell everybody that their building had been targeted for demolition," Rivera recalled. "Most of the families didn't have any place to go. Many of them were single women with children, and they felt safer staying near people they knew. So we secured the front doors and patrolled the building ourselves. Somehow we survived, though the horrors we saw in those years changed us—forever. The middle-class people moved to Co-op City and Soundview, or left the state. Some moved to the suburbs. Then the demolition began and we knew who was left behind because we could see one another more clearly as the buildings began to go down.

"Father Gigante, who was the priest at my school, Saint Athanasius, did a lot of organizing, but the great neighborhood heroine was . . . a woman named Maria Estela. She inspired women like my mother, who was in most ways a typical Latino woman—taking care of her kids, going to church—to become leaders."

Maria Estela was working with many buildings and tenant groups in 1972 when she was murdered—shot at point-blank range. In the neighborhood there was speculation that the landlords or other political forces got together and had Estela killed, and Rivera still believes that they did. "Officially, it was reported that someone she had contracted to do some work for her who hadn't been paid killed her," Rivera said. "The man was never caught."

Rivera, who graduated in 1976 from Lehman College, where she majored in health education, went on to describe how all through the 1970s the buildings in her neighborhood were burning. "Two or three times a week at night you would be awakened by the fire engines. Then you'd go to the rooftop and see where the fire was. But even when the building was saved and you went behind the apartment doors, that was the horror—when you saw the conditions people were living in. In our building, someone stole the boiler one winter. It was obviously someone who had the key, and it was obviously something planned to get us out of the building. We went without heat that entire winter. My mother boiled pots of water all the time, but it didn't matter how many clothes you wore, you always felt like the cold was running through you. In school the first two hours in class were really to thaw out—for many of us. But the nuns were relentless. They would not let us use our situation as an excuse for not performing."

Rivera married the same year she graduated from college. She and her husband had two children and moved to Old Saybrook, Connecticut, where she worked on housing matters for the Connecticut Superior Court. The marriage broke up in 1990. Since then Rivera had divided her time between the Bronx, where she lived in a small apartment on Intervale Avenue furnished with a futon, a table, and some chairs, and Connecticut, where a housekeeper took care of her children until the weekend. Even when she had lived in Connecticut full time, however, Rivera worked for Banana Kelly, and she became its chair in 1985. By then it had expanded far beyond the confines of Kelly Street. "We began to think how people walking down our street were going to feel in the years to come," Rivera told me. "We knew that we had yet to crack the one problem that kept the people we worked with from leading full lives—the lack of jobs."

When I met her in 1995, Banana Kelly managed forty-one buildings and was helping residents buy and rehabilitate apartments; it had an excellent reputation. Despite its successes, and those of other South Bronx community development groups, anyone walking along 161st Street toward Prospect Avenue, or along Longwood Avenue—streets that abut Banana Kelly's main office—could not fail to grasp that the South Bronx still had far to go. The renovated buildings and patches of grass were there, but so were the festering piles of garbage and the boarded-up buildings. According to the 1990 census, the South Bronx, with its almost 20 percent unemployment rate for men, was the poorest part of New York. Rivera expressed considerable bitterness about the South Bronx Clean Air Coalition's opposition to the mill. Initially, she had hoped that there might be a way to work things out with the project's opponents, but she no longer believed that. "They're entitled to their opinion, so I listen to them," she said. "They told me they hated Galesi. They said that he belonged to the Mob. I told them there was absolutely no indication that this was so. I've fought the Mob all my life; they've threatened me on construction sites and when we moved into areas where dealers were. I'll *never* have anything to do with those people. But I said, 'Okay, you don't like Galesi. You're an advocacy group. Do you have a plan?' No, they didn't have another plan. Not one of them has been involved in developing anything. It's intelligent to question things, but you're supposed to test your doubts rationally." (One state senator, whose district includes the mill site, responded to the project's critics by taking a practical approach. He invited two professors who teach paper-making technology at SUNY's College of Environmental Science and Forestry in Syracuse to report on the kind of technology to be used at the mill at a community meeting at his office. When the professors gave the mill's technology high marks, the senator decided to give qualified support to it.)

Earlier, Rivera suggested to me that one reason for the strong opposition to the project was gender related. "The problem in general I think is we can't have a *woman* come up with a project that benefits so many when we've been able for so long to do so little with so much. How can *she* pull this off and do so much with so little?" Another longtime South Bronx Latino politician and veteran of political turf wars characterized some of the opposition more bluntly. *"Quitate tu, ponerme yo,"* which translates, roughly, as "You get out of the way so that I can take your place."

But while the mill's opponents may have had their own reasons for continuing to fight it, it was also true that ever since Rivera had taken over Banana Kelly it had had serious management problems, and although Hershkowitz and the rest of the development team, not to mention most people in the outside world, were unaware of it, the organization that had been celebrated for its integrity and good work for more than a decade and a half was suffering from ongoing demoralization.

Although they still talked nearly every day, and sometimes several times a day by phone, Hershkowitz and other people on the mill team were finding it frustrating that Rivera often didn't respond to important faxes or voice mails. To remedy the problem, Hershkowitz took to regularly sending messengers with papers that needed Rivera's signature up to Banana Kelly's headquarters and asking them to wait until the papers were signed and return them by hand. Rivera tended not to show up at crucial meetings, or to arrive with extra people who were unknown to the others at the meeting—which made a lot of her project-mates, especially the business people, nervous. He found himself frequently making excuses for her but continued to want to believe that her attention was probably more fully focused on Banana Kelly's everyday business.

But big problems were surfacing on Banana Kelly's own turf, problems so worrisome that Anita Miller, who had recommended Banana Kelly to Hershkowitz so highly, had dropped the agency entirely from her Comprehensive Community Revitalization Program. When I asked Rivera why she was no longer in Miller's group, she answered vaguely, suggesting that it was too bureaucratic and "interfered too much" with the way Banana Kelly liked to operate. But Miller's program was a bottom-up organization. It was not at all bureaucratically overloaded and Miller had a reputation for being fair, supportive, and good at what she did; the real problem, according to Miller, was that CCRP's advisory committee, made up of their funders, began to see audits of Banana Kelly and they discovered big auditing problems; the management of the buildings was "horrendous," and there were too many disputes with tenants saying they'd paid their rents and Banana Kelly saying they hadn't. The advisory committee found out that the man who was supposed to be doing outreach for the mill project—and the organization had received grant money for that purpose—had actually been told to work in housing management. At one point, CCRP offered the services of a well-regarded consultant to help them clean up their management act. Rivera seemed to accept the idea, but when Miller suggested that Rivera meet with the consultant and outline the scope of work that needed attention, Rivera suddenly stopped answering her phone calls. By the end of 1993, the second year of Banana Kelly's participation in the program, it also became apparent that they weren't coming up with a strategy for the community plans they wanted to develop as part of the overall mill project. Miller also worried that Banana Kelly's computers were inadequate to handle the millions of dollars that poured in and out of the organization. When CCRP offered to replace the computers, Rivera said they didn't need them.

By 1994, Miller's organization had spent many thousands of dollars trying to help Banana Kelly with their neighborhood projects, but unlike all the other groups receiving CCRP's support, Banana Kelly didn't seem to be able to use the money to solve their problems. For a while, a woman with strong managerial skills named Wendy Seligson was brought in as president of Banana Kelly, but she, too, was soon gone. Then, toward the end of 1994 a theft of some money occurred at the headquarters. Miller asked Rivera if they had reported it to the police. Rivera at first told Miller that they had and then said that actually the suspected person was out of the country. They'd report it when he came back. For the people at CCRP, that was the final straw and Banana Kelly was formally dropped from its list of grantees. "You have millions of dollars in rent receipts around and someone steals from you — unless you report it to the police it's open season for anyone tempted to do the same thing," Miller, recalling that period, said in a phone conversation several years later. "It was a difficult, disappointing experience. She was simply not able to build a sense of teamwork, unlike her predecessors, with whom my relationship went back twenty years."

I must have had four or five long talks and several meals with Rivera, and on none of those occasions did she mention those predecessors. One was Harry DeRienzo, a Bronx-born, blue-eyed neighborhood youth worker who was Banana Kelly's first director and left in 1981 to run another nonprofit housing foundation, which he still heads, and the other was Getz Obstfeld, a community organizer who took over from him in 1982 (after a brief period when someone else ran it) and ran it until 1991. Rivera didn't actually say that she'd been responsible for all of Banana Kelly's past successes, but if you didn't know that DeRienzo had helped start the organization and made it into a vital nationally admired community development group and left it with $100,000 in the bank free and clear, or that Obstfeld turned it into an equally well run but far larger organization which, when he left, had $1 million in unrestricted cash reserves and a million more in foundation or development fee receivables, you might conclude, as many reporters who interviewed Rivera did, that most of the credit for Banana Kelly's successes belonged to her.

Rivera is an articulate, passionate woman and few people she encounters in the course of her travels in the business or nonprofit world fail to be impressed by her intelligence and eloquence. When Jim Black was working on the project with her, he said he was amazed at her ability to turn hard-nosed business types around. At one meeting about the mill with some of his paper company colleagues who had arrived "basically thinking this was some kind of ultra-left-wing experiment," she looked around and began her remarks by saying, "We're a nonprofit company, but what you don't understand is that nonprofit doesn't mean we don't make any money, it just means that we don't pay any taxes." Black laughed. "And, bingo, all the business types just sat up in their chairs. She could do that."

But former employees of the organization and people familiar with Bronx politics paint a picture of an epically disorganized leader who couldn't admit mistakes, someone who tended to fire competent people who worked for her and hire incompetent people because she thought she could count on their loyalty, someone whose pride consistently got in the way of addressing serious management problems that affected her organization and the people it served. According to DeRienzo, Rivera assumed her position after a threatened takeover of Banana Kelly by someone associated with Ramon Velez, a major Bronx housing and social-network kingpin, who along with Father Gigante controlled and ran fiefdoms as absolutely defined (and in earlier years nearly as bitterly contested) as any medieval city-state. Banana Kelly's turf lies in between that of Gigante and Velez, and in 1985 Velez, casting his eye hungrily on Banana Kelly's burgeoning government and foundation patronage, tried to edge his way into Banana Kelly and take over the organization via one of his operatives. He failed. Apparently the Velez people approached a number of board members stressing Obstfeld's lack of Latino street credibility, and told them that if they voted to fire Obstfeld, they could then hire Velez's man and run Banana Kelly themselves. Instead the board ousted the Velez-friendly people, and on Obstfeld's recommendation made Rivera the chair. Obstfeld remained as executive director. Harry DeRienzo himself is half Irish and half Italian, but he was born in the neighborhood and is married to a black woman, and nobody would have considered challenging him.

The Velez episode had made Obstfeld realize, DeRienzo told me, that though he had experience doing community work in Rhode Island and his mother was a Brooklyn landlord, as "a white guy from Westchester, he was vulnerable and he needed somebody local to come and be part of his leadership structure so that he could continue doing what he was doing, which he was doing *very* well, especially at that time—he was developing the concept of sweat equity in the buildings he was working with, and he was the one that made that happen." Rivera, a Latina, seemed like a good candidate. Shortly after she began her new job she asked for and was granted a salary, so she could take a more proactive part in the organization and in running certain programs that were not board responsibilities. Until then, she had served as one board member among many and had only appeared intermittently from Connecticut. According to people who were around at the time, however, Obstfeld began to be edged out little by little. Obstfeld claims he left because he felt it was time to move on, but many saw it differently.

Shortly after the attempted Velez coup, Banana Kelly called in a Washington-based group, the National Center for Housing Management, to make sure, Obstfeld told me, that the organization would be better protected structurally from similar moves. A group that stressed self-reliance and tenant responsibilities (as did Banana Kelly) and "giving back to the community"—which included mandatory attendance at regular meetings for house owners who had been given their houses through sweat-equity contracts—the National Center for Housing Management was regarded as useful by some community development groups but despised as phonily touchy-feely and quasi-fascistic by others. Banana Kelly used their services three times: the first time was after the Velez incident when they did an internal analysis of the organization, organized some staff retreats, and made a series of recommendations that included the suggestion that Obstfeld be included among the board members. Most of the staff thought it was a waste of time but Obstfeld thought their advice was "of some value."

Then, in the early 1990s, Banana Kelly was growing so fast, he said, that he felt they needed to do some serious restructuring. They called again upon the National Center for Housing Management, and an "antidependency" pilot project was set up, financed and hosted by the Morgan Bank. This project attempted to help Banana Kelly deal with a whole range of social services as it got more involved in working with clients who needed them. At the same time it stressed the value of discussing the ills of the welfare system and the importance of contributing practically to the community. These tools were intended to avoid the kind of demoralization associated with the welfare culture among Banana Kelly's former homeless clients who had been given houses. This was well before Newt Gingrich and company began sounding this credo as a cornerstone of their policy but it was even then considered politically incorrect. Everyone said to Obstfeld, he told me, "'Don't do it—the dark side is going to use it'—and the conservatives did co-opt and subvert some of those ideas, but I still feel there was an important component of that project. You can't build a strong community without the help of more of its numbers." In the late 1980s Banana Kelly had agreed to provide housing for some families who had previously lived in the city shelter system. Some had drug problems and none had ties to the neighborhood, as previous tenants had, so integrating them into the Banana Kelly community was a serious challenge. Recognizing this, the city and other funding sources began to offer the agency more money for social services. By the time Rivera took over, there were already in place programs for drug counseling, early childhood education, immunization, and many others. Rivera hired mostly neighborhood people who at first had close ties to local residents, but eventually, as the buildings began to deteriorate and Banana Kelly failed to respond to complaints, the agency's general relationship with the community began to go downhill as well.

A South Bronx–raised man named Aureo Cardona, who had

grown up with Rivera, oversaw the National Center's work with Banana Kelly. Over the coming years, Cardona was to play a role in Banana Kelly's affairs that was ever more central.

In the early 1990s, in its third sortie with Banana Kelly, the National Center organized a major overhaul of the community development group. As part of a radical reorganization and restructuring of Banana Kelly, many people were fired, and the people who were brought in to replace them, according to staff members who were there before *and* after, were far less competent than those who had been let go. "A lot of people got hurt," says Obstfeld. After Obstfeld left, there continued to be, as DeRienzo described them, "a number of purges where, wholesale, people were fired and new people brought in."

The issue, he suggested, was control. Periodically, in nearly all small community groups, there are problems with corruption or ineptitude and both DeRienzo and Obstfeld were faced with them. But, as DeRienzo put it, "You take responsibility for what happens . . . if you're so firmly in control that you're continually firing people and hiring new people . . . you basically destroy institutional memory. . . . You rewrite your own history, plus you want to make sure no one gets too vested in outside contacts and relationships because in the end . . . you've got to be the one—people have got to deal with you . . . But you can't have it both ways. You can't have absolute control and then turn around and blame other people."

Obstfeld said something similar and suggested that many of the problems that would grow exponentially over the next years were related to the frequent putsches: "The turnover was extraordinary, and she brought in people for positions in which she needed highly professional people, and they were instead people whose only qualification was loyalty. You can go down real fast doing that. We were doing fairly sophisticated work with complex government contracts and it's very staff-intensive, particularly in two areas where you have to be on it every day—management and construction. Those two areas required highly skilled people."

One of the highly skilled people who worked under both DeRienzo and Obstfeld and briefly under Rivera is Felicia Colon, who now runs a private South Bronx housing management firm.

At Banana Kelly, where she was an employee for nearly thirteen years, Colon held a number of key jobs, one of which was as bookkeeper. She is known for her terrific memory. Obstfeld told me that she "could give you today, to the penny, what the bank balance was in 1977." DeRienzo, too, mentioned Colon's capacity to remember facts and figures. "This is a lady where you can say, 'Felicia, did you send their check?' And she'll say, 'Oh, yeah, I sent it out. It was check number 35863522 on January 22.'"

An energetic, cheerful woman who is now in her late forties, Colon spoke with nostalgic pride about her earlier days in the organization, its *esprit de corps,* and the way DeRienzo turned a shoestring operation into a national success story. She remembered him "sitting in bureaucrats' offices all day not taking no for an answer" when he needed some help for Banana Kelly. DeRienzo embodied all the traits Hershkowitz rather too optimistically assumed would be shared by any grassroots leader. He was, Colon said, someone who tended to put the needs of the people around him before his own. When Obstfeld first arrived, she recalled, he seemed nervous about his white guy-ness among so many Latinos and blacks and tended to try to act "a little tough." But he soon relaxed, she said, smiling, and the staff worked very well together, "and we still work together in business today." Everyone I spoke with, including Colon, praised Obstfeld for his leadership in helping the organization expand so successfully and for his attention to details, including the books.

The National Center for Housing Management's efforts on behalf of Banana Kelly cost the organization over $100,000, Colon told me, and in the opinion of several ex-staffers I spoke with, left a sense of disarray and lack of focus that never got better. But most people attributed the growing woes of the organization not to any outside factor but to management problems within. A former staffer, who worked as a legal specialist and lived in a Banana Kelly–managed building, told me that over the next years the organization's houses on Westchester Avenue, on Beck Street, and even on Kelly Street, started to deteriorate seriously, and tenants complained that repairs, despite court orders from judges, were left undone. The litany of complaints from Banana Kelly tenants I spoke with sounded all too familiar: ceilings collapsing, huge garbage piles festering for months in unrented apartments, rats, insufficient heat, and drug addicts, formerly so carefully screened out, occupying apartments in what recently had been well-run buildings. Moreover, around the office there was a suspicion that money that was supposed to be going to the houses was being used for other things and allegations that some of the money was being used for Rivera's personal expenses. None of this was known at the time by Hershkowitz or anybody else on the mill team, but, by the mid-1990s word was beginning to trickle out that something was amiss with the former shining star of the community development world.

On the one hand, Rivera's association with NRDC and the multimillion-dollar industrial project was garnering Rivera favorable press coverage (including mine) and national and even international speaking invitations. On the other, tenants' complaints seemed to fall into a black hole and a number of Banana Kelly's buildings lost tax abatements worth many thousands of dollars because standard application forms weren't completed. By the end of the decade Banana Kelly would lose most of what DeRienzo and Obstfeld had worked so painstakingly for: its home-weatherization program (because it failed to produce the audits the state demanded), its youth program, its good name with creditors, and, little by little, the very core of its reason for being—its houses.

But none of this came to the public's attention until the late 1990s. Unaware though Hershkowitz may have been in 1995 of the internal turmoil at Banana Kelly, the continuing problems everyone had just getting Rivera on the phone or wresting important paperwork from her office began to become a more and more serious issue. Rick Campbell, working with Bruce Pulver on the financial structure of the project and, as a lawyer, seeing the necessity of having a more orderly paperwork processing system, suggested to Hershkowitz that a more available operating officer needed to be installed in the Bronx Community Paper Company's structure. Thus it was that, instead of being co-chair with Rivera, Hershkowitz became the BCPC's president and could sign off on some documents on his own.

As that year went on, however, juggling the demands of more

than fifty city and state agencies and scores of project companies and trying to shield Rivera from the steady hum of grousing about her that was coming at him from many directions, Hershkowitz began to worry about her basic incapacity to respond to what was being asked of her. Toward the end of 1994 the development team had brought in a mediator to try to help address some of the communication problems. Jonathan Rose's staff at Affordable Housing Development Corp., based in Katonah, New York, tried to work with Banana Kelly's staff to better organize their files and improve management skills. For months the project team had been asking to see Banana Kelly's business plan and pro formas for the community projects—the joint learning and health care center, the dormitory for homeless high school students, the daycare center, and the others—but they never showed up. Rose prided himself on the high degree to which the community he worked in was included in his own development projects; at a recently completed building his company had worked on, his team had just hung around a local luncheonette with their blueprints open on the table, and people were invited to scrutinize them. Early on, he had sounded a note of alarm because he'd noticed that Rivera seemed to be more interested in consolidating her power than in sharing it, as they so crucially needed her to, and he had the theory that her opponents were expressing their own power in the only way they had traditionally been allowed to, by trying to stop the project.

A new computer helped a little and the mediation cleared the air a bit, but, as time went on, the full-throttle enthusiasm that Hershkowitz felt for Rivera dampened as what had at first seemed to him a kind of benign ineptitude gradually began to look more serious. It took a long time, however, for him to relinquish his early high regard. Then one morning he got a call from a U.S. Treasury Department official, who wanted to confirm that Banana Kelly had a contract to receive some money from MoDo and asked him exactly when the agency was going to receive it. Rivera was apparently applying for grants from the federal government as if the mill were a done deal. Although at that point MoDo was still planning to market some of the mill's paper, this was long after they had pulled out and Rivera knew it. Hershkowitz had to tell the official that there was no contract and, furthermore, whatever money would be flowing to Banana Kelly would come at closing—an event that was not even remotely on the horizon. Rivera had been trying to leverage a federal grant against nonexistent income from the project. As he carefully explained the facts to the man, who maintained a neutral tone, Hershkowitz stared out over the rooftop cityscape outside his Chelsea office. Disappointment and unease followed him all the way home on the train and, when he talked to Meg about the conversation that evening, various unpleasant legal terms came into his head, hung there for a moment, and gave him a bad night's sleep.

7

Looking for Mr. Good Paper

THROUGHOUT THE SPRING of 1995, the lawsuit challenging their landlord's lease had not yet been resolved, and the appeal of the lower court's finding had not yet even been scheduled to be argued before the appellate court. Although these uncertainties left a huge cloud hanging over the project as well as a question mark about its viability for an already leery investment market, it also provided a great excuse for the state of limbo MoDo's and S.D. Warren's departure had left things in. While Hershkowitz and Co. scrambled to find a new owner and operator, they could proclaim with a certain amount of justification that it wasn't that the project per se couldn't attract a paper company or investors but rather that the enterprise was in a state of suspended animation because of its legal status—soon, they all hoped, to be favorably resolved. When anyone asked, "How's the project?" Hershkowitz could answer, truthfully, that it was on hold until the judges ruled. This was extremely convenient, because at the moment they hadn't the faintest idea who might take over from the two companies.

On February 10, 1995, Bruce Pulver and a few others, including Hershkowitz, made a presentation to the president and executive vice president of printing paper at International Paper (IP), the largest paper company in the world, based in Purchase, New York. (They got in the front door because IP's senior vice president in charge of environmental affairs had once been a government regulator and NRDC board member.) But IP wasn't interested and said that its issues were "political." What exactly "political" was a catchword for remained unclear. It could have meant that in the escalating war between paper producers and publishers about prices and supply, they simply didn't want to add any capacity; it could have meant that the complications of South Bronx politics seemed to them too daunting, and their view of the borough was the same as Ogden Nash's: "The Bronx? No thonx"; and it could have meant that in the conservative cartel-like paper industry the idea of a wild-card, enviro-spearheaded mill with socially progressive attachments was simply too far out of the range of their normal practices. As was his custom when he met with emissaries from the high empyrean of the paper industry, Hershkowitz had prepared for the International Paper meeting by having his longish, dark mane of hair cut rather short, and he forswore his normal plumage of elegant colored shirts, dressing as conventionally as he could. It hadn't made a bit of difference. In his diary entry about the meeting that day he wrote, "No eye contact."

Not long afterward, Hershkowitz received a phone call from Michael Koplik, the New York paper broker who he'd heard had turned Van As, SAPPI's owner, against the project. Since the call came a mere two months later, Hershkowitz was stunned to hear Koplik say that he thought the project was doable and offer to help bring in another paper company, Bowater. Koplik, of course, would be involved in the paper acquisition process. Hershkowitz had met Koplik before, and until the SAPPI affair, he liked him. Afterward he had been furious, but for the sake of the project he concealed his feelings. "Sure," he said, "if Bowater is interested, that's great." After a long time, it turned out that it wasn't, nor was Weyerhaeuser, nor Georgia Pacific.

At the end of the summer of 1995 the New York State Supreme Court Appellate Division voted unanimously, 5 to 0, to reverse the lower court decision. In its decision, the court found, "Clearly, petitioners, in commencing this proceeding, were less motivated by environmental concerns than by economic, political or other factors" and stated bluntly that the petitioners' claim (that the Department of Transportation had pulled a fast one by not working harder to make a full freight railyard) was baseless, since "the DOT had every right to reject petitioners' alternative proposal which had been fully aired in public debate."

Fritz Schwarz, NRDC's board chairman and chair of Cravath, Swaine & Moore, one of the city's top law firms, had argued the case pro bono before the court, under the beautiful stained-glass dome of the Appellate Courthouse in lower Manhattan; he pointed out that "the price of this suit has been damaging delays of an incredibly worthy project." And, he added, "The more subtle price has been the perception on the part of the business community that if you can't rely on the stability of a lease like this it is going to deter people from doing business with the government or from entering into leases that involve government." Because it had been a unanimous decision, it was widely agreed that an appeal was unlikely. Rivera told a reporter from the *Times* that she was grateful for the decision and relieved. She'd been convinced from the beginning that the lawsuit had once again more to do with outsiders' interests than with the people who lived in her neighborhood. She'd first understood that, she told the *Times,* after an early meeting with John McHugh, the lawyer for the suit, and several members of the South Bronx Clean Air Coalition. McHugh kept arguing that they should find another site for the project, but both Hershkowitz and Rivera repeatedly explained there were no other economical sites in the South Bronx. At the same time, McHugh mentioned the potential bad environmental effects of the mill. "It became clear to me," she told the reporter, "that this had nothing to do with environmental issues or what was best for the community. . . . I told them that I found it incredibly maddening to think that they would stand in the way of the welfare of everyday folks. I told them, 'I hope the community never discovers what you've done here.'"

Rich Schrader, who by then had left the city's Consumer Affairs Department and was serving as a project consultant, celebrated with Hershkowitz over lunch; he, too, had spoken with the *Times* reporter, saying that he thought McHugh's arguments against the mill were an all-too-easy sell in the South Bronx. "I think the South Bronx is emblematic of all the broken promises that the government has made and never come through on," Schrader was quoted as saying. "They don't trust outsiders who promise gold and deliver snake oil."

As with many complex development projects, including those less freighted than this one, the people working on it were plowing quietly on, even while the legal issues remained unresolved. As a team, everyone was working to prepare a "book," as it is known in business — a prospectus-like feasibility-and-marketing document — to show to potential investors: Philip Sears and Mike Gerrard continued to work on the permitting; Jonathan Rose was helping open doors around the city (he was particularly helpful working behind the scenes with Marilyn Gelber, the Department of Environmental Protection commissioner, with whom he had worked before) and finding ways to work with Rivera and her director of economic development, Madeleine Marquez, on pushing to get some detailed paperwork establishing the projected costs and plans for the community projects; Pulver and Campbell were also working on business plans and feasibility studies; and Schrader continued to offer Hershkowitz the benefit of his knowledge of the way the city ticked.

Having the lawsuit off their back was a great relief for everyone and there was much clinking of glasses and congratulatory telephoning in the week after the decision, but now, of course, the pressure was on again. Among the things Hershkowitz was anxious about were two promised state grants from the Office of Recycling Market Development of $400,000 and $700,000 that were taking too long to come through. Back when the lower court's adverse decision against the mill had come down in mid-March, Hershkowitz had begun to get a sense that the state, once enthusiastic about the project, was now wavering. The fact was that at the highest level in Albany there were now widely differing views of the mill. The new governor, George Pataki, possibly the state's most aggressive conservation leader since the Roosevelts, and his general counsel, Michael Finnegan, were serious environmentalists who strongly believed in the project's goals. The governor also believed that environmental protection and economic development were two sides of the same coin and had not infrequently been known to say that to have one at the expense of the other was a failed policy.

But Charles A. Gargano, or Ambassador Gargano, as he liked to be called (he was a former construction industry executive who had been appointed ambassador to Trinidad and Tobago under President Reagan), a strong ally of Alphonse D'Amato's and a generally more conservative politician, had very different views. Gargano was chairman of the Empire State Development Corporation (a new name for the old Urban Development Corp., although both names continued to be used), through which all large state development loans and grants had to pass for approval, and he didn't have much truck with environmentalists. Like many of his more conservative colleagues who regard environmental protections as a symbol of government's overreaching power and who hold a more or less unchanging view of the environmental community as long-haired, antiwar protesting, antibusiness goo-goos, the ambassador regarded business and environmental interests as irreconcilably in conflict. Hershkowitz fervently wanted to change that view (at that point he was declaring to nearly everyone he met that "investment banking is social policy"), but Charles Gargano remained deaf to the song he was singing. Banana Kelly's long association with Democratic politics didn't help either.

According to one observer of the Albany scene, though there was honest disagreement between the Pataki and Gargano factions about the viability of the project—about, for example, how the level of equity contribution was being calculated and what the market for the paper would be—the real difference between the two camps was that the governor badly wanted the project to succeed and Gargano didn't. Certainly Gargano never shared the governor's attitude of "Let's roll up our sleeves and help make it happen." In the project's early, shaky phase, Pataki consistently went out of his way to keep it alive. People familiar with the events of the time recall that Gargano came to his very first meeting with the governor about the project with the idea of persuading him to kill it, but failed. The governor was firm in his conviction that the project deserved state help and pointed out that neither Vice President Gore nor President Clinton, who had both supported the project, had been able to help it much, and it would be a feather in the state's cap if such a large industrial project worked out. A signal, the governor decided, should be sent to Wall Street. He also wanted to let New York City know that the state was seriously behind it so that the city would be confident about giving the mill the paper contracts from the Department of Sanitation. Accordingly, the governor began working toward reserving for BCPC a portion of the state's bond cap allocation (a certain amount of tax-exempt financing allocated each year for the state by the federal government for large projects that need financial assistance to get going, such as hospitals, low-income housing, and solid waste projects).

Ambassador Gargano had arrived on the Albany scene ostentatiously and publicly criticizing his Democratic predecessors for wasting bond cap money by showering it on projects that never materialized. Toward the BCPC project, his attitude was "show me the full line of investors and we'll show you the money"—despite the fact that by their very nature, the bond allocations were intended to help stimulate interest in projects. Hershkowitz many times pleaded with state officials to give him a letter saying that the cap would be there if investors were found; after the Giuliani administration took over in January 1994 and Emily Lloyd not long afterward left the Department of Sanitation, the city was the same way about the paper supply—demanding that a paper company be locked in before they'd commit to promising to supply the paper. But the paper companies wouldn't sign up unless they knew the paper was there and wanted a letter saying at the very least that if they came in the city would deliver. There were, in fact, as many positive assurances from the appropriate city officials as there were from the state—but no letters had yet been handed over.

One of the more darkly comedic moments in Hershkowitz's ongoing unhappy relationship with the ambassador occurred at their very first briefing meeting at Gargano's New York office. NRDC's executive director, John Adams, had gone along to lend his support and Bruce Pulver was there, too, to report on the financial issues relating to the project. That morning, Pulver and Hershkowitz had met with a waste hauler named Angelo Ponte, who, as far as they knew, was untainted by the kinds of allegations that swirl around the industry, and Hershkowitz happened to mention that he would be meeting with Gargano later that day.

Ponte said, "Charlie? Charlie and I are good friends. Charlie's coming to my party. I'm hosting a party tonight at my restaurant. Will you come?"

"Sure, we'd be happy to come," Hershkowitz said.

"Great, if you see Charlie, tell him I said hello."

Adams told Hershkowitz that he'd thought that the first meeting went along moderately well until the end, when Hershkowitz happened to mention that they were exploring a role for Ponte in the project and that he sent Gargano his greetings. Recalling that moment several years later, Hershkowitz was still struck by the look of frozen horror on Gargano's face. "It was as if I'd said, 'Your mother turns tricks in hell'; that was the look I got. Then he said, 'I don't know Angelo Ponte and don't know what you're talking about.' And the way he looked at me was like, if he'd had a saber, it would have been through my body. It was unbelievable, the reaction."

After they left the room, Adams, who'd never heard of Ponte and had no idea who he was, said, "Well, whatever you just said didn't work." Back at the office, Hershkowitz brooded about putting his boss in an embarrassing position with a key state official. Maybe Gargano really didn't know Ponte, and now he'd gotten NRDC and Adams affiliated with a bad guy? After all, Schrader had cautioned him that though many carters had clean records, the industry was undoubtedly involved in a conspiracy to keep out competition. Maybe he had been overly disarmed by Ponte's grandfatherly charm. (As it turned out, he had. In the late spring of 1995, Ponte's was one of twenty-three carting companies indicted by the Manhattan district attorney's office—the result of a five-year investigation—and he was one of those who later pleaded guilty to racketeering charges and was sent to jail.)

Still, unaware at that point of any such eventuality, he went to the party that night, thinking maybe Ponte was a bad guy, but thus far no one had offered any proof that the rumors about the haulers pertained to *everyone* in the business. Ponte had never been indicted. Maybe "all haulers are in bed with the Mob" was just another one of those stereotypes like "enviros can't work with industry."

When he arrived at the downtown family restaurant, F.illi Ponte, which was close enough to the Hudson to afford a view of river traffic, he noticed a few familiar faces from the city's real estate world and then—surprise! Seated comfortably at the bar was Charles Gargano. He couldn't believe it. Pulver, standing next to him, uttered, "Holy shit!" Hershkowitz immediately went to a phone and called Adams and told him about his sighting. "Son of a bitch," Adams said. Then, as Hershkowitz tells it, he went to the men's room and who should walk in but Gargano, who took his place at the next urinal. "'That was a good meeting,' he said, all casual friendliness," according to Hershkowitz. "'Well, thank you for your time, Mr. Ambassador,' I said, and then he said, 'Keep up the good work' and he's out of there. There was no mention, nothing, about that afternoon's exchange," Hershkowitz recalled. "Is that weird? That was weird."

Throughout late 1994 and early 1995, more meetings about state involvement with the project had taken place in Albany, but somehow as time rolled by the state development grant of $400,000, the first of the two grants promised to the project in February 1994, had still not come through more than a year later, though it was badly needed. On March 15, 1995, five days after the unfavorable lower court decision about the mill had come down, Hershkowitz had received a phone call from a woman named Carolyn Bachan, the Urban Development Corp.'s vice president for loans and grants and, as such, the official gatekeeper for the grant. He and his financial advisers, Pulver and Campbell, had had a less than fruitful meeting with her the week before. Although Bachan had said that in principle she supported the project, his diary note for that day was "the least cooperative meeting of the entire project." In her call Bachan now suggested that they should try to find another site.

This suggestion was, of course, tantamount to the state's dropping its commitment to the project as it was presently conceived, and Hershkowitz fired off a passionate letter to Gargano, who probably approached it with as much pleasure as he would a rabid dog. The strategy Bachan had outlined, Hershkowitz wrote, "would absolutely assure the termination of our development efforts. BCPC has spent the past eighteen months and $2.4 million organizing extraordinarily complicated lease agreements, infrastructure engineering agreements, utility agreements . . . *all tied to this site on the development schedule Urban Development Corp. itself told us would be followed.* . . . We have been asked by UDC to bring in our development colleagues from as far away as Sweden and Boston . . .

now I'm learning that UDC's own commitment to the development plan approved at the yard might be under reconsideration."

After outlining for his correspondent his imminent travel plans in Europe for a "series of meetings with important executives of major European paper companies" (an assurance which surely fell short of having its desired effect since, as Gargano well knew, between a "meeting" and a "signed contract" lay many a mile), Hershkowitz delivered a frustrated quasi ultimatum. "It is absolutely crucial that I know immediately whether or not UDC and the State of New York plan to continue with its efforts. If this is not the case, please be advised that the BCPC will cease its development efforts and investigate all legal remedies to compensate the investors. . . ."

Although Hershkowitz never received a response from Gargano (if he had, since the letter was so provocative, it probably would have ended the project), he did receive a call not long afterward from Frank Mahoney, a former investment banker and a top aide of Gargano's and one of Governor Pataki's economic aides as well, assuring him that the state was still behind the project and that he personally wanted to be as helpful as possible. Hershkowitz had the impression, reading between the lines of their conversation, that Mahoney, like the governor, was trying his best to be helpful in a highly politicized, unfriendly milieu. There were reassurances during that call about the promised grant, too, although it would actually be another year before the checks arrived.

Throughout 1995, Hershkowitz continued to try to interest paper companies in the project, even those that had turned them down already — Bowater, Weyerhaeuser, Georgia Pacific, and Pratt (which was in fact by then building its own fiberboard mill in Staten Island). Sometimes he would meet only once with a company, sometimes he would meet many times, but for a while none bit. Most of his time and attention was now turned toward the mill, but he continued occasionally to attend conferences, both national and international, relating to his work. One of these took place in Vienna, October 15 through 19, 1995, where a pride of international waste warriors (the International Solid Waste Association) assembled at the elegant Hofburg Palace to contemplate the deeps of world garbage problems. Still cleaving to Per Batelson's dictum that CEOs didn't want to meet with him in youth hostels and that he should try to stay in the kinds of hotels they felt comfortable with, Hershkowitz had booked a room at the swank Sacher Hotel—though once he'd arrived he was given a jolt when he learned that during World War II the hotel had lodged high Nazi officials. Toward the end of the conference, Hershkowitz was preparing to leave for Stockholm to meet with officials of SCA, a large Swedish paper company, to try his luck with them, when he received a note from Eric Deutsch, the well-respected vice president of New York City's Economic Development Corp., asking him to call him immediately. Hershkowitz was in the palace basement, where the cloakroom and the organizational staff of the conference were, when he was handed the note, and when he reached Deutsch, he was struck by the excited tone of Deutsch's voice: "I have a paper company for you! A real one!" he shouted across the ocean.

Hershkowitz was by now considerably more cautious than he once was about new prospects, so he didn't quite respond in kind to Deutsch's enthusiasm. "Yeah? Great. But I'm going tomorrow to Stockholm to explore the interest of SCA." "Explore the interest of" was a phrase Hershkowitz tended to use whenever he talked about paper companies that didn't shut the door in his face after his first inquiry. In the case of SCA, the "expressions of interest" were actually very strong, involving many people traveling between continents and countries. One of those people, SCA chairman Svenker Martin-Lof, was the brother of MoDo's former president, Roland Martin-Lof, whom Hershkowitz had often met with and liked, so they were positively predisposed toward one another.

The company Deutsch was referring to was Stone Consolidated, a major Canadian paper company based in Montreal. Word of Stone's interest had been brought to Deutsch by an elegant, well-known figure in the international paper industry, Niilo Hakkarainen. Hakkarainen, a slender man with elfin features, was then in his early seventies. He had a charming, quietly authoritative air, and had run a Finnish paper company, United Paper Mills, the third largest newsprint company in the world, for twenty-one years; over that period, he had built seven paper mills and, though theoretically retired ("Niilo isn't the least bit interested in *actual* retirement," someone in the industry who knew him told me), he still kept his contacts primed and, as an independent agent, his interest in new mills alive. Hakkarainen entered the scene as someone eager to build a newsprint mill in New York and had good contacts in the publishing world, especially with the *New York Times,* and with Lord Rothermere, chairman of the London *Daily Mail,* on whose board he served. Hakkarainen had been looking around for a while for a site in the city, and had also received an expression of interest in such a New York newsprint site from Roger Stone, the major shareholder of Stone Consolidated. Hakkarainen had reached the stage of casting about seriously for a site when he had met with Eric Deutsch, who told him that there was an excellent, already permitted site in the South Bronx.

Deutsch had been handed the file for the Bronx project in early 1995 by a colleague who was enthusiastic about it when she left the agency, and despite the bad luck that dogged the project over the next months — the first unfavorable lower court decision on the lawsuit, the indictment of the haulers who were supposed to be bringing commercial paper from office buildings to the plant, the loss of the two paper companies, and the collapse of the de-inked pulp market — Deutsch remained an ardent champion of it. Time and again he returned to offices close to the command-control core of the mayor, to try to persuade City Hall to really get behind it, but thus far he had not succeeded. Perhaps the South Bronx seemed to Mayor Giuliani too far from his political base to be considered important and he had no desire to have its Democratic borough president and political rival, Ferrer, credited with any major economic coup; perhaps the fact that NRDC kept suing the city for its lax enforcement of its recycling law was too much for this famously grudge-holding mayor to stomach; perhaps, like Gargano, his irritation with enviros was too strong to overcome. In any event, when the project went on hold after the first judge's ruling, Deutsch turned his attention to another mill. The other project, a Staten Island recycling mill to produce linerboard — the kind of paper used, for instance, for shoe boxes and one of the staples of the world economy — was being built by Richard Pratt, whose family paper company was one of the largest privately owned firms in Australia. The Visy mill, as Pratt's project was called, broke out of the gate at a gallop. The city had competed hard with South Amboy, New Jersey, for the project in early 1995; by August of the same year, Visy had signed a deal with the Giuliani administration to build a $250 million plant on Staten Island. Under the terms of the deal, Visy got $28 million in city tax breaks and won a contract, without competitive bidding, to process up to 50 percent of the recycled newspapers and other wastepaper in the city.

Visy also got what some local observers considered fast track environmental approval. The plant was up and running less than two years later, though a cloud surrounded it in early 1997, when it was discovered that two weeks after the company had won the contract it had given $77,500 to Mayor Giuliani's reelection campaign—far exceeding the legal limit under the City Campaign Finance Law of $7,700. The corporate record showed that Pratt began making campaign donations in its corporate name and those of its affiliates, and because the donations were given through ten different companies, it was not immediately grasped that the money actually came from a single corporate source. Although campaign officials returned the checks without cashing them, a spokesman for the company quoted in a *Daily News* article insisted that "electoral officials . . . advised that those were legal contributions."

At first a spokesman for Visy said the contributions had been solicited, but when the Giuliani campaign official denied that there had been any solicitation, the spokesman, in a subsequent interview, said he "could not be sure such a request had been made." Giuliani's Democratic challengers in that year's election, who included Bronx borough president Ferrer, made much of the matter, and Ferrer even went so far as to say that it looked like "the worst kind of government quid pro quo since the corruption scandals that U.S. Attorney Giuliani uncovered nearly a dozen years ago." Although unlike the Bronx project the Staten Island mill did not represent a significant step in industrial ecology (linerboard, unlike newsprint and glossy paper, is generally made from low-grade recycled materials, so its mill would not be displacing any timber mills) and had no particular socially progressive, esthetic, or industry-changing environmental bells and whistles attached to it, it was still bringing a lot of money to the city and would clean up a brownfield in the process.

A spokeswoman for the Economic Development Corp. said that the Pratt deal was "based on providing jobs and economic stimulus to the city and particularly Staten Island. To suggest anything else is absurd." To justify the level of help the project got from the city, the EDC intimated that an enormous number of jobs were going to be created by the mill. In fact, the mill turned out to be so highly automated that only some 161 permanent jobs were created, and since it didn't need its paper to be sorted, as the Bronx mill did, it "actually put a lot of frontline processing workers—perhaps several hundred—who had formerly been needed to sort paper around the city, out of work," according to one city official familiar with how the city's paper supply operated. Counterbalancing this, as Deutsch pointed out, was the reality that for the first time Visy turned what had only been a recycling cost for the city (paying people to carry away its paper) into a recycling revenue. Most of the paper being delivered to the mill was waterborne from Manhattan's 59th Street pier and would thus cut down on air pollution from trucks, and because Visy accepted "mixed paper" (unsorted), it was expected to (and did) help the city save more than a hundred thousand tons of additional paper from going to landfills.

When the Visy deal went through, Hershkowitz and everyone else working on the BCPC project could well have fallen into another funk, but they didn't because Deutsch and officials of the city's Department of Sanitation were reassuring: Get this thing real, they basically said, and we'll get you the paper. The problem was that no matter how hard he tried, Deutsch seemed unable even to wrest from anyone a "Letter of Intent"—a piece of paper that assured investors that when all the project's ducks were lined up, they would provide the paper. This was another Catch-22 conundrum of the project. Investors needed to absolutely know that the paper was there—as the project's feasibility study showed it would be—before they would get involved, and the city bureaucrats wanted to be assured that the deal was there before they committed themselves to giving the project the paper.

Hakkarainen, who lived in Europe, met several times with Deutsch while the lawsuit was still keeping the BCPC in limbo and things were going into high gear with the Visy mill, but once the appellate court decision came down Deutsch understood that the one element needed to jumpstart the stalled project was a credible paper company operator. When Hakkarainen came again to his office in mid-October and said he knew of one — Stone Consolidated — that was interested in building a New York newsprint mill, Deutsch was more than pleased. As soon as Hakkarainen left his office, he placed his call to Hershkowitz in Vienna. Hakkarainen and the CEO of Stone Consolidated, Jim Doughan, had actually tried hitching up with the Visy people — suggesting that they would take the white paper the Visy people got and use it for a newsprint mill, possibly nearby, while Visy would keep the brown cardboard needed to make their linerboard. But Richard Pratt, whose strong Republican party connections reached unto George-the-father, was uninterested.

Another sharing plan was also floated at the time that was environmentally laudable (and strategically brilliant): it involved barging and trucking all the paper to the Bronx mill, where it would be sorted, and then barging the separated paper that was needed for linerboard from the Bronx to Staten Island — significantly reducing the use of trucks. But the Visy people were also uninterested in that plan. When they first announced that they were building the mill, they suggested the strong possibility that a few years down the line they might well want to build another mill, and sources familiar with Visy's business mentality told me that basically they simply wanted to keep all the paper away from the Bronx, just in case they one day needed it. People who knew a lot about the city's paper market said that in order to clinch the deal with Pratt the city had made no distinction between higher and lower grades of paper and had downgraded and priced down the higher-priced white paper going to the mill. This allegedly irritated the Department of Sanitation's director of recycling, who thought his agency — and the city — were being cheated by the arrangement, even though certain complicated financial adjustments had been made to compensate for the downgrading.

One week after Deutsch's transatlantic call to Hershkowitz, a meeting was held at NRDC's offices attended by Hershkowitz, Hakkarainen, Pulver, John Wissman, who worked for Jaakko Pöyry, the paper industry consulting firm (Wissman was preparing a pre-feasibility report about the city's paper market), Frances Beinecke, NRDC's deputy executive director for programs, and others. At the end of the meeting Hakkarainen said to Hershkowitz, sticking out his hand, "We're going to build this mill." Hershkowitz said, smiling a bit ruefully, that he'd heard that before—to which Hakkarainen responded, "But not from me." Hope-fueled, the project's engines once again started chugging; just enough money to keep everyone going was coming in from foundations like the Pew Charitable Trusts, SURDNA, and the Educational Foundation of America, and though the state grants still had not come through, Hakkarainen announced that Stone Consolidated was going to contribute $75,000 a month to cover development costs. At a second meeting, Hakkarainen brought up pollution problems his fellow Scandinavians were discovering in the Baltic Sea, and once again Hershkowitz's spirits rose—another businessman who actually worried about environmental issues! In November, Hershkowitz met with Hakkarainen in Paris, and by the end of that month Morse Diesel International, a large construction company that Jonathan Rose's family had worked with, was also approached in an exploratory way. At that point Deutsch also got them a $75 million tax-exempt allocation, though it came with a proviso: use it in three years or lose it.

When Hakkarainen saw the site he was a little worried because he realized there was no room for expansion—mill developers like to have room for a second machine that can take over production if the first one breaks down—but all in all, he decided, the time that would be saved because all the permits were in place and the other favorable aspects of the project made it worth the risk. Over the next weeks and months there was a great deal of shuttling back and forth of people connected to the project between Montreal and New York and Europe, and the project—which just a few months before had looked so threatened—was taking on a decidedly positive shimmer. It was occupying every moment of Hershkowitz's day and large parts of his night—since transatlantic calls during European business hours often came when he should have been fast asleep. An enthusiastic soccer pop and a Little League organizer, he was seeing his children less and less and was so tired from trying to keep all the project balls in the air that he found it difficult, if not impossible, to talk much about what was going on with Meg because he was so wrung out by the time he got home. A generous woman, Meg saw full well the complexity of the demands on her husband, but she sometimes wondered why additional people from NRDC weren't stepping up to the plate to help him more.

The fact was that despite all Hershkowitz's efforts to e-mail and meet with various members of the staff of NRDC, the independent way that people operated at his office continued to foster at every stage of the project the sense that this was his thing, his rather *experimental* thing, and no one else knew much about it. Some of the lawyers and investment bankers on NRDC's board, aficionados of risk aversion, admired Hershkowitz but had felt far from confident about the project from the start. They supported him, but by and large had the view that what he was doing was not exactly what NRDC did or was there to do. In a modest way the ideological rift between him and all of them was not entirely unlike the debate that developed in the Catholic Church after Vatican II when Pope John XXIII urged his nuns and priests to engage more fully with the world and more practically address the needs of the poor people in it. Some factions of the Church were horrified by that shift, convinced that a more activist, less purely sacerdotal role for the clergy was inappropriate; that's what social workers were for. Similarly, in the environmental world, there was strong resistance to crossing over the line between business and advocacy—to going beyond the role of advisers—a step that Hershkowitz so passionately believed had to be taken, lest the movement become irrelevant.

The project attempted to create something tangible from environmentalist rhetoric. It challenged the idea that government should do ever less. Endeavoring to counter more than a century of unsustainable trends in an industry that has been supported by retrograde government regulations, bureaucracies, and subsidies, the mill team tried to reduce the risks and raise the rewards for in- vestors in order to overcome the deep-seated market resistance to industrial ecology projects.

It was also true that accomplishing this was a lot harder than Hershkowitz had imagined. The suspiciousness many of the busi- ness people felt about community groups was surely not going to be helped by a full understanding of Banana Kelly's management problems, so he tried to shield his business associates from too much knowledge about it; the resentment Pulver and sometimes Rivera felt about the advice Rose gave them—though Hersh- kowitz considered him a crucially important adviser on the proj- ect—was not something he felt he could share with Rose; the ani- mosity many of the engineers and bottom-line financial types felt toward Maya Lin, who was designing the mill, however much she kept her costs down and tiptoed respectfully around their concerns, was so out of whack with Hershkowitz's pride in the esthetic heft and prestige her participation brought that he tried to shield her, too, from some of the more virulent opposition to her ideas. Some of it, of course, she could not help but be aware of.

Before MoDo and S.D. Warren pulled out, when the plan was to build a coated paper pulp mill, a tense relationship developed be- tween the southern-based Rust Engineering & Construction, the project's engineering company at the time, and Lin. Lin told me that she'd been interested in environmental issues since she was a girl growing up in Ohio and that, along with pleasant walkways and vistas, she wanted to incorporate water into her design to reflect one of the most technically innovative aspects of the project, its use of so-called gray water (cleaned up but not potable) from the Ward's Island sewage plant to provide clean water for the plant's de-inking and power needs. But the engineers, who were used to putting their machinery in the architectural equivalent of a brown paper wrapper, balked at having to deal with what they regarded as the time-and-money-wasting esthetic considerations Lin brought to the table. Her gender and race had indisputably been factors in the heated public controversy that preceded official acceptance of her design for the National Vietnam Veterans Memorial, and here, too, she felt that extra-professional issues were playing a role in her relationship with the engineers. Hershkowitz also told me that one paper company executive on the early team showed great resistance to Lin and felt so strongly about her participation that he threatened to resign from the project. At a meeting about the design for the plant, one of the Rust engineers asked Lin to repeat every comment she made, because, he said, he couldn't hear her—though he seemed to be able to hear all the other people at the meeting and I, seated next to him, could hear her perfectly well. After the fourth time he asked her to repeat herself, Lin offered no further comments. Not long after this the mill's board of directors decided they would ask Rust to take that particular engineer off the project and replace him with a woman at the firm who got along with Lin.

From the start Lin, whom most people probably think of foremost in terms of her intense esthetic vision, was in fact acutely mindful about the dangers of adding too much burden to the project. Hershkowitz encouraged her to do artistically what she did best and was always supportive, but she was leery from the outset of having anyone say, "Oh, this thing didn't get built because an artist got involved and that doubled the project's budget": "If it was going to happen . . . it had to happen in a way that would be so cost effective and cost efficient that I figured that whatever I did in the way of design could not prevent a factory such as this from getting built," she told me. "So from the beginning my goal was to make something better design-wise . . . but not impact on the overall cost. That wouldn't mean I could get it for free." To some of the development crews she encountered who didn't know much about her, she was a genuine mystery. "They were puzzled," Lin said, "and thought I was there to make the offices a different color."

In the end she came up with a series of what she called "interventions," which included maximizing daylight and using a lot of glass—since the Triborough Bridge bisected the site and actually split the two-story plant into two sections, Lin hoped to turn that to advantage by letting the people going by in cars see what was happening within and generally exposing the process to public viewing. She also included a cascading wall of water to call attention to the major role water played in the process, and a garden, a glass steam stack, and some trees—a symbolic bow to the 5.1 million trees that would be spared each year by the recycling and to the economic hopefulness the plant represented in its congenitally impoverished part of the city. Commenting on a show featuring a scale model and drawing by Lin of the mill at the Municipal Art Society a few years later, Herbert Muschamp, the *New York Times* architecture critic, described it admiringly as "low-rise, low-down . . . visually spare, conceptually rich." He noted that the design elements were "at once formal, functional and symbolic. Air heated in the glass stack powers the building's cooling system. Cool air drawn from the water wall circulates in the offices. The water itself . . . is used in the recycling. Energy is also saved by the use of skylights and louvered clerestories, which admit natural light and ventilation throughout."

Muschamp observed that Lin, who studied architecture at Yale, described herself as a designer or artist rather than an architect; many of her works, he said, could be placed in the category of public art, one that generally tended to "fall outside stylistic genres." The Bronx design, however, recalled for him the work of Charles and Ray Eames, designers whose work also tended to spill over the borders of easy definition. When someone once asked Charles Eames to define the boundaries of design, Eames replied, "Where are the boundaries of problems?" The Eameses focused on building a model for low-cost housing for the postwar suburb. "Nearly fifty years later," Muschamp mused, "Ms. Lin's clients face a different set of problems. Suburbanization has drained parts of the city of people, jobs and stability. The Machine—industrial production—has been exported overseas. Landfills are full. Clean water and air turn out not to be limitless." Solutions to these problems, he pointed out, rarely reside within the province of the artist; without her client's experience in economic and environmental matters, she would be unlikely to have a way to address them. Nonetheless, she operated, he thought, "at the place where visual metaphor and material reality intersect" and wanted the building "to send the message that the forest is now urban. It is the newspaper you are reading and millions like it, there for the harvesting every day."

Notwithstanding the effusions of the *Times*'s architecture critic (and those of one City University professor, writing in a catalog for the Bronx Museum of Art, who called her design for the project "the most important work of art ever created for the Bronx"), Lin continued to encounter resistance and irritation throughout the period of her involvement with the project. I asked her how aware she was of the problems she posed for many of the business people, and she said, "They feared that I was going to design something unsympathetic to their bottom-line operations of the paper plant."

"How masked was their opposition?" I asked her.

"I knew what they were thinking of me. They were like, Get out of here. It was frustrating at times. Information was never just handed over . . ."

One of the people on the team who was helpfully mediating between Lin and the businessmen was Jonathan Rose, who is both comfortable in the business world and more than sympathetic to Lin's environmental concerns, which he shared and focused on in his own construction projects. "Sometimes they *couldn't* listen to me," Lin said, "but they could listen to Jonathan." Lin says that because she knew with whom she was dealing she didn't really take offense, although she was wary. Rose thought that some of the problems Lin had with her detractors could have been addressed better if there were more face-to-face discussions, more trying to see things from each other's perspective. Hershkowitz, who may have been shown a more naked face of the opposition, disagreed; he thought the problem went deeper. Worrying about the potential for cutting Lin out, he had protected her inclusion in the project in the crafting of the development agreement. Because of similar fears, he had done the same for Banana Kelly, making them, in fact, the legal owners of the BCPC development project. Reflecting on Lin's experience as well as the resistance some male executives had shown to working with a Latina, Hershkowitz remarked to a friend, "The only toxic chemical this project suffers from is testosterone."

With the entrance of Stone Consolidated as a possible industry partner, and Hakkarainen signed on as co-developer, everyone associated with the now-three-year-old project felt as if the clouds had parted and the sweet day of closure was, if not in sight, at least looming. More than ever before, Hershkowitz felt that if the operation was like a flailing, tentacled beast that often got out of control, it was important that as many people as possible felt it could be tamed. So he continued to keep quite a few of the problems he encountered and some of his own doubts to himself. One of the people he had come to count on over the past year at Banana Kelly was Madeline Marquez, its director of economic development and environmental initiatives (the last part of her title had been added when the BCPC project started to get off the ground, thus far its only foray into the enviro world). Marquez had her detractors around the Banana Kelly office—some people thought she was too strictly guided by Rivera's wishes, but Hershkowitz, Rose, Pulver, and Sears found her more responsive than Rivera to their calls and faxes, far prompter in dealing with paperwork, and a generally helpful teammate. Philip Sears worked with her a lot and thought especially highly of her. A well-organized person with banking experience, Marquez always arrived at meetings prepared and could promptly come up with needed numbers. When she first showed up, the assembled suits might have looked at her masses of dark hair, long red fingernails, and purple lipstick and listened to her heavily accented speech with more than a little condescension, but they, too, soon learned to respect her, and from the point of view of economic development for local businesses (from a revolving loan fund) her part of the Banana Kelly enterprise was still doing well.

So it was with some consternation that as the project entered its new hopeful phase, Hershkowitz began to notice that Marquez, his best link to the Banana Kelly pipeline and his main hope for preparing documents and getting people up to speed about whatever topic needed to be discussed, had been showing up less at team meetings. In her place, Aureo Cardona, who'd been appearing on the Banana Kelly horizon off and on for years, at first as a representative of the National Center for Housing Management, then as someone whom Rivera brought in on her own, began to show up. Cardona had neither a banker's background nor the familiarity with the project or the consultants that Marquez had, and the only hint Hershkowitz had about the larger role Cardona would play was a strange phone call from Rivera the day before the two men first met. Hershkowitz had just returned to his office from lunch and, for the first time in months, had begun to feel that his vision now had a good shot at realization. He was staring at his photos of Meg and the kids, whom he had been working hard to give more of his time to, and the masses of papers around the office, when the phone rang and he heard Rivera's voice.

"Look," she said, "I'm bringing someone to meet you tomorrow, but don't laugh when you see him."

"Why would I laugh? Who is he?"

"Just someone who'll be helping me," she replied.

Rivera didn't offer any further explanation. When Cardona showed up at his office the next day, Hershkowitz saw a large, wide man with a major weight problem, a long ponytail, and a pale jacket, who exuded a kind of cheerful, relentless unstoppability. He certainly didn't look like anyone else associated with the project, but Hershkowitz was not the kind of man who would laugh at someone because of his appearance, and Hershkowitz wondered about Rivera's warning. Two other people Hershkowitz hadn't met before arrived at NRDC's ninth floor conference room along with Rivera and Cardona, an older and a younger man, both Latino, who headed two different Bronx housing rehab companies. At first they said they belonged to the same company, but it turned out that they had never worked together but had been encouraged by Cardona to believe that they could build the paper mill and had decided that they would do that as one company.

Hershkowitz had never heard of either of them before, had no idea that they would be showing up and, as politely as he could, explained that the hiring of the construction company wasn't his call; that it wouldn't be he, but a paper company or its representatives that would choose the mill's construction partner; that mills were a highly specialized kind of job utterly unlike housing rehab; and that industrial-scale construction, in general, was a whole different animal. He explained that the paper company would certainly be looking to a construction company for equipment, vending guarantees, and possibly some equity, which definitely suggested the need for a much larger business than they were. He felt bad for them and fervently wished he'd been given a chance to have a phone conversation about them beforehand. But nothing he said seemed to carry any weight; the men kept assuring him that they could handle the job, and the more Hershkowitz demurred, the more positive they became about it. Rivera would not meet Hershkowitz's frantic glances, and it was clear that Cardona was not happy about the way things were going.

By the end of the meeting, which lasted about forty-five minutes, Hershkowitz thought he had convinced the two housing rehab men that their hopes were unfounded, but he hadn't. When they all pushed their chairs back from the conference table and stood up, the older man kept trying to shake his hand to seal some imagined deal, and several times repeated, "I can really help you out locally, politically." Normally, Hershkowitz would shake anyone's hand and he felt deeply embarrassed, but it seemed apparent to him that the handshake was not a realistic possibility. So he just kept saying things like "Well, thanks for coming," "Glad to have met you," and backing away from the proffered hands, sidling toward the conference room door, and then bolting outside it into the safety of the office hallway.

Although he was only subliminally aware of it, Hershkowitz seemed to be joining the ranks of those whose loyalty Rivera questioned, and Cardona, whom she presumably perceived as someone tough, someone cunning, someone who would protect her interests, had, according to those who saw them together often, become the leader of her personal cadre of front-line loyalists.

Even though the community projects—the learning and health center, the daycare center, the dormitory, etc.—were an important part of the plan, the money for them was going to come at closing; meanwhile the team's attention was on environmental issues and finding investors. What to everyone else connected to the project seemed like a necessary shift in focus, however, apparently to Rivera looked like a lapse and a slight. Madeleine Marquez, who had worked together with Rivera on the project from the beginning, remembers a growing unease at Banana Kelly at the time, that "it stopped being a community project, and all of a sudden it was just business." As the project kept growing in size—in its new incarnation as a newsprint mill, it was now estimated to cost about $450 million—there was also the reality that various people—financial advisers, the lawyers issuing the bonds—would profit handsomely at the end, and according to Marquez, the subject began to come up that Rivera wouldn't be one of them. Hershkowitz had always assumed that Rivera was simply interested, as he was, in the bigger picture—of doing her community good—and that she probably knew that the $6.2 million that was going toward community projects was not an easy sell in the conventional business world. He wasn't getting any money out of the project nor was NRDC—having the mill up and running would be the payoff. But now, like some kind of dissonant background noise, there emerged an unease with arrangements as they were, and at the forefront of the new—tone? mood?—stood the somewhat enigmatic figure of Aureo Cardona.

When Niilo Hakkarainen, who was trying to sort out who the players in the project were, asked Cardona what his job was, he murmured that he "worked for Banana Kelly"—and Hakkarainen could not elicit anything more explicit, though he tried. But in fact Cardona was brought in to do what Madeleine Marquez had been doing—though for a long time she wasn't told that. At first they would both show up at meetings. Then, after a while, without explanation, she disappeared.

8

Incrementalism and a Simple Lesson in Economics

ON JANUARY 19, 1996, buoyed by Stone's interest in the project and the encouraging talks he was having with Jim Doughan, the company's CEO, Hershkowitz met with Michael Finnegan, Governor Pataki's chief counsel. Finnegan assured him that "the word no did not exist in the governor's vocabulary for this project," and that he himself would do his best to help with whatever state issues he could. Four days later Hershkowitz noted in his diary that John Adams had also just met with the governor. But back downstate, Eric Deutsch at the NYC Economic Development Corporation was still having problems coordinating the support that was desperately needed from the city. The project had already been allocated $75 million in tax-exempt bonds and needed at least $180 million more, and Deutsch had promised to ask for it. But something was holding that request up.

On January 24, Hershkowitz, exasperated that the local leadership—faced with the upcoming closing of its last remaining garbage dump, Fresh Kills—would not embrace a project that would affect the city so favorably, wrote in his diary: "Eric Deutsch couldn't get me a simple letter indicating the additional amount of tax-exempt financing EDC was requesting from the state because his boss was concerned about what its impact might be on Gargano. So I couldn't tell potential investors about this in an authoritative way; he couldn't get me a letter from the mayor or the deputy mayor to give to the president of the United States before my meeting last week at the White House with Katie McGinty, the president's chief environmental adviser, and he can't get me a letter from Fran Reiter [the deputy mayor for planning and economic development] to help coordinate support out of the VP's office." Despite all of Deutsch's avowed good will and favorable view of the mill project and the entrance onto the scene of a major paper industry player, he still could not get the city to seriously champion the project.

One of the strong bureaucratic points of resistance to the mill was the low number of jobs created (depending on the year, the estimate was 150 to 600 permanent jobs) for the amount of investment needed—especially since the city's recycled paper was already being exported. Even the Visy mill, with its owner backing and incredible political clout, had initially met a certain amount of opposition because it was never going to generate many jobs. Most of the city's bureaucratic purse strings holders were familiar with nonindustrial real estate deals. There was so little industry coming to the city that they were unfamiliar with the economic realities of industrial projects, and, it is probably safe to say, unaware of the real economic value added to paper by a mill. The sorting and baling involved in preparing New York City's paper for export basically took a $10/ton material and turned it into a $50/ton commodity. The Visy people were taking that $10/ton paper and turning it into a $300–$400/ton commodity—and the rate for newsprint was even higher—$600–$700/ton. Even leaving the larger environmental issues out of the equation, the mill investment obviously would have a far greater ripple effect on the economy.

Because of the shot in the arm brought by Stone's participation in the project, everyone was working with a renewed energy. An upbeat piece had appeared in the *Times* in December, noting that the project had signed on Prins Recycling Corp. of Fort Lee, New Jersey, to build and operate a $25 million wastepaper sorting plant on the site. In the piece Randy Daniels, a former deputy mayor under Dinkins who had become a senior vice president and deputy commissioner of economic revitalization at the Empire State Development Corp., and who consistently gave Hershkowitz a hard time and usually acted skeptical about the project, was quoted as saying, "The agreement is a demonstration of serious interest by an established recycling company and formalizes the negotiating process." Everyone at the middle and upper-middle management ranks of the city bureaucracy now seemed to be enthusiastic about the project, but a granitically resistant mood still prevailed in the highest quarters, where support was most needed.

At a January 21 meeting at the Department of Sanitation in the office of John Doherty, the well-liked commissioner of the Department of Sanitation who succeeded Emily Lloyd, there was a discussion about raw material availability, how they were going to negotiate, the kind of paper that was needed—could they take mixed recyclables, could they take other recyclables with the paper? At that point the answer was yes, since a sorting plant was part of the plan for the site. And if the state was supportive, could they help with more trucks for the DOS's increased demands for recycling? Doherty and his head of recycling and his head of waste reduction seemed genuinely eager to work with the mill team. They had been unhappy with the way the city deal with Visy had been handled: they didn't like that the contract did not specify which borough the paper would come from (and therefore wasn't dealing sensitively with traffic impact issues), they thought that the paper price Visy was given was far too low, and they generally resented being left out of too many negotiations.

The Sanitation people liked Hershkowitz and through back channels tried to keep him up to speed on current City Hall attitudes toward the project. Eric Goldstein, as part of NRDC's urban program, was at that point suing the city over its lack of enforcement of local law 19, the city's recycling statute. In Goldstein's lambasting of the mayor, who was no friend of recycling, the Sanitation people, who favored it, resented being often tarred with the same brush. In 2001, a study commissioned by Goldstein for NRDC would conclude that the department was lax in its efforts to educate the public about its recycling programs. But the Sanitation people whom Hershkowitz was working with felt that they never got credit for how far the department had come, or how complex the New York City recycling program was to run. Its public education brochures, for instance, had been published in six languages, and its operations included overseeing truck- and waterborne garbage, as well as marine- and land-based transfer stations.

To make his court case Goldstein did not stress the department's accomplishments, but rather the ways in which it was falling short of its goals. The side effects of NRDC's successfully waged law-suits—six of them, all paralleling the period of the mill project, and all against the city—will probably never be fully known. The people at the DOS claim the suits didn't affect it that much, but Goldstein thinks they were significant. As environmental advocates, NRDC often bumped heads with city, state, and government officials, he told me, but in this project they were trying to be partners with government and specifically with City Hall. "There are some places," he said, "like the U.S. Environmental Protection Agency, where you can both be in the midst of bringing a lawsuit against the federal government and working cooperatively. With Mayor Giuliani, if you're suing him, it is impossible to be a friend."

Goldstein also later came to believe that NRDC's organizational structure, which was itself in the process of transition as the New York staff grew from about 40 people to 125, was not at that point giving Hershkowitz the help—whether or not he was asking for it—that he badly needed. Hershkowitz filed regular reports about what was going on and talked to his colleagues, but ever more the coordination of the project's thousand-and-one moving parts fell on his shoulders alone. As the person coordinating the organization's urban program, Goldstein blames himself for not recognizing what was happening. Then, too, so many things had either already gone wrong or had the potential for going wrong that Hershkowitz had gotten into a mindset of Preemptive Total Alert. Even people on his own team, who were capable of handling whatever they were charged with—like Tim Martin, the former Greenpeace activist, when he was coordinating NRDC's part of the project's outreach effort—would find Hershkowitz peering over his shoulder. Martin has huge respect for Hershkowitz, but he said, "Allen was so worried about the potential for disaster that he found it hard to yield control." From Hershkowitz's point of view, of course, he felt he was already overburdening his organization with too many demands in an area, industrial ecology, into which they had never ventured and which he hoped they would embrace as a strategy in the future. On several occasions he thought he was letting people know he could use more staff help, but somehow this message was not getting through. If he minimized the level of stress and slipperiness of much of what he was going through it was partly because he didn't want to alarm them. Above all, he wanted to make this thing happen. But as Goldstein pointed out, "He was the central spoke, totally, but the spoke was being overwhelmed. It's almost like an air traffic controller—at some point you've got to go to your boss at the FAA and say too many planes are coming in."

One of the subtle realities that Hershkowitz encountered at his meetings with city officials like DOS Commissioner Doherty and his colleague Bob Lange, who was in charge of recycling, was how much the operating style of the mayor affected the way you could do business with anyone. Under Giuliani's predecessor David Dinkins, who was in office when the project was launched, the commissioners of city departments or agencies had had far more decision-making power. Now, every important decision came from one man alone. Some people in government believed that for the mayor there were, as one city bureaucrat said to me, "Only two boroughs—Queens and Staten Island—those that had voted solidly Republican. The other three were all considered outer boroughs." People such as Marilyn Gelber, the innovative and well-liked commissioner of the Department of Environmental Protection, whom Hershkowitz was talking to about acquiring the city water needed for the plant, were struggling with the transition and still tended to act as if they had control of their own bailiwicks—which eventually they found out they didn't (especially Gelber, who was fired, many think, because of her innovations and independence of spirit). At that January 21 Department of Sanitation meeting, all the parties were discussing pricing—there was never any question about the paper's *availability*. In fact, at that point, with Stone Consolidated in the wings, they were discussing moving to contract negotiations on the wastepaper supply. The next day, however, when Hershkowitz and a Stone representative showed up at the offices of the Economic Development Corp., they were informed that the Economic Development Corp., whose charge it was to bring new business into the city, and not the Department of Sanitation, would be negotiating the contract. An interagency war was obviously developing over whose baby it was. What was not understood until much later was that whenever the Bronx mill project seemed to be edging closer to realization, the Visy people would "bring in the troops from Australia or wherever they were doing a paper mill project, sit down with their good contacts at City Hall, and express alarm because their own plans for an additional future mill, they would claim, were getting more developed and they wanted to be sure of the paper," according to one city official, and somehow the availability of the paper for the Bronx project would then once again be called into question. Every city official who'd ever been connected with negotiations for the Visy project mentioned with awe the name of Helmut Konecsny, Visy's technical director and a man who was unlike Hershkowitz in any way you could think of. Konecsny seems to have possessed the kind of ultimate, driving, hard-core business mentality and cool singlemindedness that was optimal, they suggested, for steering a complicated industrial project safely into harbor.

One day later, Hershkowitz was back again at Mike Finnegan's office with the Stone representative discussing the economic benefits of the new kind of mill that they were now planning to build for newsprint—and also some of the obstacles it was facing—to reinforce the need for state support. The Stone executive noted that both on the acquisition and the "off-take" or delivery side, the savings could be considerable for his company. At that point, it cost the company $30–$40 more per ton to get the recycled paper from New York to Quebec than it would cost them to get paper and take it to the Bronx. Similarly, to deliver the newsprint from their mill in Quebec to publishers in New York cost around $50 a ton compared to the less than $20 it would cost with the Bronx project—so, in total, there would be roughly a $60–$70/ton advantage to locating in New York. As a newsprint market, too, it was pointed out, the New York City metropolitan area was peerless, consuming 1.5 million tons of newsprint a year; the entire nation of Canada consumed less: 1.2 million tons a year. As part of yet another study produced for this stage of the project, they were also figuring out job characteristics for labor negotiations, and they discussed the range of costs that Stone's executive committee had given them and that a Jaakko Pöyry pre-feasibility study had satisfied: the next step was for the project to go for approval to Stone's board of directors. While they waited for that to happen, everyone in the team went into overdrive. Phil Sears speeded up on his work getting the water acquisition issues sorted out. Tim Martin and another specialist at Jaakko Pöyry Consulting, who knew her way around the waste-paper world so well that Hershkowitz once described her to me as "the Yoda of the wastepaper supply worldwide," were struggling to obtain an assessment of the realities of wastepaper availability.

Smelling blood, the team began to try to accelerate the pace of everything they were working on even more; there were an increasing number of group meetings, and team members who had mostly been focusing on their own corner of the development plans began calling one another up more. All along the process had been evolutionary, and the question was always being asked: Who's the next player we need, the next company that is the best at what it does that we can afford? Valmet, a Finnish company and one of the largest paper mill equipment vendors, was brought in by Hakkarainen to work with Jaakko Pöyry on the mill engineering, Merrill Lynch had been chosen to be the project's bond underwriters and to work with Pulver on financial advising, and Mike Gerrard was gathering all the permitting data to have it readily available. Hakkarainen, with his several decades of experience building paper mills, was a great asset, now meeting with the project's landlord, now meeting with the Stone people, now weighing in on a discussion about the sorting plant.

Hakkarainen's good contacts at the *New York Times,* it was hoped, would help the group not only in its effort to get the publisher to take its newsprint but to put some equity in the project. Possibly because of the hoped-for *Times* input, but unbeknownst to Hershkowitz or any of the other team members, Hakkarainen had also signed some kind of agreement with a company called NAB Construction Company, owned by Gary Simpson, the son-in-law of the chairman of the New York Times Company and brother-in-law of the *Times*'s current publisher, to work on a construction feasibility report. During the same period Mary Cesar (the "Yoda" woman, who was Jaakko Pöyry's recovered-paper specialist), Wissman (the same company's paper cost analyst), Hakkarainen, Pulver, and Valmet were also busy evaluating the way the mill's sorting plant would work.

In his diary of that month, February 1996, Hershkowitz began to struggle to come to terms with Rivera's shift in attitude toward the project; one entry at that time notes that "the project was as successful as it was because it was never really about itself. Certainly never about any one of us . . . it was about commitment to the idea of doing something good. Yolanda's decline began . . . when she started to think more about herself than Banana Kelly." Somehow, Rivera now no longer brought up the community projects or the community's needs with him or talked the way she used to about her neighborhood; and more and more, with Cardona at her side, the warmth that once marked her collaboration with Hershkowitz seemed to be absent. Jonathan Rose felt that Cardona was at least a better answerer of calls and faxes and generally showed up at the meetings he was supposed to be at; Rose even had a certain sympathy for what he imagined might be Rivera and Cardona's perception that perhaps they, like the Wall Street people, deserved to have their fingers in what was getting to look like an expanding pie. But most of the other people on the team who encountered Cardona were hard-pressed to understand what he was contributing to the process. Basically, Hershkowitz believed that Cardona was a storm the project could weather. The important thing was to keep going.

At another meeting toward the end of February 1996, in Albany, Finnegan, responding to Hershkowitz's ongoing worries about not getting a solid commitment letter from the city for the wastepaper, suggested alternative supply sources: the project might be able to get the Metropolitan Transit Authority's paper, for example, which was under the control of the governor and possibly also the State University of New York's. In political circles, Finnegan was known for creative problem solving, and that same day he came up with what Hershkowitz considered a completely brilliant idea: there was an as yet untapped state revolving fund for clean water projects; with it you could get 50 percent subsidized interest for anything having to do with water *and* you could get an advance on some of the money. An estimated $42 million worth of technology investments would be needed for the mill relating to its water use and cleanup plan—and according to Finnegan there could be separate financing arrangements for that piece of the plan. Moreover, the law also allowed for some of that money to be allocated for development costs, so Finnegan arranged for a $3 million, zero interest advance for all costs associated with designing the mill's water system. Since paper is essentially water and fiber, it was possible when the money came through the next fall to use it to pay the many members of the team whose fee payments for legal, engineering, or design work, all relating to water issues, had had to be postponed as the coffers emptied.

When Finnegan went to the Environmental Facilities Corp., the state money issuing agency, which is quite strictly audited by the federal government from which it receives its funds, they were dubious, however; they were worried about defaults, especially since three or four recycling mills—though not *newsprint* mills—around the country were failing. It had turned out that the supposedly great new de-inking process that they'd used wasn't as efficient as many people thought it was going to be, and it also became clear that there was as yet no glossy magazine paper made from recycled fiber that was as bright or as cheap as timber-based paper. Beyond that, there was overcapacity in the industry. Undeterred, Finnegan then went to the state legislature and, with the help of John Adams, who assumed the role of BCPC representative and whose nationally known name carried far more weight than Hershkowitz's, worked to enlist the help of the majority leader of the state senate, the speaker of the assembly, and the governor, and they got the loan guaranteed by the state legislature.

By early March 1996, everyone was working late at their desks, the hope of getting paid was alive, and the feeling of exhilaration was intense. On March 11, at Stone's headquarters in Montreal, a sleek steel-and-glass building next to the posh Queen Elizabeth Hotel, at a meeting with Supro Mukherjea, the company's senior vice president, Hershkowitz, despite the prevailing all-team feeling of optimism, noticed two things that made him a bit uneasy. The first was that Mukherjea was looking out the window as they talked; except for Per Batelson, an unwillingness to make eye contact seemed to be one of the signifying attributes of the paper industry's captains and their lieutenants. The second was that employees of the company had to pay for their own coffee, which was sold from a vending machine, an extreme of corner-cutting that seemed pathetic to him. Somewhat enigmatically, Mukherjea also said he thought that they should publicly announce new plans for the project soon, since industrial forecasters were predicting a virtual collapse in the price of newsprint the following year. Although

Mukherjea said this calmly, the statement so unnerved Hershkowitz that that night in his diary, he wrote, "Could this be the end of
announcing the project?" and in his distress appended a misquote
from *Don Quixote:* "Fortune always leaves the door open for disaster." The actual quotation conveys, in fact, the diametrically opposite sentiment: "Fortune always leaves one door open in disasters,
to admit a remedy."

When Hershkowitz arrived back in New York, Hakkarainen,
who had seen the price of paper alternately plummeting and shooting to the sky his whole life, told him not to be disturbed by industrial forecasts; he'd learned, from his own experience, that the best
time to build a mill was when prices were low and old mills are
closing. "By the time prices rise again," he told Hershkowitz, "you'll
be on line with your cost advantage and new state-of-the-art technology." A few days afterward Hershkowitz spoke to Mukherjea
again. This time he seemed sanguine enough and told Hershkowitz
that soon the moment would come "to get all the parties" collabo-
rating on the project—which one city observer had begun calling
The Beast—together in the same room now that it looked like a
go, pending approval from the Stone Consolidated board of directors, who were voting on March 26.

The all-team rally never took place, however. On the twenty-
sixth, upon returning from the yoga class he had started attending
to help him get through the project's vicissitudes, there was a message waiting for Hershkowitz from Mukherjea. Stone's board had
voted against the project. The reason they gave was twofold: they
had originally hoped they could get all their fiber from the city's
wastepaper program but now thought they'd have to buy some on
the open market, which they didn't want to do, and more funda-
mentally, they didn't view the overall return as sufficiently attractive—it was too low. The next day, Doughan, the company's CEO,
called Hershkowitz at home to offer a further explanation. They
had decided to go to South Korea. With the Bronx project, according to the most optimistic projections, they could get a 36 percent
return; in Korea it would be 40 percent. Many months later, Hershkowitz found out that they'd lost by one vote.

9

Dancing with New Partners

SOMEWHAT DAZED FROM having plummeted so quickly from development heaven to hell, the battle-weary soldiers began to once again gird their loins and take stock of where they were. Where were they? In conference rooms, restaurants, and bars around the city, that question was at the center of a lot of earnest conversations. For some, there was a depressing sense that the hostility of the paper industry and its desire to control the paper supply was so all embracing that there was no way they were going to allow any new capacity in. Though she is not a cynical woman, Mary Cesar, the former Jaakko Pöyry recovered-paper specialist who is now the general manager of an online company that provides news and other resources for the forest industry, wondered if, in fact, any short-term interest the paper companies demonstrated in the Bronx mill wasn't simply to keep their eye on the project. "It's an incredibly old-fashioned industry, and it's not beyond the people in it to say, 'I'll throw a little money at the project and then it will go away.'" Although the sums then being "thrown" at the Bronx mill were not inconsiderable—were in fact in the millions—Cesar still thought her theory might be plausible.

"If you look at the scheme of things, if you invest ten or twenty million dollars in development costs, that's like pocket change for their capital budgets; I mean we're talking about paper machines that cost a hundred million dollars—capital budgets of billions of dollars every year. For them to throw in twenty million dollars to make a project go away is not beyond imagining—it makes it look like they're doing something and then they just shuffle their feet. I've no evidence of that here, but I've seen it often enough." Eric Deutsch of the Economic Development Corp., contemplating the project's many highs and lows from his vantage point in the financial district, had begun to have suspicions along similar lines: "Paper companies would come around and show some interest," he said, and then "they'd walk away ... they really didn't want the project to happen. They didn't want the competition." In his diary on April 15, 1996, the day that Bowater, too, formally turned the project down, Hershkowitz recorded something that one of the consultants had said to him that day. "There seems to be some sort of a pact among these producers not to add any new capacity," which was, Hershkowitz added in response to that thought, possibly illegal. A few years later, it would emerge publicly that an ever-escalating war between newsprint producers and newspaper publishers was indeed stimulating what one newsprint analyst characterized as "an intense street brawl" and "a huge game of chicken." After several decades of consolidation in the newspaper business that gave publishers like Gannett and Knight Ridder leverage that made paper companies nervous, a *New York Times* article on May 14, 2001, noted a major and swift consolidation among paper suppliers. For a while, between 1992 and 1994, supplies had outrun demand and newsprint stayed below $500 a ton. But then, as the *Times* reported, paper producers had "sudden urges to clean, repair, revamp and otherwise temporarily shut their mills for a week or three, idling hundreds of workers and reducing the total supply more than 100,000 metric tons. Call it supply-side economics." Unsurprisingly, newsprint prices began to skyrocket, going up $100 a ton from October 1994 to April 1995, and up $50 more by May. By the following October the price had soared to $740—a 50 percent jump from the previous year. By February 2000, the Justice Department would begin an investigation of possible collusion on newsprint prices, but it closed it in the spring of 2001.

At first the publishers reacted to the spike by cutting staff, closing down parts of their operations, and even cutting the dimensions of their papers by an inch or more; eventually they would try to beat the mills at their own game by accumulating stockpiles of paper and telling suppliers they would not be taking deliveries for some months. And so it went. The Beast, of course, was caught in the middle of this. But whatever whiff of it was caught by the team in 1996, it wasn't enough to scare them off. Niilo Hakkarainen stuck to his position—he had seen it all before and advised against panic and kept repeating his mantra to one and all: Build and be ready with a better technology when the upswing comes.

A somewhat more elusive problem that also seemed to be afflicting the project was the temperament and manner of Hershkowitz himself. The people who worked alongside him had nothing but admiration for his passion, his do-or-die energy, his capacity for comebacks, his prodigious mastery of every technical detail that was thrown at him, and even his sometimes unfathomable optimism. But many of the business people he encountered—cool players in an unforgivingly tough game—distrusted his ardor and positively hated his eloquent descriptions of the important environmental and social benefits that The Beast was—as they thought of it—saddled with. They might be willing to put up with it all if they could make enough money at the same time, but they rarely were that keen on hearing about it. At the hub of the project, whatever the paperwork said (and it plainly said that Banana Kelly was the owner of the development company and that various other people had important jobs), was this fast-talking, obvious LIBERAL, an ineluctable fact that most of the paper company types were uncomfortable with and Hershkowitz knew it.

Even people who genuinely liked him, like Eric Deutsch, found it frustrating that Hershkowitz didn't seem to grasp how overburdened, from a pure business perspective, the project looked, and felt that his insistence on not compromising even the smallest of his progressive goals made a good project a harder sell. Deutsch noted, approvingly, that the Visy mill's environmental review was nothing like the painstakingly comprehensive Environmental Impact Statement that the Bronx mill had prepared, and that Visy had erected the plainest of plain buildings around its machines. "From the business community's point of view, when you're building a factory, you're building a factory—the mill on Staten Island is made of corrugated metal. We would have these fights because Allen felt that their air permits had to be more stringent than even the law allowed, and so on." And though Deutsch admired Maya Lin and agreed that the burdens she placed on the project were slight, the perception was that "she was one more premium we can't afford, if you really wanted to get the thing done." He felt strongly that "it wouldn't have been such a bad idea to compromise on a few of those points, but Allen can be an incredibly difficult person . . . because he had to have it his way . . . and it was the right way. . . . Just every little thing." On at least one occasion, Deutsch's frustration with Hershkowitz reached a pitch so high that a co-worker found him literally standing on his desk, screaming at him. One of the ironies of people's reactions to Hershkowitz's habit of waxing enthusiastic about the project to nearly every person he bumped into on the street, according to Deutsch, was that a lot of people didn't really get the point of the whole thing. "They didn't understand that it wasn't that he wanted to make a name for himself and a ton of money; his underlying vision was to put all the pieces together — to put recycling and urban development together."

A lowering sense of defeat hit Hershkowitz after the Stone deal fell through, but he didn't spend much time licking his wounds. A few weeks after the turndown he was working on a Hakkarainen suggestion — to see if he could interest a consortium of publishers, including the *New York Times* and the *Wall Street Journal* with possibly some help from Central National Gottesman, a major paper marketer whose owner Hershkowitz knew, in taking over the project. Hoping to enlist a few NRDC heavy hitters at the first meeting with the publishing representatives, he phoned John Adams, Robert Kennedy, Jr., and Larry Rockefeller. He wanted to see if they could lend him support at the meeting he'd arranged at the *Times* with yet another family member, Stephen Golden, who at the time was vice president of forest products, health, safety, and environmental affairs — but no one was around. Although the consortium never happened, Golden became an important supporter and eventually the *Times* said it would put $20 million into the project.

As soon as they'd heard the news that the mill had changed its spots and would now produce newsprint, Golden told me, it became interesting to the *Times*. They liked that for a lot of reasons, "because new production means higher quality paper, because the newest machine has got the newest technology, the highest quality . . . and frankly, new capacity means . . . more competition, and that means that prices will be moderated a little bit. . . ." It was also favorable for them, he said, "to have more rather than less production, because we use so much newsprint." Then, and later, Golden was certain that to succeed the project had to cost no more than $400 million and said that the *Times*'s participation as an investor would depend on keeping the cost down to that level. Compared to the cost—$200 to $300 million—of building a mill in the boondocks, $400 million was already high, but with other supply advantages and after doing due diligence on the project, the *Times* decided it would be a low-cost producer. If other investors could be found, they thought it was doable.

Although the deal that Hakkarainen was supposed to be putting together with Stone had collapsed, the project still had a written agreement with him that ended in April 1996, shortly after the Stone deal had folded; because he still seemed interested in helping out and had good credibility in the industry, the contract was extended in writing to June and then verbally extended until September (during that period, with everyone hoping that he could still flush some paper company out of the woods, Hakkarainen explored bringing in a company called Donahue). Hershkowitz liked Hakkarainen and considered his expertise invaluable, but recently he'd found out from team members that Hakkarainen seemed to have stirred up a little storm of suspicion around himself by advising a number of people on the team not to tell others about certain conversations they'd just had. Initially, Hakkarainen's vague secretiveness had been a kind of joke; his business card, for example, had nothing but his name on it.

But this was different—an uneasiness was developing about it and Hershkowitz worried about the effect it was having on everyone's morale at such a vulnerable moment. After a meeting with Hakkarainen on April 22, 1996—Earth Day—he wrote in his diary: "Niilo has got to stop thinking he can tell me or Bruce or Riccio or Galesi or anyone that they shouldn't tell us things, it makes him look untrustworthy. . . . He must understand he can't go around us. Trying to have people working on his project and not telling each other things says a lot about how he views relationships that involve trust and says he doesn't value trust, and so no one will trust him."

Some people, like Mary Cesar, thought that Hakkarainen's secretiveness stemmed from an attitude that she'd encountered with many Europeans she had worked with—a rather lordly "they know what they know and don't need to explain themselves mindset." The NAB Construction Company had been secretly hired by Niilo to offer an estimate of labor construction costs. According to the terms of Hakkarainen's agreement with NAB, moreover, Gary Simpson, NAB's owner, had a right until the fall of 1996 to come up with an acceptable price for the project. Since no one knew about this but Hakkarainen, other construction companies were sought out over the next months and Hakkarainen never suggested to anyone that it wasn't a good idea. He even arranged a meeting with a dozen or more members of the team on June 26, 1996, at the 51st Street and Broadway headquarters of Morse Diesel International, the large construction company that Jonathan Rose's family had worked with, which had been involved with scores of major projects, including the Sears Tower in Chicago and the rebuilding of some terminals at J. F. Kennedy Airport.

At the meeting Hakkarainen said nothing about NAB nor did he mention them afterward. Neither NAB nor Morse Diesel had ever built a paper mill before, but Morse Diesel was a far larger company. It had invested in paper mills, it had just been taken over the year before by a vast British consulting, construction, and engineering conglomerate called AMEC and, most important, Morse Diesel's COO worked a lot in New York and had good labor relations in the city. In fact, he was then the chairman of the New York Building Congress, an amalgam of unions and construction companies. Although the ideal construction company would have been one with expertise in building a paper mill, none of the companies that worked in New York City did—but a company that knew its way around large projects in the city seemed like the next best thing. People left the meeting feeling good about Morse Diesel. Perhaps Hakkarainen understood that he'd backed the wrong horse. What no one but he understood at that point was that NAB believed it had some kind of exclusive on the project and that it had already worked on an estimate of construction costs whose numbers had come in way too high.

Toward the end of the summer of 1996, Hershkowitz met with Marty Gold, who had helped negotiate the lease agreement, Rick Campbell, who continued to work with Bruce Pulver on financial issues, Rivera, and Cardona, who again put forth a small rehab contractor he knew as a candidate for the project's construction company and was again rebuffed. The need for construction guarantees, performance guarantees, investment obligations, and the resources to hire industrial experts from around the world was reiterated. The company Cardona was suggesting was far too small and too inexperienced and had far too few resources to be qualified, it was generally agreed. Cardona, clearly irritated, then said in what Hershkowitz felt was a retaliatory spirit, that "Maya had to go." She should be removed from the project and an architect whom Banana Kelly had worked with in the past should be hired instead. Although Cardona's choice was a good architect and well respected, no one thought he'd be a better choice than Lin and everyone said so.

In fact, on October 30, 1995, Lin had more than earned a glittering place in the project firmament by testifying on behalf of the mill at the City Planning Commission, whose approval was one more hurdle that needed to be crossed. The Commission had at first seemed reluctant to give the Harlem River land-use plan its blessing, and for a moment the fate of the whole enterprise looked bleak indeed, partly because of the Regional Plan Association's ongoing conviction that the space should be saved for a future full railyard. When Lin began to speak about the mill, however, the commissioners' body language perceptibly shifted; they were obviously impressed by Lin and by her passion for the project and everyone agreed that she turned the moment around and probably was responsible for their getting the commission's approval.

As it happened, the firm Cardona mentioned was owed a lot of money by Banana Kelly—money which they never got. In general, financial problems at Banana Kelly seemed to have been mounting and Cardona had been calling Hershkowitz up and saying in a somewhat truculent way, "We've got to get money for Yoli" (a term he alone seemed to use for Yolanda Rivera), and often he salted his conversation with racial epithets. When Hershkowitz tried to talk to Rivera about it, she would turn the subject elsewhere.

He wasn't the only one having a hard time with Cardona. At Banana Kelly's headquarters, Madeleine Marquez, who had been Rivera's trusted ally since 1992, was not only being edged by Cardona out of her job as liaison for the mill project, but was gradually being pushed out of the organization as well. Marquez watched in amazement as Cardona began to assert his control and power over the organization. His influence over Rivera was "immense," she said.

From the start she had been wary of him—through the grapevine, she'd heard that "he burned every entity he'd been around," and when he was present everything "happened too fast. He was involved in everything, the Youth Program and the BCPC project and everything at Banana Kelly." Watching him, she said, she had the sense that he was "a two-faced get-over artist" who "thrives in chaos." Marquez felt cautious about opening up Banana Kelly's financial records, which Cardona wanted to see. "If he wanted answers to the financial statements of Banana Kelly, I would say ask Yolanda. Stuff like that." In July 1996 she was asked by Cardona to fly to Puerto Rico to give a seminar in Spanish at the office of Cardona's business, Crescendo, Inc., about how to create a business plan. But Hurricane Bertha hit the island when she arrived, and no one showed up, nor did much happen over the next two weeks. She came back with the impression that Cardona's company, staffed by Cardona's daughter, seemed to be a business in name only.

Over the next months, a time of heavy negotiating for the project, Cardona apparently moved to get Marquez out, and Marquez believes that it was his determination to "control, divert, and sabotage" Banana Kelly's understanding with the BCPC that led Rivera to cease treating the development team as collaborators. "The next thing you know," Marquez recalled, "I was told Allen and those guys aren't going to know anything." It was during the fall of 1996 that she was told that her presence would no longer be required at the BCPC meetings, and in January 1997 she was fired. "I was accused of being disloyal; to this day I don't know what that is and what I did. I've never been told." Ten other people, including the firm's lawyer, were laid off in the last weeks of 1996 and early 1997, in what became known around the office as "the Christmas firings." Rivera also sent a memo to her staff in that same period, announcing that as part of Banana Kelly's "internal restructuring," the organization would now be divided into three institutions—Banana Kelly, Inc., BK International, and Banana Kelly Community Improvement Association. Everyone knew that Rivera had some kind of ambitious international plans that had evolved from the good reception that she'd received at various conferences, usually in connection with the BCPC or as a result of publicity she'd had because of her association with it. (In March 1996, at the Habitat II: U.N. Conference on Human Settlements in Istanbul, Banana Kelly had received the prestigious Dubai Award for "Best Practices in Improving the Living Environment.") But no one knew anything about those plans and no explanation of them was offered when Rivera made her announcement. At the time of the firings Banana Kelly's self-help, self-scrutiny employee program called "Health Realization" was in full swing, and when Madeleine Marquez tried to find out what she did wrong and how she had been disloyal, she was told, "You're 'health realized,' so figure it out." Marquez was in the middle of applying for a mortgage just then, and losing a job she had not long before considered stable and rewarding was frightening, but she soon landed on her feet; by March she was working as the managing director of the Brooklyn Economic Development Corporation and is now the director of the Bronx Initiative Corporation at the borough president's office. She still bumps into Rivera from time to time, and despite all that happened between them retains a degree of sisterly sympathy for her, though she is always surprised by the way Rivera acts as if nothing unusual had transpired between them.

One might wonder how much Marquez's assessment of the demoralization afflicting Banana Kelly in 1996 was related to her dismissal were it not for the fact that so many people who worked at the organization with no reason to hold a grudge shared it. Former board members, housing managers, social service heads, and staff members I spoke with—including many who left the organization in good standing—recounted how they had all watched in dismay as too much of the money coming into the agency seemed somehow not to get to the people it was supposed to be serving. It was widely believed that Rivera used Banana Kelly funds for personal expenses. Robin LeBaron, an idealistic young Canadian urban anthropologist, who had written his master's thesis about the South Bronx, began working at Banana Kelly in the summer of 1996. LeBaron had a research grant and volunteered to work for free (Banana Kelly gave him a dorm room to live in) so that he could observe life at the organization as "field work." Serving at first as a general factotum, he eventually wrote the material for their Web page. For LeBaron, who was twenty-six at the time but with his bright expression and shock of blond hair looked younger, it was a chance to see how a great organization he'd heard only good things about worked day to day. His plan was to write a Ph.D. dissertation about "the good work community groups were doing." But he left after only six months. "It became clear," he told me, "that I couldn't write anything favorable about them as an agency, though I could write favorable things about some of the individuals who were working there, and I didn't want to do work that just slammed community groups, so I decided to get out of it."

Almost as soon as he arrived he became aware of the frustration of many staff members at not being able to carry through on their work because of lack of support. "A lot of good people were not being given the resources to do their jobs and yet, at the same time, there seemed to be plenty of money for traveling around," he said. In an article he wrote about the organization a few years later, he pointed out that the once active and strong Banana Kelly board of directors had gradually lost all its power. Board meetings became infrequent, and for the most part, according to one former member, "the board was serving as a rubber stamp"—though Rivera told LeBaron it was as strong as ever. Cardona, LeBaron said, was around all the time but no one was sure what he did. He threw a great party, LeBaron recalled, but around the office he instigated a kind of reign of terror, calling in employees who were working hard and were committed to the organization and taking them to task, telling them that they'd be fired if their performance was substandard. He functioned "sort of like the godfather." From LeBaron's point of view, although a few of the people who were fired were deadwood, in general, he said, "They seemed to target the best people with the most integrity in the firings." LeBaron searched a bit to find the right words to characterize both the experience of those who'd been fired and his own, and finally settled on "traumatizing" and "soul destructive."

Hershkowitz's diaries of that period have a certain rueful tone. He reflects often on what he has been learning about some of his preconceptions, and those of the project's opponents: "Political ideology," he wrote in one entry, "does not elevate us above the facts of science, nor do good intentions elevate us above the ruthlessness of the market."

The team was now aware that NAB Construction, at Hakkarainen's behest, had been working for a while on construction feasibility specs for the project—though as far as everyone but Hakkarainen was concerned, the company had done so in a purely exploratory way for which they would be paid by Hakkarainen as consultants—and they knew, too, that its numbers were coming in far too high. Jaakko Pöyry and Valmet, the paper machinery vending company, also at Hakkarainen's request, had worked on their own studies, focusing respectively on mill design and water and energy needs (Jaakko Pöyry) and equipment costs (Valmet). It was the construction company's job to translate their numbers into local terms, with estimates for labor and materials added. In November a meeting was held at Hakkarainen's lawyer's office that Gary Simpson, NAB's owner, also attended.

At the meeting Hershkowitz, certain that a mill with construction costs as high as he'd heard Simpson was proposing—rumored to be more than $600 million—could never get built, said that he knew it was too far above the $400 million that the *Times* had asked for and suggested that Morse Diesel be brought in to do an independent review of NAB's numbers, as well as Jaakko Pöyry's and Valmet's. Jaakko Pöyry and Valmet had no objection to the review and had, in fact, privately indicated that they, too, thought that NAB's numbers were too high, but Simpson, a man with gray-ish-brown hair and an angular face, would not agree to the review of his company's work. Simpson defended his high numbers by say-ing that wage rates in New York, among other costs, were three to four times higher than anywhere else. However, by then the team had been told that NAB didn't have the best relations with unions in New York and for that reason suspected that they probably couldn't get as good a deal as Morse Diesel's John Cavanagh could.

What wasn't being said was that in order to avoid paying con-sultant fees to Simpson—whom he, acting alone, had hired for the feasibility study—Hakkarainen had promised NAB an exclusive on designing and building the mill and signed an agreement to that effect. However, that agreement, like Hakkarainen's, had an expiration date: Simpson's was November 1996—that very month. For reasons Hershkowitz couldn't figure out, Simpson's attitude seemed to be: "I'm putting up with all of you, but soon you'll be gone and I won't." Like Hakkarainen, he also seemed secretive.

The early "racist" accusations—against the project, against NRDC, and against Hershkowitz himself—that had surfaced before the lawsuit but quieted down for a while after the favorable Appellate Court decision, had resurfaced again over the past year in a par-ticularly nasty way. One of NRDC's lawyers, participating in an en-vironmental justice conference held at the Rutgers School of Law in Newark, New Jersey, in March 1996, had been pained to hear her organization attacked repeatedly. A few of the conference speak-ers—community activists, advocacy groups, academics, government representatives, and foundation representatives from the North-east—praised NRDC for its recent work in West Harlem, in Puerto Rico, in the Brazilian rain forest, and on an Albany incinerator. But far more, the organization was singled out as one that had not dealt respectfully with communities of color. The South Bronx mill was the target and obvious reason and the South Bronx Clean Air Co-alition the main attacker, and it was clear that their word had been taken as gospel and spread to other groups from other communi-ties and into a general critique of NRDC. Fanning the flames of all this was a pamphlet being distributed by someone who seemed to have no community affiliation that also severely criticized NRDC, in terms that the lawyer felt wouldn't have been taken seriously were it not for the South Bronx Clean Air Coalition's allegations.

The NRDC lawyer left the conference embarrassed and upset by what had happened and later wrote a long memo to her colleagues (including John Adams, Vernice Miller, and Fritz Schwarz) in which she said that although she didn't know that much about the specifics of the project and though she had always thought it sounded like a good idea, the controversy over it—which focused nearly entirely on the process by which the organization had pursued it—was seriously compromising NRDC's reputation in environmental justice circles and threatened to undermine all of the organization's environmental justice work. In recent years, environmental justice issues had been raised in many of NRDC's successful lawsuits. The lawyer added that Vernice Miller's presence on the staff had heretofore given them some credibility, but that while it went far in helping, it wasn't enough to convince the community that NRDC was acting in good faith.

But how could it when, as it turned out, Miller was one of the conference planners who seemed to have helped engineer, or at least not discourage, the anti-NRDC agenda? As Ricardo Soto-Lopez wrote in a furious letter to NRDC several weeks later, Miller had once again worked against her own organization's best interest. Soto-Lopez, who was now in law school at Rutgers and working full time as the national coordinator for the Puerto Rico–Northeast Environmental Justice Network, initially had a good experience with the conference organizers, working closely with them to make sure that the Puerto Rican environmental justice perspective was adequately presented. But then he had also asked that the Bronx project be highlighted as an example of "what national environmental organizations could be doing in coordinating with community-based organizations to deal with brownfields." Soto-Lopez had been told by a member of the planning committee that the project was considered "too controversial . . . and would be . . . too divisive if presented." In his letter, Soto-Lopez wrote, "I argued strenuously that the project should absolutely be presented in order to bring out any controversial issues for debate and that any environmental issue concerning this project should be presented to ensure that nothing be 'swept under the rug.' I was told that if I wanted to get the project on for the conference, I should join the planning committee headed by Vernice Miller." Because he was working full time and attending law school, Soto-Lopez told the conference coordinator he couldn't do that, but he was assured several times, he wrote in his letter, that "opponents of the project would not be given any opportunity to make any representations concerning the project without the opportunity for a balanced presentation ... by the project's proponents."

Soto-Lopez says he took these reassurances at face value. He thought he'd be able to attend the conference himself, but a sudden medical emergency of his father's kept him from it. When a written evaluation of the conference arrived on his desk several weeks later, however, he was furious to discover that there had not been "a balanced presentation" at all: "During the Plenary Session, Vincent 'Panama' Alba had made strong representations against the project." Despite his father's illness, if he had known that Alba, one of the inflammatory South Bronx Clean Air Coalition speakers at earlier public hearings about the mill project, was to be allowed to make such a one-sided presentation at the Plenary Session as a "featured speaker," he wrote, he would have done "everything humanly possible to get to the conference." As someone who had been involved in the project from its conception, as a fellow environmental justice advocate, as someone who, in fact, was studying law at the very school where the conference was being held, he went on to say, he took strong exception to what had happened. "This is not the first time representations have been made against the project without rebuttal from its proponents," he continued. "It is not the first time either, directly or indirectly, that the director of NRDC's environmental justice initiative has not been helpful in public ..."

Both the lawyer's letter and Soto-Lopez's disturbed the people who read them at NRDC, but it is probably fair to say that of the two, the lawyer's letter had a far greater effect by casting seeds of doubt about the mill enterprise within the institution and arousing a subtle level of skepticism that Hershkowitz at first experienced as a slight wind riffle, but, in time, as a gale force.

10

Once More into the Fray

FOR SOME MONTHS NOW Hershkowitz and Jonathan Rose, who lived not far from one another in northern Westchester, had been meeting fairly regularly for Sunday morning walks around a certain lush meadow near Rose's house. During these relaxed constitutionals, they would exchange ideas about the project's developments (or non-developments), assess its current dilemmas, and attempt to figure out future moves. The multiple-moving-parts problem was such a constant that it wasn't always easy to look at the project as a whole, but somehow during these walks they felt they gained a beneficial perspective. It was during one such walk that they agreed that Morse Diesel, with its wide big-project experience and New York savvy, seemed like the best choice for a construction company.

According to Tony Winson, a vice president of New York operations for Morse Diesel International, he and his colleagues had been keeping their eye on the project for years. Winson, a broad-faced Brit who is a civil engineer by training and a construction manager by trade, had even talked to some of the out-of-state engineers who had worked with the project early on, but had felt convinced that "if they were going to build something in that locality . . . you had to have New York expertise." While the mill team's efforts to find an owner and operator continued to go through various ups and downs in 1993, 1994, and 1995, Morse Diesel tracked the project from afar, waiting for the time that it would look right for them to step into the picture. If Hershkowitz and Rose thought they had chosen Morse Diesel, it also seems that Morse Diesel had chosen them. When they heard about Niilo Hakkarainen's participation, Morse Diesel's interest quickened, and they went to talk with him several times. They somehow knew he was talking to other construction companies as well, including NAB, but they set about wooing him by doing a lot of research about who he was and what he had done. It was obvious to Winson that the idea of the mill was a good one, even though at that point the development team didn't have the financial capability of doing it and was still looking for equity investors. Nonetheless, the project still looked promising to his company and they continued their sleuthing.

As a result of the profile they gathered, they went to Finland and met with a Finnish contractor who had worked with Hakkarainen. They also met with people from Valmet, his preferred supplier of paper machines, and with Jaakko Pöyry, his favorite engineering company. Although Hershkowitz says he explained the way the project was structured quite early on to the Morse Diesel people, Winson claims, "We didn't know who else was in the picture . . . Niilo came across as being the person who had been elected to develop the project." Though he says he didn't understand her role in the deal, he also visited Yolanda Rivera, along with his company's specialist in community relations, and told her that they were known as a "caring" New York construction contractor and had won a lot of awards from communities because of their involvement with local people. Not long after that last Sunday walk with Hershkowitz, Rose called Morse Diesel to say that things with NAB were not working out as intended and that the team urgently needed to talk with them and have them come up quickly with a cost estimate. On December 18, 1996, Morse Diesel sent Rose a proposal to engineer and build the project on the come—that is, deferring payment until closing—from soup to nuts.

Hershkowitz spent Christmas week working with Marty Gold, the lawyer who had been on the team since its early days, on a contract with Morse Diesel. On December 24, Hershkowitz wrote in his diary, "It's Christmas Eve and I'm negotiating a contract with Tony Winson . . . and Marty Gold; Jonathan is on the Caribbean island of Nevis, Niilo's in Biarritz, Bruce Pulver is away, Yolanda is nowhere to be found, and I'm in the kitchen." Hershkowitz spent the rest of his kids' Christmas vacation hammering out the agreement. Finally, in the last days of December, he signed an agreement with Morse Diesel as the engineering, procurement, and construction (EPC) contractors. The agreement stipulated that Morse Diesel would provide a preliminary cost estimate by January 30, 1997, that would be within BCPC's maximum budget limit of $400 million, subject to a range of plus or minus 10 percent.

Though Hershkowitz, along with everyone else, had learned with much annoyance of Hakkarainen's secret agreement with NAB in September, he wasn't worried about any conflict of interest at that point because Hakkarainen had told him that the agreement had expired and had even shown him and Gold a letter terminating it. NAB's Gary Simpson would not allow anyone on the team to look at the work he had done for Hakkarainen, but Hershkowitz had confirmed that his estimate came in at $635 million—nowhere in the ballpark of the *Times*'s figure. Nonetheless, Simpson, too, had been on the phone with Hershkowitz over the Christmas vacation telling him that if he signed an agreement with Morse Diesel, NAB could sue them. This rattled Hershkowitz, but when he immediately phoned Marty Gold and repeated what had been said, Gold told him that Simpson had no grounds for a suit. The idea at that point was that the effort to find an owner would continue, with Morse Diesel not only lending its shoulder to that effort but intimating that it might well find someone to finance the whole deal. Still hoping for a possible consortium of newspaper publishers to come together, Hershkowitz and others spent many months in talks to see if that might work out—and one can imagine that it might have looked like a tempting way for the publishers to get out of the war they were in with their suppliers, by becoming their own suppliers—but that plan, too, failed to gel. They did, however, get off-take letters—good-faith promises to buy certain amounts of paper—from the *Times,* News Corp (the *Post*), and Gannett, and the promise of a $20 million commitment from Lord Rothermere.

All the time the renewed struggle to push the mill forward was taking place, Hershkowitz kept going to the same sorts of conferences and meetings he'd always attended, but he was coming to feel more and more conflicted about them. At one, the 1996 Sustainable America Conference, which took place in a New York hotel, he had stared gloomily at the floor while a lengthy debate took place on how to get consensus on the proposed platform. The air of self-congratulation he sensed all around seemed too easy. That night he wrote, "A lot of very familiar talk with vague references to 'transforming the economy.' First we have to transform ourselves and our strategy, and then, if we are really successful, we can make a small contribution to the economic development of one neighborhood."

Over the same few months, there were a number of talks with New York unions about wages and scheduling uniformity (many unions have different work-hour rules—some start at seven in the morning, others at eight, etc.—and the team wanted to get all the people at the mill to basically work the same hours). There were also negotiations for breaks on some of the more eccentric regulations, such as the prohibition against "importing" into the city any pipe less than eight inches in diameter—a rule that necessitated the fabrication of the pipes in the city whether or not their price or availability was optimal.

Hershkowitz also wanted to see if he could whip up any interest in having the unions themselves invest in and even possibly run the mill, because, as he pointed out, it was they who ran the mills anyway. When a friend told him that it was probably not in his best interest to share the news of this effort with too many people, he responded, "But, you know, I think the pendulum is going to swing sooner or later. We'll look back at these days, these last ten years especially, and ask how did we so shut out these progressive options? Why do we not even allow ourselves to have a discussion of union-run plants. . . . But I believe it will come back because of the current excesses of the bottom-line mentality." Over the last months of 1997, Hershkowitz was meeting nearly every day with Merrill Lynch's Dan Donovan, a tall, rangy, hardworking man who was the director of his firm's Municipal Capital Markets Group. Donovan confirmed the choice of Morse Diesel as the right company to work with. He told Hershkowitz that a major construction company and "turnkey" operator—one that would guarantee that the plant got built and would oversee its readiness down to the last detail—were in fact critical. While Donovan was running the numbers, contacting potential investors, and trying to capture more equity, he found a group, Southern Energy, that wanted to pay for and run the mill's power plant—like the wastepaper sorting plant, an integrated part of the mill's overall design.

By then the company that had originally signed on to run the wastepaper sorting plant had gone bankrupt and a new sorter came in—Anthony Lacavalla, a small, good-natured, dynamic man then in his mid-thirties, whose company, Crystal Paper Co., was based in Florida. Lacavalla already ran prosperous paper processing plants in New Jersey and the Bronx, only blocks away from the mill site. He also kicked in $500,000 to the project when he joined the team, a godsend, because, in the seat-of-the-pants way they were now operating, the money Stone had put in—all told, $300,000—was already gone. Hershkowitz liked Lacavalla but could sense that the project's landlord, Galesi, felt nervous about him. Was it possible that his Italian landlord was suspicious of an Italian recycler because of a stereotype problem? Lacavalla, who graduated from college with a degree in criminal justice and sociology in 1985, joined his family's business, which was started in Harlem by his grandfather in the horse-and-buggy era. Hakkarainen told me he was against Lacavalla's putting in the money because his was not a very large company, and it would be awful if the project failed and he lost it.

Until Visy came on line at its Staten Island plant, Lacavalla's company had a large portion of the city contract for newspaper and curbside recycling; when they lost that (although they also had contracts in the Bronx and a joint venture paper processing plant in Jersey City with Weyerhaeuser Paper Company), Lacavalla decided to hedge his city contract by bidding for the paper processing plant of the mill and putting up the $500,000 to sweeten his bid. When he first heard about the Bronx project, he told me, "It was supposed to be built within a year or two years. In the industry, the word was that the mill would soon either be getting what Visy didn't get or a large portion of what was left. I thought what everyone else thought, that the paper would go to the Harlem River [yard—the site of the proposed mill]. . . . I thought this was ideal—to feed a news mill in the South Bronx with all the newspapers in New York and feed the newspapers with the finished product. . . . It was common sense, you know, the Bronx needed the jobs; the land was clean, as far as I knew from Allen. And I thought it was a go . . . and a great opportunity." The BCPC team chose Lacavalla instead of other bidders, including some very big companies, not just because of the half million he threw in, but because it was obvious to them that his experience in the paper world was so extensive.

One of the oddest calls that the project team received came from a man at a paper company called Evergreen, which was trying to build a mill in Poughkeepsie, New York. The man offered to pay them to *stop* trying to build the mill—by buying their development rights. He seemed surprised when they turned him down. Another end run around the project was being attempted by a large, multinational hauling company called BFI; BFI had become a major presence in the city's commercial waste-hauling industry after so many of the old established waste haulers were sent off to prison, and now the company was trying hard to get the same paper the mill was after to use in their own processing plants.

Yet another, perhaps even stronger competitor for whatever paper was left over from the city, after Visy took its share, was Waste Management, another huge multinational company, the largest waste handlers in the country, with the strongest possible ties to City Hall. For political clout, you would have to look far to beat Waste Management's heavy lineup, composed of both its staff members and its lobbyists. It included Peter Powers, Rudy Giuliani's former first deputy mayor, high school friend, fellow opera lover, and successful campaign manager, who was probably the single most influential voice in the mayor's first term—his company served as consultant to Waste Management; Dennis Vacco, the former Republican attorney general (who was close to Powers and Giuliani and was Waste Management's vice president for government affairs for New York, New England, and Canada); and Randy Mastro, Giuliani's first chief of staff and subsequent deputy mayor, who would, after leaving city government, briefly represent Waste Management in a dispute it had with the Metropolitan Transportation Authority.

A few weeks after the glad news of the infusion of Lacavalla money had reached most of the people working on the project, Hershkowitz received a ten P.M. conference call from Aureo Cardona and Rivera and afterward scrawled a diary entry about it: "Aureo argues, 'We should get the Lacavalla development money for community work.' 'What kind of work?' I asked. And he can't explain." After the call, he was concerned that a shakedown could be coming on. Cardona had already, earlier that week, mentioned to him that Banana Kelly should keep the Lacavalla money. But Hershkowitz had explained that the money was needed to pay the engineers and lawyers and paper consultants who had already done work. The first time he'd asked for money Hershkowitz asked him what the budget for the project he was asking for was. How close to meeting it were they? What obligations would they be having in the future, where else was the money going to come from (in terms of grants Banana Kelly would receive), and what resources was Banana Kelly planning to allocate toward whatever they were asking for? But no coherent plan was offered nor did there follow any focused discussion of what the money would be going for.

Although the *Times*'s Stephen Golden had strongly recommended to his board that it support the project, and its support carried considerable weight in business circles, the team was still, at the start of 1997, ownerless, and this central fact colored every negotiation—even when Golden generously accompanied them to a meeting at City Hall with Giuliani's deputy mayor for economic development, to demonstrate that the *Times* was onboard for off-take, and Hakkarainen was trotted out as a possible operator. Golden was willing to extend himself at least in part because he believed the very existence of the mill would be a powerful benefit: "If the city can demonstrate that this is a place where people can build and operate manufacturing facilities, then the city has a return—potentially—to some of the economic fuel that was so important in its early days, when so much manufacturing went on here." And that, he said, "would be great for the city of New York." Golden did not limit his efforts on behalf of the project to going along to meetings—"I wrote letters," he told me, "to various state and local officials, describing our absolute commitment to the mill as a customer."

Still, Hershkowitz had the yard's landlord, Galesi, breathing down his neck — because Galesi himself had to show the state that he still had a viable tenant, and Hershkowitz was being urged to come up with something or move over, so that somebody else could move in. According to a Memorandum of Understanding Galesi had signed, the project was supposed to be paying him $25,000 a month and $104,000 a month after construction, but he had agreed to defer the rent payments until closing.

City and state officials were also beginning to sniff ever more warily around the project, wondering if it was alive or dead. In one discouraging conversation he had with a highly placed city official, the man had said point-blank, "I don't think the project is going to happen." Hershkowitz asked him why. "Because you have no track record." At that point he had been fielding late night conference calls all week; exhausted and exasperated, he said, "So if my name were Trump this would happen?" The official looked straight at him and said, "I believe it would." Hershkowitz left this encounter feeling particularly dejected about the apparent insurmountability of this established attitude, which he had already seen confirmed — first when Visy entered the picture, and then when Galesi and other city officials had immediately offered Hakkarainen their support, even though he had nothing firm at the time to offer.

On December 12, 1996, which happened to be the birthday of his eighty-four-year-old father, now living in Florida and ailing, Hershkowitz was "reamed," as he later told Rich Schrader, at a meeting with Ambassador Gargano and Randy Daniels, Gargano's deputy commissioner of economic revitalization at the Empire State Development Corp. They reminded him in the harshest terms of the bald facts, facts that he was already painfully aware of: that he didn't have an operator; that Stone, which was supposed to be onboard by the previous April, had not materialized; that he didn't have enough equity; that he really didn't have a commitment for the paper; and that the project was dragging on and on. The drubbing he was given was so fierce that when Hershkowitz left he felt that there was scarcely anything left of him but a few bones and viscera. However, that morning, before the meeting, Mike Finnegan had called him and told him that after his meeting with Gargano was over, he should go upstairs without being seen to the governor's office, to meet with Diana Taylor, the governor's aide and trusted amanuensis.

Few people outside the state government knew her name (though she would eventually be thrust into the limelight after becoming the CFO of the Long Island Power Authority and as Mike Bloomberg's companion when he became New York City's mayor), but Taylor was a central member of Governor Pataki's staff. Wherever he flew, she accompanied him, laden with file folders. The office in which he was meeting Gargano was one floor below the governor's. Although Hershkowitz assumed there was a connecting staircase, he was told to proceed to the ground floor and take the elevator from there. So Hershkowitz left the meeting, took the elevator down to the lobby, was okayed by a security guard and, nervously looking over his shoulder, entered the elevator leading to the governor's floor. There he was met by Taylor, who Hershkowitz thought looked a lot healthier and friendlier than any of the people he'd just left, and whose attitude could not have been more different from theirs. The governor's position at that point was: Okay, your project is stalled. Let's try to get it going again. To do that, Taylor wanted a number of things: copies of the permits, the draft lease, and the letters of commitment for the off-take. She also mentioned the possibility of a letter of support from the governor to the *New York Times.* To a grateful Hershkowitz, her matter-of-fact assumption that the project was still alive, if ailing, and her businesslike focus on trying to get a government commitment for the bond allocation was manna.

On Sunday, December 29, NAB's Simpson called Hershkowitz again. This time Hershkowitz suggested that NAB might work together with Morse Diesel, but Simpson told him he wasn't interested. The evening of the day that the agreement with Morse Diesel was signed, Jonathan Rose also phoned again, from Nevis, and said, "Allen, this is the first time I think we have a greater than fifty percent chance of closing." New Year's Day found Hershkowitz once again working his phone on a conference call with Marty Gold (whom Hershkowitz depended on as a project lawyer but also now regarded as a friend), Hakkarainen's lawyer, and Simpson.

Hakkarainen was still in France, Simpson at Tahoe, Gold in New York, Hershkowitz in his kitchen. Somewhere in the conversation Hakkarainen's lawyer mentioned that his client was going to pull out altogether; he was no longer interested in the project. But that turned out to have been said for Simpson's benefit. In fact, Hakkarainen was expressing enthusiastic interest in the project's next phase and was soon to be hired as a ten-thousand-dollar-a-month consultant.

While he was fielding the call, Hershkowitz could see his kids playing in the snow outside the kitchen window and, from time to time, beckoning him to join them. All afternoon, while the world of high financial intrigue raged telephonically around him, he watched his family build a sleigh run on the hill behind his house, heard his kids shout, "Daddy!" and felt really lousy about not being able to join them. It was upsetting to him and infuriating to Meg.

As soon as he hung up, the phone rang again. It was Cardona. Pugnacious. Accusatory. Why was Rivera's name not on the Morse Diesel agreement? No acknowledgment of the huge effort that had been made to get to the point they were at. No acknowledgment of the better footing the project was now on. Hershkowitz, who was by then completely wiped out, explained that he tried many times to reach both of them but had failed and he had no idea where they were. Where had they been? "On vacation," Cardona shot back tersely. As president of the BCPC (per Rick Campbell's suggestion), Hershkowitz was legally entitled to sign the contract without Rivera's co-signature—but he would have much preferred to have it there. Cardona continued to be accusatory about the signature issue and began cursing and complaining about the way they were being treated. A snowman had gone up in the front yard. Meg, her cheeks rosy from the cold, stepped briefly into the kitchen and shot him a dirty look. After a few more attempts to explain what had been happening, Hershkowitz finally said, "What have you been doing for this project? The only thing you ever do is ask for money. Instead of always asking for money, why don't you try to raise some?" To which Cardona replied, "What do I get for it?"

"What do you get for it?" Hershkowitz shouted into the phone. "The project you signed on for, that Banana Kelly signed on for—to co-venture with NRDC."

Later that week, feeling bad about the way things had gotten out of hand in that conversation and the way his good relationship with Rivera had been deteriorating, he talked to his rabbi about the project and asked him for a story about reconciliation. The rabbi suggested the story of Jacob. Hershkowitz read the story, but it didn't help.

Or maybe it did. A few days later he scheduled a meeting with Gary Simpson and several people from Morse Diesel to make a last-ditch effort at getting NAB and Morse Diesel to work together. Morse Diesel offered NAB the prime subcontractor position, but Simpson refused it. On a personal level, Hershkowitz rather liked Simpson, but Simpson kept saying he didn't need either him or Morse Diesel, that it was not BCPC's project, but Hakkarainen's. When Hershkowitz responded that his own name and Rivera's were on the lease and on the permits, even this seemed to cut no ice. Sensitive by now to suggestions that his negotiating style was too "in people's faces," he sought Gold's help (he considered Gold a shrewd, deft negotiator) for ways to bring everyone together. He was coached by Gold to exercise his best diplomatic skills and to assure Simpson of a fair remuneration for his work to date. If there were things Simpson insisted on that he thought they couldn't accept, Hershkowitz was not to say, "I can't accept that," but rather, "I'll get back to you on that," and most of all, not to leave the room without an agreement. He succeeded in all but the last task. The two sides clearly did not like each other, and because of whatever he understood his arrangement with Hakkarainen to be, Simpson was in no mood to compromise.

By 1997, the rift in the upper reaches of the state government between the Gargano and Pataki factions had become more obvious, and, reportedly offended by the way certain moves had been made behind his back to help the project, Gargano was more hostile than ever to Hershkowitz whenever they met. One of the worst such meetings, several people recalled, took place during the second week of February 1997. It had been arranged to introduce the people at Morse Diesel to some of the state and city officials who had been dealing with the project. On seeing John Cavanagh, Morse Diesel's COO, Gargano remarked that that was a comfort to him, and that was the last good moment of the meeting. Hershkowitz had cut his hair extra short for the meeting and went fully prepared, as he told a colleague, to make a real effort to "kiss Gargano's ass," but that best-laid plan apparently went awry. Charles Millard, a Giuliani appointee, who was then the head of the Economic Development Corp., interrupted Hershkowitz for a point of clarification just as he began introducing the various parties from Morse Diesel: "Here is our EPC contractor—" "What's an EPC?" Millard shot out. Now, while the average citizen has no particular reason to understand the term EPC, or engineering procurement and construction, it is, in fact, the fundamental term in industrial development. The idea that the head of the city's Economic Development Corp., charged with encouraging business development, would not know what this meant was almost inconceivable to Hershkowitz, and at the very least confirmed his gloomy suspicion that as "development" in big city lingo had become exclusively associated with commercial real estate—the very *language* of industrial development had become archaic to some of its officials.

The meeting didn't get any better. According to one person who was there, the more Hershkowitz felt the resistance around him, the more frenetic he got. Hakkarainen says it was so awful he found himself determinedly staring at the table top. Hershkowitz also constantly corrected what he felt were certain misstatements of fact on the ambassador's part—not a good move. At one point Hershkowitz explained the Hakkarainen principle: that the latest state-of-the-art plant will always remain standing while older ones fail (as they were beginning to do around the country); then a potential investor who had put money into a mill that was still doing well tried to speak, but Gargano turned to his neighbor at the conference table and said in a whisper that everyone could hear, "This is bullshit!"

Even Eric Deutsch, a friend of the project, seemed somehow to be courting favor with the state officials by arguing against it—vividly painting the worst possible scenarios, all of which, without government support, would amount to a self-fulfilling prophecy. But Millard's question at the start of the meeting had made Hershkowitz feel "almost physically sick," he noted in his diary that evening. He went on to observe that you'd never know from the meeting that brownfield reclamation, a big boost to the city's recycling program, sewage water cleanup, and job development were what the officials were being asked to support. Rather, he wrote, it felt "more like we were trying to convince them to accept a load of hazardous waste."

The following week he received a call from someone he knew and liked in the New York state government, who simply said to him, "Gargano doesn't want this to happen." At that point Hershkowitz still had the support of the governor, so, despite the momentary chill that overcame him, he filed this unambiguous message in some back part of his brain. But that night he wrote, "Because NRDC doesn't dole out job offers or campaign funds, there's little benefit for senior staff at city and state agencies to work with us other than the inherent value of the project to the city. And compared with personal advancement or political fundraising, that doesn't count for much. That's why they want a Rose or a John Cavanagh at the helm of this project and not me." His notion of the collaborative nature of the project had always been: I'm just the guy coordinating all the experts' input. The business world didn't seem to have room for that vision. Some people could live with the idea of his coordinating the project. Many, too many, he was discovering, could not. Even members of NRDC's own board, to whom he had recently given a project update, were obviously worried about the time everything was taking. "Ah, Allen, another chapter of the never-ending story," one of them, a much respected founder of the organization, quipped as Hershkowitz stood up to make his presentation.

Once again, however, thanks to the self-assured presence of Morse Diesel, a sense of momentum was infusing the project. Because Valmet, the Finnish company that was supposed to provide the paper machines for the mill, was nervous about its earlier contractual relationship with NAB, Morse Diesel did not try to work with them; instead, they hired a company called Kvaerner Engineering & Construction, a huge Norwegian shipbuilding and industrial development firm with a net worth of about $1.5 billion, which also had a smaller paper mill machinery division.

Hershkowitz received this news a few days before he left for a Paris environmental conference and felt more or less neutral about it, until someone asked him if he would meet sometime with the executive vice president and head of their paper division, Roland Martin-Lof. Martin-Lof was in London, where the company's paper division was based. "Roland Martin-Lof?" Hershkowitz remembers repeating incredulously. Martin-Lof was the former head of MoDo, the man, along with Batelson, with whom he started the project. He couldn't believe his ears. He told me his heart "soared." Not only had he always liked Martin-Lof, who left MoDo shortly after the big management reshuffle that had accompanied their shift in strategic focus, but Martin-Lof had been a big enthusiast of the project. Morse Diesel had planned for Hershkowitz and Martin-Lof to meet several weeks later, but Hershkowitz called him up immediately and they set up an appointment for later that week. He and Tim Martin, who was continuing to work with the project as a research associate, were on their way to Europe anyway for the Paris conference, where Hershkowitz was making a speech, so they made a detour, coming back, to meet with Martin-Lof. In London, Martin-Lof, who greeted Hershkowitz warmly, told him that Kvaerner was going to offer financial guarantees to reduce the risks of the project—performance guarantees. Their strategy was to announce that they would be the operators and guarantee the project, and eventually other operators would come in and buy Kvaerner's rights.

It turned out that Kvaerner was eager to break into the global paper machine vending world in a bigger way and wanted to be the mill's operator; it was willing to put in $30 million in equity. Wall Street would be happy with this, particularly because Kvaerner was such a creditworthy company. Kvaerner's tough negotiator, a man named Tom Krieser, saw this project as giving them, in turn, good visibility in the global paper market. He, too, was eager to have his firm participate in it, but for a price: in exchange for what they were offering they wanted a 50/50 deal with Morse Diesel on profits; Krieser's posture was: "We're bringing in the crucial equipment, we're putting in equity—you're only a construction company— we're the big player here." In Kvaerner's initial negotiations they had been willing to settle for less, but that was because they hadn't realized that Morse Diesel was merely the construction company —not the developer. Morse Diesel, on the other hand, had once again begun talking to Valmet, whom they thought could provide superior paper-making machines, even if Kvaerner still brought in the de-inking equipment. If Valmet were to be once again in the picture, they, too, would be chomping a piece of the pie. Kvaerner was suggesting a brand-new structure, and setting terms that it was far from certain Morse Diesel liked. And how Morse Diesel's parent company, AMEC, might have felt about Kvaerner, which only two years before had attempted a hostile takeover, was another unknown. Hershkowitz thought they ought to accept Kvaerner's terms because it was clearly good for the project.

Not long afterward, while attending yet another meeting in Washington, he returned to his room at the Capitol Hill Hotel to find a message waiting for him from John Adams. He called back and found that Adams had congratulations and great news for him.

Adams: "You got the $180 million state tax-exempt allocation. The vote was today."

Hershkowitz: "Fantastic!"

Adams: "The vote was nine to two."

Hershkowitz: "Unbelievable!"

Adams: "*Against* you."

Hershkowitz: "What?"

Adams, laughing: "You got it anyway."

The two in favor were the governor and Finnegan. Because the governor's vote overrides any other, the allocation went through. This was a triumph for the project, but a disaster for the ego of Charles Gargano, who had been trumped on his own turf and whose raison d'être, the doling out of tax-exempt projects, had been temporarily annulled. The state had already allocated $75 million for the mill; now, with this $180 million, the equity lift (the funds still lacking) was still heavy—$145 million—but a lot less heavy (if the goal of $400 million could be reached). The *Times* was at that point talking about putting in $20 million, Lord Rothermere was still in with his $20 million and, according to Hakkarainen, the mill continued to hold the interest of a Stone-era Canadian investor who said he was still good for another $20 million, and now Kvaerner was talking about throwing in $30 million and giving performance guarantees. With these guarantees, even risk-wary investors, nervous about the many new mills that were not making it around the country, could now step up to the plate because they couldn't lose their money. That night Hershkowitz went to bed rolling around in his mind a passel of welcome thoughts: the fact of the tax allocation; the presence of Roland Martin-Lof in his corner; an encouraging phone call from Per Batelson, who had just talked to Martin-Lof and said things looked good; the presence of a new, solid paper mill–building engineering company that had recently joined the team—Harris Engineering; the guarantees and the solid input of Morse Diesel. That night he slept well.

11

All Hands on Deck

AFTER SEVERAL WEEKS of calculation Morse Diesel said they could build the project and guarantee it that day at $495 million. They thought it was a reasonable price, but it was still too far above what the *Times* said was absolutely needed and, consequently, that much harder to finance. They had also estimated that it would take 1.4 million man-hours of labor to build it (again, far below NAB's estimate, but still hefty). Hershkowitz worried about the numbers, but a week later after several key people worked on them the estimate had come down to $440 million, plus or minus 7 percent, and Morse Diesel said it would put some money into the project, too. So many consultants were now pushing to move things forward that after one big meeting where there were more than thirty people present, Hershkowitz wrote that it felt like "all hands on deck" before a big ship sailed. Issues that still needed to be worked out included an agreement with the Department of Sanitation, the acquisition of a letter confirming the recently announced tax-exempt allocation, a water agreement, possible Empowerment Zone support, and Bond Act money. Firing across the bow, of course, was their nemesis at the Empire State Development Corp., the ambassador. Gargano's animosity toward the project had now become glacially hardened. "Come back with a done deal or be gone," he advised several members of the team that month when they met with him to discuss other subsidies needed for the project.

Shortly afterward, Hershkowitz had been deeply embarrassed by a call Randy Daniels (the deputy commissioner at the Empire

State Development Corp.) made to Stephen Golden at the *Times*. Golden considered the details of his negotiations with the BCPC team private—it was important that the newspaper not alienate any of their current paper suppliers—but Hershkowitz had had to tell Daniels, in confidence, that the *Times* was a potential investor, in order to establish the project's current viability. The next day Daniels put in a direct call to an infuriated Golden, who had been burnt once before by public disclosure of a supposedly private meeting with enviros. Daniels had called to check up on Hershkowitz—a hugely insensitive move. Hershkowitz wrote a strong letter of apology to Golden, who had a pretty clear grasp of what was going on politically and so didn't hold the incident against him. On the other hand, since theirs was still far from a done deal, Golden had had to say to Daniels, "Well, we're not sure." Daniels, of course, had no idea of the many meetings and strong input of the *Times* at that point and reportedly went back to his boss with a message that the *Times* wasn't interested and that Hershkowitz was not telling the truth.

Hershkowitz had also begun once again to feel besieged by community opponents, people who seemed to be redoubling their efforts to block the mill. The South Bronx Clean Air Coalition told an aide to Fernando Ferrer that the mill would be spewing dioxins and causing breast cancer, and the aide called to tell Hershkowitz that they were concerned about the mill's chlorination process. This was the first time in many months that he'd heard anything from the borough president's office. Hershkowitz explained that because the mill wasn't using chlorine, there would be no chlorination problem. Earlier, at a presentation at the Patterson Houses, a South Bronx housing project, an entire family—a father, mother, and two sons—had come up to him and said they were unemployed and would love to work for the mill and asked if there was a sign-up sheet for jobs. He'd been so moved by their eagerness he nearly wept, and Phil Sears, who'd been there, felt the same way. But the moment was shattered by the South Bronx Clean Air Coalition's Carlos Padilla, who stood up and said it was a bad project and a polluting one. When Hershkowitz tried to clarify the pollution issue, Padilla said he was lying.

Some members of the NRDC staff continued to believe that Padilla, who kept popping up at public meetings to attack the mill project, was a concerned and sincerely motivated activist and that if Hershkowitz could only focus more on the content of Padilla's concerns and less on getting the job done, he might change Padilla's mind. But when it emerged a few years later that Padilla and some of his fellow Coalition advocates were supporting a 5,200-ton-per-day waste-transfer station that a company was hoping to locate in the South Bronx, that belief in his sincerity may have been finally shattered. At a local hearing about the transfer station, according to a *Times* article that featured a big color picture of Padilla thigh deep in the long grass of the proposed site, local residents and members of the other hardworking Bronx grassroots groups, some dressed as cartons of garbage, protested that their borough was already handling too much of the city's refuse, and "accused the South Bronx Clean Air Coalition, which traditionally has opposed such projects, of accepting money in exchange for its support. 'You are accepting money from them and playing their community partner,' Majora Carter, an official with the Point Community Development Corporation, shouted at members of the South Bronx Clean Air Coalition. 'This is obscene.' "

That past June John Tierney, a staff writer for the *New York Times Magazine,* published a much read antirecycling cover story in the Sunday magazine section, "Recycling Is Garbage," and in February Hershkowitz's ninety-page rebuttal was published by NRDC. At the New York Academy of Sciences, where he'd been invited to discuss his response, during the question-and-answer period he was interrupted by an unsmiling woman named Lorna Saltzman who accused him of bad faith in the Bronx and began distributing a broadsheet to audience members.

On one side of the paper, two bewigged gentlemen regarded each other across a desk. One of them held a quill and looked expectantly at the other, who was reading the just-penned sentence of the Declaration of Independence: "We hold these truths to be self-evident, that all men are created equal . . ." Above his head was a cartoon bubble and the words "It's a nice sentiment, Hershkowitz, but the fact is you own slaves and you can't separate the message from the messenger." On the other side of the paper was a message, which began with a general assertion of the long and painful history of South Bronx exploitation and read, in part:

> Mainstream green environmental groups (Green Color Of Money), like the NRDCC (Allen Hershkowitz), use there credentials and influence to punish and discredit community grassroots organizations for the sole purpose of personal gain. NRDCC has been giving this information about a project in which they stand to gain called The Bronx Community Paper Company. . . . The community of the South Bronx will not stand by and watch its public land be stolen, it's health destroyed more than what it already is, and lied to by poverty pimps like the NRDCC. With the budget cuts in health care services and the down-sizing of our hospitals, while at the same time the rate of asthma and asthma-related deaths is on the rise, the Harlem River Yard venture/Bronx Community Paper Company will surely mean death sentences for many of the residence of the South Bronx. We will continue to fight for we are truly fighting for our very lives and the future of our children. The South Bronx community will win for you see there is a GOD and its not NRDCC OR Allen Hershkowitz.
>
> Definition, NRDCC—National Racist Dividing Communities of Color. The last C is not silent and will never be.
>
> —South Bronx Clean Air Coalition

Saltzman, who, Hershkowitz later learned, had once worked at the city's Department of Environmental Protection and was fired for using its stationery to back a cause the department had no knowledge of, did not respond when Hershkowitz defended his project. But something about the blank stare she maintained throughout the encounter made him feel really uncomfortable.

The increasingly personal nature of the attacks on him so freaked him, in fact, that the next time NRDC updated its in-house address list he removed his home address from it, giving, instead, the organization's. Hershkowitz knew that Vernice Miller had been confronted by senior NRDC officials about her negative attitude toward the project. He and she had been asked to "work out their differences," and they'd tried. Sometimes she even spoke about the project to him in a friendly way. But recently he had come to believe that whether for reasons of past allegiance or greater community sympathy, Miller's higher loyalty, vis-à-vis his project, lay outside NRDC. The final straw for him was when he was turned down for an Environmental Protection Agency "sustainable development challenge grant," which the project seemed to meet every criterion for (the grants were targeted at cleaning up brownfields and merging environmental remediation with job creation). Rivera had called to say that she'd been told that Miller, who sat on the EPA's environmental justice advisory council, had argued against the project's receiving EPA support. Miller denies this and says that she had nothing to do with grant administration.

That feeling of besiegement from within was the hardest thing he had to deal with. Several times he noted in his journal that the complications of trying to build a mill were "trifling" compared with what his parents had had to endure in the camps. But the attacks on his integrity and ongoing fusillades from people who were supposed to be his allies made him feel ever more isolated. The unaccustomed feeling ran so deep that even Meg didn't know how to help him with it.

At one informational presentation at the NRDC for other enviros and a handful of NRDC staffers to bring people up-to-date on the project, Miller had ambushed him and attacked the project in terms so strong that several of the outsiders present, when they learned she was an NRDC staff member, found it hard to believe. It was, of course, staff policy that regardless of the differences people had with one another, they were not to air them publicly or subvert another colleague. Hershkowitz gritted his teeth and responded as politely as he could. But that night he noted bitterly in his journal that "we couldn't have paid a hostile organizer to do better."

Another time, Miller confronted him in his own office, challenging his credentials for dealing with an environmental justice initiative, which, she reminded him, was in her bailiwick—and when Hershkowitz advanced the theory that this was a very large project in which environmental justice was but one component and that he had NRDC's blessing to proceed with it, she started yelling at him.

He tried to remove himself from the confrontation by leaving his office, but Miller blocked the door. At a loss as to how to extricate himself, he phoned John Adams, who was not in the office, then Patricia Sullivan, NRDC's deputy executive director for administration, who wasn't there, either. As luck would have it, just then Frances Beinecke, the organization's deputy executive director for programs, called from somewhere outside the office. Hershkowitz hastily explained the situation and Beinecke asked to be put on the speakerphone. She told Miller to leave the office, which she did. Miller later apologized for the incident, but despite several subsequent long talks, she and Hershkowitz never came to an understanding. Hershkowitz knew of other people at his organization who had erred far less but were for various reasons "helped to find other jobs," as someone at the organization genteelly expressed it. His friends wondered if NRDC was afraid of a discrimination lawsuit if they let Miller go.

From time to time, Hershkowitz would chat with Henry Breck, the chair of Ark Asset Management Co. Inc., a mutual fund management company, and the treasurer of NRDC's board. Breck had been extremely helpful with financial advice at different junctures, though he often told Hershkowitz the project wasn't going to happen; a running joke between them was Breck's repetition, every time they met, of the suggestion, "Why not do it in Wappingers Falls?" Hershkowitz got the impression from Breck that he thought the whole deal was something of a private fantasy of Hershkowitz's, who, because of his persuasive powers, had somehow managed to pixilate a great number of people into sharing his fantasy. Reflecting on these sessions with Breck in early 1997, Hershkowitz once told me, "He kept saying to me, 'Allen, don't work too hard on this. You're very smart. You could be an investment banker, but this can't happen.' But as he's saying this, I'm saying to myself, 'Okay, let's see, the former president of MoDo Paper Company is involved in this project. He's working for a paper equipment vendor that's one of the largest firms in the world—and *he* thinks it can happen; I have the former managing director of the United Paper Mills, who's built more than seven of these things, involved—and *he* thinks it can happen; I've got the Merrill Lynch people and the *New York Times*—and *they* think it can happen. Galesi? Cavanagh? Don't tell me that I can cloud their comprehension of reality so significantly that I've got all of them in thrall. I'm not crunching these numbers on the project. Merrill Lynch is, or Bruce Pulver, or, before them, Jaakko Pöyry; I'm not doing the engineering or the water supply estimates. The engineers at the Department of Environmental Protection and several engineering firms are doing that. Have I overwhelmed their judgment, too? . . . Thank you, Henry, I'll take that under consideration.' I wasn't impolite. . . . But I had to discount his judgment because I was getting other information from people in the industry telling me it *could* happen."

Since the state revolving fund money had not yet come through, the project was again growing short on development funds. Kvaerner said it would kick in a million immediately if Morse Diesel would do the same and reiterated that it would assume the operation of the mill or assure that an operator was arranged for. But Morse Diesel had still not yet decided if they were willing to work with Kvaerner under the terms it had stipulated.

The total budget remaining to complete the development phase of the project was estimated at $4 million by Morse Diesel. Two million was expected to come in soon from the state revolving fund, and the project team hoped that the New York City Partnership, a private group, might be able to help them with a $2 million bridge loan. Started specifically to help manufacturing in New York for the public good, the group seemed like an ideal place to approach for help. Hershkowitz wrote to its CEO, Robert Kiley, in late January 1997 and said he'd like to set up a meeting. Kiley sent back a rather lowering letter in early February to Hershkowitz saying that before a meeting could be convened they would need confirmation of the commitment of a paper company prepared to serve as a co-owner and operator, and an analysis of the status and competitive position of the paper company in Staten Island. The fact was that a linerboard mill (the Staten Island Visy mill) and a newsprint mill produced different grades of paper and were not actually in competition with one another, and Hershkowitz sent a three-page letter that same day explaining that, as well as the project's current operational status, and sent copies of his letter to a number of people on the team.

Kiley had also asked that any new information on principal

commitments or other matters be forwarded to his colleague Kathryn Wylde, the president and CEO of the NYC Investment Fund, which worked together with the Partnership. In March, a meeting led by Wylde was held at the Partnership's offices, but when Hershkowitz made his presentation he detected a certain *froideur* emanating from Wylde that felt all too familiar by now. She seemed prepared to help them only if they didn't really need help. At one point, when he was explaining something, she interrupted him, pointed to Hakkarainen and said, "No, him." Once again he saw, with a kind of double vision, that what no one was actually coming out and saying was that Wall Street didn't even want to see his face. Drawing on his readings of the Dalai Lama, he didn't react at all to Wylde but tried, as best he could, to exude practical good will. It didn't seem to make much difference. To give Wylde confidence that her group's money would be secure, Roland Martin-Lof went along to the meeting. He was ready, he said, to negotiate a contract with penalties and bonuses—bonuses for more output and penalties for any paper not having the right quality. Wylde listened carefully to him and nodded, but didn't say anything, and she listened carefully to everyone else, and afterward wrote in a note to Jonathan Rose that the project seemed "important for the city" and that they'd like to be helpful in "bringing it to fruition."

Requesting certain documents, she expressed her concern that "a surrogate owner-operator, even one as capable and world-renowned as Kvaerner, might not be in a position to exercise enough control over the project to give comfort to investors as to future management and operations." Wylde commissioned an analysis of the project by Salomon Brothers Smith Barney: no analyst from Salomon, to anyone's knowledge, contacted any of the consultants working on the project, and in the end the message came back in very general terms that the industry had too much capacity, and that the mill in New York would not be a good idea.

Although an article would appear a few years later in *Crain's New York Business* asserting that the Partnership generally had the problem of finding worthy manufacturing businesses to support, Wylde did not recommend helping the mill with a loan. Moreover, after receiving the Salomon analysis she communicated her lack of interest and confidence in the mill not only to her Partnership colleagues but to a great many city and state officials as well. She forwarded Salomon's report to them, which was, to say the least, more than a little unusual and to most people associated with the project, gratuitously hostile. Several months later Rose wrote Wylde a protesting letter, describing some of the fallout from her gesture: "Because the generally negative report done by Salomon Brothers was passed to the city in isolation from other facts and materials," he wrote, "and because it was then circulated among city and state officials, we find ourselves continually having to overcome obstacles and confusion stemming from the report and from comments attributed to Investment Fund's staff. We wish that all our submissions and all your due diligence or analysis would have been kept confidential, solely at the Fund. The Salomon report is misleading in many ways: for example, it doesn't adjust for time, it doesn't adjust for transportation costs, it compares unequal technologies and, most important, it doesn't address many specific aspects of our project. In many ways, the report is raw, general data with little applicability, but people without great knowledge of this complex subject area can be influenced by it. I am not sure what at this point can be done to remedy the negative cloud that has been cast, except to request that if you and your staff are asked about our project, it would be helpful if you would simply say you decided that the project was not appropriate for the Fund." Rose added, "Since many of the facts regarding the project have materially changed since you reviewed them, we would be grateful if you referred all inquiries to our investment banker, Dan Donovan, at Merrill Lynch."

Wylde responded that she had acted appropriately and wished the project well, but gave no indication that any struggle ought to be mounted to overcome whatever obstacles Rose had identified. When the Partnership was first announced publicly, it was spun as a catalyst for investing in manufacturing that would draw on the support of a lot of wealthy people who wanted to see that sector revitalized. Instead, the process had been as superficial and narrow as any bank application.

Not for the first time in his long history with this project, Hershkowitz sensed, too, that the distrust Wylde obviously felt for him as an enviro had surely been compounded by the quickness of his speech, the animation of his facial gestures, and the enthusiasm he showed for the broader model he hoped the mill could be used for. One afternoon as we were finishing lunch at a Greek restaurant called Periyali, across the street from his office, he remarked matter-of-factly, "Business people hate enthusiasm, it seems to delegitimatize whatever you're saying," and proffered a quote from Emerson, whose dog-eared *Collected Essays* he'd been toting around ever since graduate school, and to which he repeatedly returned: "Passion heats up a room and everyone flees."

He had also lately come to grasp, frustratingly, that the very successes of the project—in acquiring the permits, high-powered players, and whatever financing they'd attracted—had changed the way they were being looked at. Whereas, at the beginning, many people saw them as civic do-gooders trying to leverage their philanthropic circumstances toward a profit-making public interest institution, in time, Hershkowitz observed, "People began to say, 'Oh, you're just like any other business, and we're going to compete with you as we would with every other business and cut your balls off as we would any other business.'" Business leaders were always criticizing environmental organizations for getting in the way of development; the project was a gesture at changing those stripes a bit and the hope was that groups like the Partnership would respond in those terms, but that would have required a mindset entirely different from what Hershkowitz and his colleagues encountered.

12

A Rolls-Royce with a Flat

ALTHOUGH IT WAS Morse Diesel that had approached Kvaerner to be their equipment supplier—contractually it was their decision as to whom they could work with—they ultimately couldn't accept the 50/50 partnership demand. Since Morse Diesel wanted more than a 50 percent claim in what *they* at least saw as a lucrative enterprise, the collaboration crumbled because of that basic disagreement over anticipated profit.

When the news came that Kvaerner was out, Hershkowitz and others were busy rooting around to find out what additional subsidies akin to the state revolving fund—for example, recycling financing, brownfield remediation financing, municipal ownership possibilities—might be cobbled together to further help the development process. Having deferred to Morse Diesel and Kvaerner to work out their negotiations, Hershkowitz had been unaware that the course of those negotiations had not been progressing smoothly. Unfortunately, urbane, kind, thoughtful Roland Martin-Lof, whom everyone liked, was in London, while Krieser, his chief negotiator, was reportedly disliked by the people at Morse Diesel. From what Hershkowitz heard, Krieser was the anti-Roland. He had also not been aware initially that neither the *Times* nor Hakkarainen was all that happy with the idea of Kvaerner as the operator, because the firm hadn't had that much experience with high-quality newsprint paper—their experience had been mostly with the kind of paper used for penny-savers and similar giveaway sheets. Hakkarainen in particular felt that they didn't have the right machinery for what the mill needed—or if they had it they would probably be testing it for the first time with the Bronx mill, and he didn't think the project could afford to be a guinea pig.

Hershkowitz was crushed when he heard the news and wondered, not for the first time, how clear a vision some of his partners had of the scarcity of unexplored avenues left open to them. Kvaerner might not be ideal, but it was certainly solid and willing; by now he was painfully aware of how capital intense the building of the mill was, especially in the city; he thought Morse Diesel was acting rashly; the departure of Kvaerner from the project with its all-important performance guarantees seemed to him like the premature sailing of a well-stocked supply ship from a hungry, besieged port. On the other hand, Morse Diesel wasn't worried, so in a perverse way this latest twist boosted Hershkowitz's confidence. NRDC itself took many risks in the boycotts and litigations it instigated, but so much in the business world seemed to be about risk aversion that without hefty support from the government, as the forest industry had in billions of dollars of taxpayer financed subsidies and exemptions from environmental laws, there was little chance of bringing about large-scale innovation. Even as the project had been moving forward in slow fits and starts, the forest industry had been vaulting ahead in its commercial logging to satisfy the world's growing demand for paper and other wood products. By the mid-twenty-first century, if current predictions are right, only 5 percent of all virgin tropical forests will remain on the planet. In the United States, where species and habitat diversity have been on the decline for more than a century, an estimated 95 percent of virgin forests have already been cleared and logged. Globally, less than 20 percent of the world's virgin forests now remain intact, and most of them are threatened. Nonetheless, as the EPA has reported, "the overwhelming bias of federal tax policies and program outlays favors extractive [virgin] industries and their beneficiaries over recycled markets." Examples of those policies and programs, apart from the federal donation of forest roads, include below-cost timber sales from federal lands, United States Forest Service research provided free to industry, and write-offs for timber management costs. Furthermore, along with the growth of the industry, the technologies for timber harvesting, timber processing, and paper-making continue to spew forth deadly discharges of hazardous waste, greenhouse gases, and effluents, and its products have contaminated lakes, rivers, and landfills with phenol- and heavy-metal-laden discards that break down into billions of pounds of toxic organic compounds, dioxins, acid gases, and climate-altering chemicals. Wood-based pulp and paper mills, besides being famously malodorous (the result of their "cooking" process, which produces major emissions of sulfur compounds), have also long been known to produce significant quantities of hazardous air pollutants.

For a while Hakkarainen had been talking about the possibility of forming a management group to run the mill with others like himself, experienced in the paper world, and this idea was now discussed with greater interest. So was the obvious lack of political support from the mayor's office, which, at meeting after meeting about the supposedly available municipal wastepaper supply, was beginning to loom as a major stumbling block and one that the group seemed unable to succeed in overcoming. Now overseeing the people who were looking for financing for the mill, now talking to the engineering construction team, now dealing with the unions, now divining the latest paper supply figures, Hershkowitz was able to concentrate on this problem only fleetingly. Each one of the things he was doing was pretty much a full-time job, and even working flat out seven days and most nights a week, there always seemed to be one more big task that needed attention immediately.

The human resources person at the office called him to say that unless she had calculated wrong, with sick days and not taking a vacation in over four years, he had accumulated 147 days off. And they both laughed. But the number of night meetings, small-hour-of-the-morning transatlantic calls, and overnight hotel stays in the city continued to steal precious time from his family. Meg had started her own electricity-brokering and energy-conserving business and began working at home, and in order to make that work his childcare responsibilities grew.

Perhaps Hershkowitz, who once took heat from a Democratic bureaucrat when he stood near Governor Pataki as he announced certain significant legislative and environmental gains at a press conference, should have understood how much the project could have used a dedicated political strategy committee. NRDC's unequivocal nonpartisan policy, for instance, was an obvious liability in the shark-infested waters of big development politics. And unbeknownst to Hershkowitz, the dispensing of Bond Act jobs was part of the ongoing struggle between the governor's office and Charles Gargano. The act provided a lot of money for constructing better sewage treatment plants and for capping landfills and perforce would create many construction and other union jobs, and the ambassador reportedly assumed he would control those jobs as part of the Empire State Development Corp.'s normal largesse-doling function. But it turned out that Mike Finnegan, as head of the governor's environmental team, would control it and allocate new patronage, and once again Gargano was said to have been more than displeased. Hershkowitz sensed that the two men were not that fond of one another, but he had no idea of the depth of their differences. At the meeting to introduce Morse Diesel to the state officials where he so irritated Gargano in every other way, he had also, in his Candide-like ignorance about the symbolism of the Bond Act, said proudly, "Oh, by the way, I spoke with Michael Finnegan. Finnegan says he thinks we can get Bond Act money to support this!"—and was utterly confounded by the baleful look his glad tidings elicited.

By the spring of 1997, Marilyn Gelber, the progressive and well-liked commissioner of the city's Department of Environmental Protection, to whom Hershkowitz had been introduced by Jonathan Rose in 1994 and with whom he had had a happy and productive relationship, was gone. Gelber was that rarity in bureaucratic circles, an experienced civil servant who had the capacity to think innovatively. A holdover from the previous administration, Gelber was fired by Mayor Giuliani for "bad management," at a particularly awkward moment in her prolonged, delicate, and successful effort to work with entrenched opponents—the upstate watershed towns and the environmental community—to establish controls on the upstate reservoirs that provided the city's increasingly threatened water supply. People familiar with the inner workings of city government said that she was ousted because she balked at hiring patronage appointees foisted on her by the mayor. An unusual editorial in the *Times* (which generally accepts political beheadings and appointments as standard operating procedure) protested that Gelber "was forced out of office before her task was done."

Without Gelber's participation it would have been far harder to channel state revolving fund money to the mill. The loans were earmarked only for municipalities, not private institutions, so Gelber, working with Hershkowitz, had figured out a way for the city to technically own the water cleanup plant, though the BCPC would pay for its construction and operation. Gelber admired Hershkowitz's idea from the start and found him "brave and smart." He, in turn, had found her, nearly uniquely in the city bureaucracy, as enthusiastic about the novel environmental aspects of the project as he was. And insofar as they applied to her bailiwick—the city water supply, its machinery, staff, six thousand miles of water mains, and its sewage water treatment plants (including the Ward's Island plant, just across the Bronx Kill from the Harlem River yard), which treated 283 million gallons a day of wastewater—she was eager to find a way to turn them into reality. As one of the members of the team observed, "If Gelber had been mayor, the mill would have been up and running in two years."

As far as the state government was concerned, the project qualified for subsidies mainly because the project's sewage-water-into-clean process involved radically reducing (from fifteen milligrams per liter to less than two) the nitrogen discharge coming from the mill's share of the Ward's Island sewage treatment plant water, which normally ends up as an algae-creating pollutant in Long Island Sound. To learn about the hundreds of billions of gallons of the city's effluent discharge every year and the chemical content of the water they would be dealing with, and to find ways to clean it up, was as difficult and complex a task as any Hershkowitz and his team had to take on. Five different engineering companies labored on it. This work was made infinitely easier, however, by Gelber's promptly cutting through miles of red tape to make the right people available quickly. Sifting through her directory of senior staff who oversaw effluent management—people who served on the Water Utility Board, engineers who were designing future systems, and people currently operating the system—she called them and

put them together in one room from the very start with Hershkowitz and his team with instructions to try to make the plan work.

When I spoke with her, Gelber was modest about what she'd
done. "I fully anticipated that we would come to an agreement
here. I never doubted that if the engineering worked—and we saw
eventually that it seemed to—and if we could come up with some
range in terms of price tag for this thing, I was confident that we
could work it out—and there was a real public benefit to it."

Hershkowitz says that Gelber's input in terms of leadership
was monumental, and Phil Sears, whose environmental planning
firm was one of those working on the water process and who by
then had been dealing with the DEP on various projects for nearly
twenty years, said he had never before witnessed that degree of cooperation and coordination by a commissioner for a project. Despite all the help, however, some early engineers working with the
BCPC team screwed up when they set out to assess the characteristics of the water to make sure there weren't too many persistent
toxins in it. In other words, *could* it be cleaned up?

That was a crucial question, since the idea that the city used
more than a billion gallons a day of this increasingly precious resource only once and then discarded it seemed like folly from an
environmental point of view. It was a fundamental principle of the
project that it would not go forward if they had to use fresh water.
He knew the Visy mill was using a million gallons of fresh water
a day; with droughts and water shortages plaguing so much of the
globe, that seemed a travesty. Because the city didn't have a lot
of industrial dischargers, though, Hershkowitz had a pretty good
idea that the tests would have a positive result. He had served on
the New York City Citizen Advisory Council's Sludge Advisory
Board—sludge is the byproduct of water treatment—and he was
an avid reader of *Sludge News*. What the engineers, who weren't
from New York, forgot when they took their fresh water samples
from the East River, however, is that it flows both north and south,
because it is tidal. Initially they took a sample only when it was
flowing south, when almost no ocean salt was flowing into the sewage treatment plant, and found that the pollutants were mostly bac-
teriological rather than more persistent organic toxins.

They discovered their mistake by sheer dumb luck: Tim Martin, who was working with Sears on a lot of the day-to-day water matters, was having a conversation with one of the DEP engineers, who just happened to mention in passing the oddity of the two-way flow of the river. Martin, realizing at once that their sample was obviously all wrong because of that, raced back to NRDC and called everyone working on the water system to tell them that they had to quickly get another fresh sample. When they took the new sample, from the river's northward run, they naturally found that the now-brackish water had chlorides from sea salt that ranged from 700 to 800 parts per million. The cleanup system would reduce that to under 30 parts per million—a more than satisfactory level.

Under Gelber's watch, her staff, working together with the BCPC staff, found a way to design the cleanup system in the most compact manner possible (a reverse-osmosis-system plant—one that uses electric charges to dechlorinate water—was going to occupy half an acre on Ward's Island next to the sewage treatment plant), in the most technically reliable way possible, and the least costly way possible. After Gelber was fired, BCPC also had to design a pipe transport system from Ward's Island to the Harlem River yard. As a result of the close collaboration that developed between DEP senior staffers and the BCPC team, Hershkowitz also came to know more than a little about the people who served Gelber. Though BCPC was going to operate the mill, Hershkowitz knew that it was really important to the senior engineer at Ward's Island that city employees who worked with him would run the reverse-osmosis plant and no one else.

Gelber's successor was Joel Miele, an engineer who had been the city's Department of Buildings commissioner. When he took over, the whole project got suddenly lowered like a boat on a lock, dropping down several levels in terms of senior staff availability and decision making. In a day-to-day way, Miele delegated the project to his deputy commissioner, Robert Adamski. Adamski was a seasoned DEP employee, but he balked at hiring municipal employees for the plant when a private company could foot the bill, and Hershkowitz had the impression that he hadn't really discussed the issue with Ron Wallace, the senior engineer at Ward's Island.

When Hershkowitz next spoke with Wallace, his impression was confirmed. Moreover, Wallace was really ticked about the idea of outsiders coming in to operate on his turf. "No way," he said, which Hershkowitz thought was understandable, but suddenly the whole project seemed in jeopardy because of the way DEP communication had broken down.

To Hershkowitz's regret, Gelber's chief of staff, Ben Esner, with whom he had spoken many times a week, left shortly after she did, and Hershkowitz never again had the same access he had under her stewardship. The process of planning continued to evolve after she left, but it lost the momentum it had when she was monitoring the effort. He and Miele attended several meetings together, but Hershkowitz never actually spoke separately with him, even about the water rate they were going to be charged—a crucially important matter still unresolved when Gelber left. The "gray" water was going to be a lot cheaper than fresh; industry paid about $1.39 per 100 cubic feet (or about 760 gallons) for fresh water; the BCPC needed a new rate structure for their gray water because none existed (there never having been a market for it), and they were fighting to get it knocked down to about 50 cents per 100 cubic feet. Gelber believed that a satisfactory rate would eventually be worked out. "The easiest thing in government is to say no," she told me. "It's much harder to say yes and figure out a way within the very complicated government context to work things out." But whereas she was willing to push things along so that most of the water problems would be solved by the time the ownership issue was resolved, Miele's withdrawal as enthusiastic collaborator and the subsequent ascendance of lawyers and engineers slowed matters down considerably. Sears told me that putting a new rate structure into place is a big deal, and "they are very careful about it because it is a precedent for a long, long time. . . . And *any* rate changes are watched fearfully by some very powerful interests." But Ben Esner, Gelber's chief of staff, who was gone by then but heard about what happened, and was all too familiar with the process, had a somewhat different take: "Lawyers and engineers will negotiate forever—they need somebody to stop the lawyering and tinkering. They need somebody who can sign off."

Despite the new "keep your head down" tone that characterized the Department of Environmental Protection, in time, Sears says, because of all the work that had been done under Gelber, they had a negotiated agreement. "Not a total agreement, but we were in place and it could have been signed off on as soon as there was somebody to sign off for it on the project side." The Water Board, which is under mayoral control and therefore a highly politicized body, had not yet approved the new rate. Had the mayor been strongly behind the project, said Sears, "We would have had the gray water contract all signed and sealed and taken care of." But, to Gelber, even the Cerberus-like Water Board did not seem like an insuperable obstacle. "It could have gone through, even without the Water Board, as an interim pilot project—one plan, one time—as an experiment, which it was. And then, if it succeeded as a business, we'd set a rate."

One of the innovative changes Gelber had made at the DEP was to establish for the first time an Environmental Economic Development Assistance Unit, to try to help bridge the widening gap between economic development and environmental concerns. "I was really thrilled with the idea when Allen came in, that here was this environmental organization that got it in terms of green industries—it wasn't just to say no, to sue, to stop something."

By the late spring of 1997, Hershkowitz had finally worked out the structure of a paper contract with the city with a deputy mayor, though the commitment letter, confirming that the city's wastepaper was actually going to be made available, was still not forthcoming. In truth, the paper acquisition process had begun to look rather zany, or even surreal to a number of people on the team—and even to some people who were not part of the team. In the same way that Hershkowitz was shielding helpful bureaucrats like Eric Deutsch at the city's Economic Development Corp. and other city officials from his increasing worries about Banana Kelly as a partner, Deutsch was shielding him from discouraging news: though he was continually knocking on colleagues' doors at City Hall to try to get the city's commitment to the project locked in, he was getting nowhere.

Still desperately trying to lower the construction costs, Hershkowitz, Rose, Pulver, and Donovan were told at a meeting with Morse Diesel's project director, Charles Ludlow, that they couldn't go down any more, basically because of labor costs. "If you were building to achieve the lowest cost, you'd build in Indonesia or Brazil," Ludlow said at one point. Hershkowitz knew that was true, which was why he continued to argue that the government had to step up to the plate—if for nothing else than as an alternative to the city's incinerator program. Until the environmental community had prevented it, the city was going to be spending $3 billion on five incinerators to get rid of its garbage. Why not pony up just a fraction of that to help a project that so beneficially dealt with some of the city's waste?

That spring, too, he had attended the annual dinner of the League of Conservation Voters. He had been on hand at the dinner many times before, but this one was different. On this occasion Richard Pratt, Visy's owner, was honored and Visy was given the League's annual environmental award for building their recycling mill. The Visy project had also cleaned up a brownfield, of course, and was recycling city paper, but—call him nitpicking—it did seem to Hershkowitz a bit ironic that they should be singled out for an environmental award, considering the cursoriness of their environmental review and their earlier utter lack of interest in a plan that would have cut down enormously on the city's truck traffic.

For the much needed state revolving fund monies to be channeled through the state's money-dispensing Environmental Facilities Corporation and released to the project, that agency needed a small mountain of engineering, legal, and financial reports to be sent its way. Marty Gold, along with various people at Morse Diesel, was working nearly round the clock to satisfy their demands, but was driven nearly crazy by a particular senior engineer at the EFC. Hershkowitz laughed wildly whenever anyone brought up the engineer's name and told me that he actually had Kafkaesque nightmares about the man, whose bureaucratic zealousness seemed boundless. It was around that time, too, that Gold helped negotiate an arrangement with Morse Diesel: against the soon-to-be-awarded state revolving fund money, Morse Diesel would take an amount of money equal to the amount being paid for water-related work and loan it back to BCPC to pay people who were not working on water-related issues.

With all this whirling around him, the central missing component of an owner was now looming larger every day, and Hershkowitz was beginning to feel more than a little depressed as what seemed like every paper company on the planet declined to work with them. At a meeting at Merrill Lynch, Dan Donovan had stressed that they *had* to find a way to close before the end of the year, that the tax-exempt investor market was a disaster, and that three or four de-inking projects around the country were in default. The idea that time was running out and that they'd better move faster was now being expressed in many quarters; Hershkowitz had received a call not long before from the city Department of Sanitation. The department needed to know soon — if it was going to be giving them its paper — that there was something there to give it to.

Hershkowitz began noticing that he was answering on the average about twenty-five phone calls daily about the project. He rarely put down the phone without his assistant telling him that two or three people needed him to call back immediately, and he was sending or receiving at least as many project-related e-mails that required his urgent attention every day. There had also been such an intense effort over the past few months coordinating so many technical financial analyses, addressing so many political issues, and dealing with the demands of so many city and state agencies that he was at the point of total exhaustion — and it was far from clear that they were moving any closer to closing. Just when his despair had begun to shift into overdrive, he and Meg happened to attend a local landowners' council semiannual dinner. There he bumped into Ken Wallach, the president of Central National Gottesman, one of the largest mill representatives in the world, who had been following the project's progress for several years and had some interest in marketing the mill's output. Over drinks at the bar, Wallach asked what was happening and listened attentively as Hershkowitz gave him an update. When he finished, Wallach said he might be able to help him. The following week Wallach met with the team (which was now about forty strong and included not only most of the original consultants and advisers but also about twenty engineers and construction people) at Morse Diesel's midtown office and was given a more elaborate description of the project's evolution to date.

In that same period, recognizing that despite all their negotiations they were encountering some nearly insurmountable resistance from City Hall vis-à-vis the paper, the team decided to hire a lobbying law firm that was famously well connected in the city, especially with the mayor. It was hoped that the lawyers would help them find a way to vault past whatever obstacles stood in their way. They paid the firm a huge retainer, and at one point were assured that the city had agreed to their proposal and a Memorandum of Understanding was all but on its way; but not only did their efforts prove useless, the lawyers they worked with kept pressing Hershkowitz to pony up money for Mayor Giuliani's war chest and continued to press him even after he explained that he was unable to oblige because of NRDC rules. At a lunch with a former chairman of NRDC and Ed Costikiyan, another New York power broker with strong ties to the mayor's office, Costikiyan promised, too, to try to intervene on the project's behalf. That day he put in a call to the mayor's office. Deputy Mayor Randy Mastro told Costikiyan, "Others want the paper," but asked for a two-page memo. The memo was duly sent but joined the blizzard of previous memos sent to City Hall in, apparently, political black-hole-dom.

Then, on July 10, 1997, Hershkowitz's eldest son Dylan's tenth birthday, Ken Wallach from Central National Gottesman phoned Hershkowitz. "Allen," he said, "I think you've got a Rolls-Royce with a flat tire and I'm going to supply you with a spare — I may have found an operator for you — Joe Kruger." Kruger, who in 2001 was named "Supplier of the Year" by Dow Jones for the third year in a row, ran one of the largest paper companies in North America — its principal product was toilet paper — and he was the third generation of his family to run the privately held company, which was based in Montreal. Kruger's name had, in fact, been mentioned a couple of times before, but for reasons Hershkowitz was unsure of, nobody went after him. It might have been because Kruger was known, as one executive familiar with the paper industry put it, as "a bottom feeder" — that is, known for buying cheap facilities in bad shape and rehabilitating them as opposed to building new greenfield plants or acquiring top-of-the-line ones. Hakkarainen had seemed, at an earlier date, not to want to work with him, Hershkowitz sensed, because Hakkarainen was a bit of a snob—he was always talking about "the big boys," like the *New York Times*'s Sulzbergers, with whom he liked to do business—and Kruger was cut a bit rough for Hakkarainen's taste.

Now, however, Kruger looked like the train's last stop and nobody was thinking of reasons not to like him. By the end of the month the team was setting up meetings with Kruger's chief financial officer. In the midst of the enormous burst of energy and paperwork gathering for the briefings that accompanied this happy development, they finally closed on the $3 million state revolving fund advance. The closing took place on September 4, 1997, at a downtown law firm, and to Hershkowitz's horror Rivera did not show up—although he'd called several times to remind her about the closing. Her non-appearances had by now become a common occurrence—sometimes she'd show up for important meetings, sometimes she wouldn't, and she rarely called to say when she wasn't going to make it—but this was obviously such an important moment for the project that Hershkowitz found her absence difficult to fathom. When the papers were drafted, both his name and hers were on the document; in order to close, the lawyers had to white out her name.

Five days later, on September 9, 1997, Hershkowitz, along with several people key to the project, met with Joe Kruger and George Bunze, Kruger's CFO, at Merrill Lynch's midtown office. A short, thin, confident-looking gray-haired man, who spoke in a far more animated way than any paper company executive Hershkowitz had yet met, Kruger had come to offer his services and to give the project just what Hershkowitz said was needed to keep the mill alive, but no more—and especially not enough to make Wall Street happy. Kruger seemed to know just how desperate the project was and strode into the situation with all the finesse of a Mack truck.

In a memo he sent to several of his NRDC colleagues after meeting Kruger, Hershkowitz wrote, "Kruger offered to operate the mill and invest $10 million, a very low amount by Wall Street standards. So low, in fact, it might not be adequate to get the mill financed, since it will raise questions in the minds of other potential equity investors as to why the operator is putting in less than one-tenth the amount of equity the project needs. Kruger wants a one-year payback on his $10 million—that is, he wants $10 million in fees and profit in the first year alone. That would be possible if newsprint prices were at their 1995 historic high levels (about $800/ton), but it's hard to do. I told him that we would try to see if BCPC could construct a capital structure that might allow for that. He wants government subsidies to make up the difference if we can't meet his demands."

Hershkowitz reported that Kruger, like so many of the paper company officials, had a real aversion to New York. He went on to quote Kruger as saying: "'Frankly, I'm very afraid of the city and I don't want to go near the Bronx.' And he said, 'What can your organization do to help me sell more toilet paper? Maybe if you helped that market, I'd be more helpful here in the Bronx.'" Hershkowitz suggested, pokerfaced, according to someone else who was at the meeting, that perhaps they might start a campaign touting the benefits of eating prunes.

After Hershkowitz laid out the basic financial arrangements of the project, he continued in the memo, "Kruger said, 'Let me get this straight. You've raised $8 million for this project and you're not getting it back?' I told him our return was to see this project succeed, since it would be good for the city and help some very poor people find jobs, that's our mission.' He looked around the room like I was the dumbest moron in the room (which, as you all know, may be true). It is rather sad to see a guy with so much wealth be such a pig. He also said, quite seriously, that he 'wants a medal from the vice president' if he helps make the deal happen."

The response to his memo that Hershkowitz most treasured was from Pattie Sullivan, NRDC's witty, elegant, auburn-haired deputy executive director for administration. She wrote: "I personally really want to meet Joe Kruger and hope there is not a MRS. Kruger as he sounds like my kind of guy. Keep up your good spirits, Allen."

In addition to his $10 million in fees and profits in the first year, Kruger also said he wanted a guaranteed $10 million a year for ten years after that, from operating fees, sales, or return on equity. While on the one hand, this would be a ridiculously sweet deal for Kruger, on the other, the consensus was that without Kruger the deal would fall apart—get him onboard, was the general idea, and we'll negotiate a better deal. We'll build on what's there. At that point, every last-ditch effort to enlist other paper companies—Bowater, Weyerhaeuser, IP, Georgia Pacific, SCA, Donohue, McLaren, Japan Pulp and Paper, Oji—had come to nothing, and Hakkarainen, his good connections notwithstanding, was not coming up with anything either. Before Kathy Wylde had requested the Salomon Smith Barney report and circulated it to the greater metropolitan area, and after Stone had pulled out, Hershkowitz had talked to several analysts himself at Salomon over breakfast in their executive dining room; the Salomon people had said that there were probably only two paper companies who would do the deal at that point when there seemed to be so much overcapacity in the industry: Pratt and Kruger. Both companies were privately owned and, the way the market looked, that was crucial because there was no way a publicly traded company would do it—their stock would plummet if they had to justify new capacity to their stockholders, no matter how valuable the project was environmentally or socially. Also, publicly traded companies couldn't at that point justify building any domestic mills when Asian mills were suddenly becoming extraordinarily cheap and easy to buy. They had actually asked Pratt, but he wasn't interested.

Kruger was the BCPC's last best hope—and there was only a little more than five months to go before they lost their permits. Their state loan agreements specified that they had to have an operator who would use them by February 28, 1998, or they would forfeit their permits, and that, as everyone knew, was about how long it would probably take to negotiate and finalize a contract. Hershkowitz ended the meeting by telling Kruger that he would try to get him what he needed. Kruger seemed a bit stunned; he asked him if he'd actually understood his terms, and Hershkowitz told him he had.

13

Signed, Sealed, and Deconstructed

THE DAY AFTER THE Kruger meeting Hershkowitz and three colleagues paid a visit to Ruben Kraiem, the chair of the Legal Committee of NRDC's board and a partner at one of the city's leading law firms. Kraiem ran his firm's Latin American investment practice. Because of his position on the board, Hershkowitz had briefed Kraiem periodically, and this visit was an important one because everyone on the NRDC board who knew about the project was wondering if it was really going to happen. Kraiem was one of the board members—who he believed were in the majority, he told me—who had felt "enthusiastic" about the mill project and thought it was "a terrific idea." But as chair of the Legal Committee, he was, in a sense, NRDC's lawyer, charged with scrutinizing the risks the organization was presented with. As he understood his role, he couldn't "think too hard about the merits of a particular action." Rather, he told me, "I have to look at what the risks are and be extremely clear about them and then have other people, who are program people, decide—well, notwithstanding the risks, it's the thing to do." Like everyone else, he thought the Kruger deal was too sweet. But after his visitors left his office, he seems to have been marginally persuaded that they could eventually work to make it a better deal, by the necessity of Kruger's participation to save their lease with the state and by the argument that Kruger was, in fact, going to be a catalytic force, an operator the *Times* could accept and a strategic, significant investor. He also saw how many directions Hershkowitz was being pulled in, and like so many others before him, strongly suggested that people be found to help him more.

Kraiem advised them to find an additional investment banker to help structure the next phase of the project. Of course, from Kruger's point of view, he, too, was taking risks by moving forward; their five years of steady effort notwithstanding, there was still a great deal of uncertainty hovering around the deal. What the project had were the permits, the lease, and a good idea that several important companies had signed on to; but neither the paper agreement nor the off-take agreements had been locked in, and they were still a long way from closing. It was not as if there were a mill in place that Kruger could just take over and move into production. So while more than a few people saw the Kruger offer as insubstantial, Hershkowitz, who that day had been told that there was a possibility that the governor might try to talk to Kruger and try to get him to ante up some more, was thrilled.

Whatever the deficiencies of Kruger's offer, the team gratefully felt as if they would finally get to cross the finish line. Maya Lin was working hard preparing her model and drawings of the project for the Municipal Art Society show, which would be taking place during the Christmas season, at a time when thousands of tourists would be milling around Rockefeller Center, a block away from where the show was going to be held on Madison Avenue. For once, her input and the good publicity that it was expected to generate was universally understood to be an important benefit.

Then, on October 7, 1997, Gary Simpson's NAB Construction Company announced that it was suing BCPC, NRDC, Banana Kelly, Morse Diesel, Valmet, Jaakko Pöyry, Hakkarainen, and New York City Paper Mill, Inc. (a corporate vehicle established briefly by Hakkarainen) for *tortious interference,* a fancy way of saying that all of them had unfairly breached their contract and kept Simpson's company from its rightful market opportunity.

As soon as Hershkowitz received news about the suit, he trudged, shaken, down the hall to John Adams's office to tell him about it. He was particularly stunned because, a few months earlier, when Simpson was threatening to sue, Hershkowitz had checked with Marty Gold and some other attorneys and asked if Simpson had a case. They asked him if BCPC itself had an agreement with Simpson, and he told them, "No." And the lawyers were unanimous in their opinion that there was no case and not to worry. He'd also bumped into Simpson at another League of Conservation Voters celebration. Simpson had been more than friendly at the party, Hershkowitz told me: "Gary comes over. 'Hi, Allen. How are you doing? Let's let bygones be bygones. How is the project going?' I told him it was going great. 'Oh, you think it's going to happen?' 'Yeah.' Two months later we get this lawsuit levied against us, claiming that we stole his project." Although the sums involved were large—NRDC alone was being sued for $80 million and the total amount of the suit added up to some $600 million—Adams reacted calmly to the news. NRDC's annual budget at the time was only $30 million, and if they lost, they'd be wiped out. But he simply said to Hershkowitz in his usual affable way, "Go tell Pattie" (Sullivan), and directed him to call Charles Koob, an NRDC board member and partner at Simpson Thacher & Bartlett, who would handle the matter. "The NAB lawsuit seems to be in good hands," Hershkowitz wrote in a note to Adams a month later. "It could take a while—nine months or so—to get rid of it; my diaries were Xeroxed by the lawyers last week."

Once the lawyer and other NRDC board members began looking at the suit, however, and considered the organization's vulnerability and weighed its key role in the development process, it was soon decided, to the project team's horror, that a radical bailout was in order. Whatever the viability of the project at that point, the lawyers and investment bankers on the board who looked out for NRDC's interests felt that the organization had to withdraw from its leading role in it. At a meeting of the board's legal and financial committees and a few other board trustees on January 7, 1998, there was, as Pattie Sullivan later characterized it, a "rush for the door." With Henry Breck, the board's treasurer and never a project enthusiast, taking the lead by saying emphatically, "It's time to move on," the ad hoc committee that had been created to consider the organization's position, composed of men who had served as Hershkowitz's advisers throughout all the years of the project, decided that NRDC had too vulnerable a role in the project and should no longer be so centrally involved.

Breck, who describes himself in his NRDC board of trustees bio as "an economic and social conservative who is also committed to NRDC's ultimate goals," observed that although the project was obviously still being worked out, they'd already spent too much time and money ($2 million) on it and the lawsuit was telling them that it was time to withdraw as expeditiously as possible and let others carry it forward. It was further agreed that Hershkowitz, who was characterized as being "too close to the project," would also have to withdraw.

Marty Gold, who was there along with Adams, Beinecke, John Cavanagh of Morse Diesel, and Sullivan, said, "If you take him out, this project is going to die." At that point, Hershkowitz, Marty Gold, Bruce Pulver, Dan Donovan, Jonathan Rose, and others on the BCPC team had just spent four months negotiating *mano a mano* with Joe Kruger and George Bunze. They had to deliver an operating agreement to the state by February 28, 1998, or the project's permits would be gone and they'd default, and at that moment, though the Kruger deal was miraculously close to being finalized, there were a mere six weeks until the permit-default date. So Hershkowitz went into shock when the board said to him, "Get out."

Some years after the meeting, he told me, "I couldn't speak, because, if I spoke, I would have cried. What was going through my mind was all the work I'd been doing and all the work that still had to be done. Even then, it took me a year to stop working on the project. But it wasn't a deliberate exit strategy. The single biggest mistake we made was not bringing in my colleagues from the programs at that point." Hershkowitz had been talking to his NRDC program colleagues, the organization's advocates, people like Eric Goldstein, who was sensitive to the social issues, and others whose advice he sought on water issues, air issues, transportation issues, brownfield cleanup issues every step of the way. There were perhaps twelve different colleagues he'd had to check with all along. "Eric was the first guy I talked with because he's in charge of New York City. He was dealing with sewage water cleanup and emission policy—these are the people who knew the stakes for the project. These are also the people who are normally *consulted* to work with the board people to figure out an exit strategy."

He continued, "There was no discussion, no debate, no program, no rational plan about how to make the program succeed while we protected the institution. It felt very haphazard. Ad hoc. Abrupt. We just figured out how to get out. I said, 'Wait, there are nineteen contracts I signed—with Morse Diesel, Marty Gold, Mike Gerrard, Jonathan Rose, Maya Lin.' I had hired people. Money from the state, grants. They said, 'Okay, well, we have to get out of those. We have to make sure we have no liability.' It did not seem to me to be the smart way we normally do things."

Had there been any precedent for this, any other lawsuits? I asked.

"Sure," he said. "A similar situation occurred with the apple growers and alar, but then there had been a deliberate, thoughtful retreat. Normally what we do is convene program people and board people and review what our objectives are and how we might still achieve them. But this did not feel like a strategically considered exit, it was really Henry blowing steam, which became NRDC policy."

Hershkowitz believed at first that the main reason for the rapid exit, which took over a year to finalize, was the lawsuit. All the more because Adams, while being generally gallant and supportive, not long afterward allowed himself to say, "If this suit brings down the organization, I'll never forgive you." On one of their Sunday walks during that period, Jonathan Rose was moved to comment, "Boy, you guys sue everybody, but when it happens to you, you just can't handle it." Hershkowitz thought there was some truth in that, but nonetheless he had many sleepless nights thinking about what Adams had said. He told himself guiltily that whatever he thought about the disastrous way the exit was taking place, it was understandable, considering the jeopardy in which the suit seemed to place NRDC.

But he was wrong about the organization's motive for wanting out. Although the possibility of losing a suit is always there, none of the main movers of the organization's withdrawal—not Henry Breck or Ruben Kraiem—thought that it placed the organization in much danger. What they thought, I discovered when I interviewed them, was more like: Well, here's just one more nail in the coffin of this thing that has gone on too long. Breck, a straightforward, influential, and forceful board member, had wanted the project to work, he told me, though from the start he didn't believe it had a chance, because it was economically dicey. And he thought the lawsuit was "absurd." I had noticed, too, from an Internet search that NAB had been involved in many lawsuits. About the current one, Breck said, "I never took it seriously. First of all I thought that the number was ridiculous and I thought that if we ended up losing . . . one way or another we might have to settle it for a couple of million dollars. Eighty million was crazy. The mere fact that the number was so large made me think of it with derision." But, Breck added, "I also felt enough's enough. I didn't want to be around the project anymore. It was generating lawsuits and it was burning up one of the most talented people in the environmental movement." The organization had already invested enormous amounts of money and time and effort in the project, and, unlike Stephen Golden at the *Times,* who still had confidence in the project, Breck felt convinced that "it was not going to happen."

Ruben Kraiem was given the task of finding a way to end NRDC's role in the enterprise. "The idea was," Hershkowitz said, "to get us out, period, and it took him four months of work when he tried to do that. . . . This was a nearly half-billion-dollar project NRDC wanted to get out of. Fine. But no one who was actually working on it wanted the project to end." After a while Hershkowitz understood that none of the board members involved, because of their worries about the organizational role in the development process, cared much if it died or not. Even as he saw that he would not be allowed to continue doing what he was doing, however, Hershkowitz argued strenuously that a way should be found to protect the project, and one was, but from his point of view, not a way that ultimately served it well.

What Kraiem found when he looked into the project worried him so much that it just seemed crucial to beat a retreat. "What I learned . . . was that NRDC was perceived, rightly or wrongly, as having responsibility to develop the project which exceeded the role that NRDC was qualified to perform. We were perceived as having the lead role in areas that exposed the organization to considerable risk. However important the project was, the overall health and solvency and reputation of NRDC are much, much, much more important and so my first reaction to that was — that's kind of alarming. . . . People think that they can come against us for business deals that go sour. That's not a good thing."

During the next weeks, while regularly visiting the Simpson Thacher lawyers and telling them everything he knew about the project and especially about the NAB affair, Hershkowitz continued in a kind of hallucinatory spirit to finalize the agreement with Kruger. At the beginning of December, Dan Donovan, the investment banker who'd been working on the project along with Bruce Pulver, reported to Hershkowitz late on a Friday that he had lost his job at Merrill Lynch, and by the following Tuesday Donovan had an office and a job working as a BCPC project consultant with Hershkowitz at NRDC. Meanwhile Maya Lin's show at the Municipal Art Society had opened and been received with great fanfare, bringing the project much favorable public attention, and around that time, while giving a program report to the NRDC board of directors, Frances Beinecke, John Adams's second in command, spoke with genuine admiration about the show. But, even as the architecture critic Herbert Muschamp was lavishing praise on the project in the *Times,* Hershkowitz's confreres at NRDC were working toward relieving themselves of its burdens.

Once again Hershkowitz had worked straight through the Christmas holiday, and for the second year in a row, on New Year's Day. Part of the ongoing development negotiations, which were being handled by Gold, Pulver, Donovan, and Rose, as well as Hershkowitz, involved a certain amount of wrestling with Morse Diesel and with their landlord, Galesi. Although all of them were theoretically working together, Hershkowitz pointed out, "Donovan and Pulver and Rose were trying to get Morse Diesel to come to a better price. So they were not necessarily in tandem with Morse Diesel; and they were also working on Galesi to refine their long-term lease deal, so they were not necessarily in tandem with Galesi." Seeing the scimitar falling rapidly toward his neck, he tried to call Yolanda Rivera but couldn't reach her. He consulted with Per Batelson, who though in Sweden was still on the four-person BCPC board along with Rick Campbell, Hershkowitz, and Rivera. Both of them felt strongly that optimally the project should be taken over by those who knew it best—namely Rose, Donovan, and Pulver. But they knew that Galesi and the people at Morse Diesel wouldn't be that keen on the idea. "If the project is going to be tossed up, if it's going to be a jump ball," Hershkowitz told me at the time, "*they* want it, right? But I've been working on this thing six years, I know who has got the vision. I know who *knows* everything . . . and I say, okay, what I am going to try to do is finish the Kruger agreement, get it signed, and then try to get an agreement to give the project to Dan and Bruce and Jonathan."

But the NRDC board had other ideas. They did not want the project being passed to a "consortium of advisers," as Kraiem characterized the BCPC team. They wanted the project to go to a *company,* to men who run businesses. And even when Hershkowitz reported that Anthony Lacavalla, who would be running the sorting plant and had already put up half a million dollars, would be willing to kick in up to two million more to work with the team Hershkowitz was proposing, the board's ad hoc committee engineering NRDC's withdrawal did not warm to this idea. They thought that Lacavalla's was too small a business.

Back in early January, Aureo Cardona, who had somehow come to speak for Rivera at crucial moments, told Hershkowitz that he'd been talking to a banker at Credit Suisse who said he was interested in the project and "wanted to do the whole deal," and Cardona asked Hershkowitz and Donovan to look into it. A letter was produced from the Credit Suisse man in which he asked for various documents about the project, but when they put in a conference call to him, it immediately became clear that he wasn't in a position to do what Cardona said—his was a relatively modest position; he was not managing director for project finance. Even if he could have, moreover, he wouldn't have wanted to, he told them, because he just didn't do those kinds of projects. He had talked to Cardona, he said, out of courtesy to someone at the bank who knew Cardona. Furthermore, the Credit Suisse man said, "Banana Kelly is involved in a rogue effort that is not good for your project."

Sometime later, Hershkowitz was told that Kraiem, too, checked with Credit Suisse and confirmed what they'd found. When Hershkowitz and Donovan next talked to Rivera, they told her that the Credit Suisse man wasn't interested and they told her what he'd said, hoping that that would be the end of the matter. But on February 10, Rivera came into the office clearly upset. Cardona had apparently flipped the message from the Credit Suisse man. He told Rivera that the banker had said that it was Hershkowitz who referred to Banana Kelly as "a rogue company" and that Hershkowitz had used a racial epithet to characterize them. "Yolanda," Hershkowitz said, "do you believe that?" "I don't know what to believe," she told him.

Ironically, even as Kraiem was exploring NRDC's situation and figuring out ways to gracefully disentangle, Hershkowitz was making real progress with Kruger and was allowed to coast for a while because things were going so well. Despite all the to-ings and fro-ings and melodrama, and against all expectations, by February 13, 1998, Kruger was ready to sign. The final agreement had been reviewed by about half a dozen people, and on that day Donovan and Hershkowitz flew up to Montreal to meet with Kruger and his CFO, Bunze, in their two-story, factory-like office building just outside the city. Kruger's attitude toward the project and toward Hershkowitz had, over the past months, shifted by degrees from Here I am. What are you going to do for me? to Well, this is really a rather interesting critter, to Okay. Let's do this! In Hershkowitz's words, Kruger had gone from being an "intrigued skeptic to an almost enthusiastic collaborator" who in the end, Hershkowitz believed, would, because of the philanthropic uniqueness of the project, be persuaded to dig into his deep pockets for more money.

Kruger welcomed them warmly and after the signing introduced them to the president of the company, the vice president, and the team that had been picked to journey down to the Bronx to oversee construction at the mill. He also took them on a little tour of the office and with some pride pointed out photo-portraits of his forebears hanging in an office gallery. With only two weeks left to deliver the agreement to the state, the deal was finally done. Because Kruger was the sixth largest producer of newsprint in North America, a supplier to several New York publishers (including the

Times), and a creditworthy multibillion-dollar company, Hershkowitz could not help feeling as he flew back to the city that it looked like they were actually heading toward closing. Arriving at home he walked in the door looking so happy that Meg jumped in the car and came back a little while later with a bottle of champagne. But he declined. They'd drink it later.

The way the BCPC board decision-making process had been set up all those years, *everyone* on it — Campbell, Batelson, Hershkowitz, and Rivera — had to sign off on the agreement. So, as soon as he returned to the city, he sent a copy to all of them. Campbell's copy came back signed; Batelson's copy came back signed; but a few days passed without anything coming back from Rivera. On February 18, five days after Kruger signed, and with only ten days to go before their permits would be taken away, Hershkowitz and Pulver went to see officials at the Empire State Development Corp. to let them know that they at last had an operator onboard. It was a strategic visit designed to buttress their shaky position with the state agency. When they arrived and told Randy Daniels that they had an agreement, Daniels said, "No, you don't," and gave them an exasperated look. Apparently Aureo Cardona had called to tell him that Banana Kelly had not yet signed the agreement, effectively sabotaging their effort. Hershkowitz phoned Rivera as soon as he got back to his office. Her voice sounded strangely flat. "I don't know about this agreement," she said.

"What do you mean?" Hershkowitz said, trying not to sound panicked, and asked her why she hadn't called him, instead of having Cardona phone Randy Daniels. He remembers repeating that question, but she didn't answer him and the conversation got nowhere, so they agreed to meet for lunch. It was clear that Rivera knew that without her signature there was no deal.

At the lunch, Hershkowitz pleaded in vain with Rivera to sign the agreement. "Yolanda, it's been over six years," he said. "If this happens, it's over. Why are you doing this?" Not for the first time, he told me, a little speeded-up movie passed through his head of all the times he had to set his clock for two A.M. to talk to Per and all the midnight calls he'd had over the last months of hell negotiating with Kruger, and not for the first time he broke down and wept. He didn't know what more he could say—"Yolanda, please, this is what we wanted . . ." Rivera looked everywhere but at him, then told him, "If Aureo approves the agreement, then I'll sign it." Hershkowitz said, "Wait. Per has approved it. Rick has approved it. I've approved it. Our advisers say we should sign it. Marty Gold approved it. Jonathan's approved it. What does Aureo know about this agreement?" Rivera said nothing. Then she turned to leave, repeating, "Aureo has to approve the agreement."

"So that seemed to be it," he told me. "I am bouncing off the fucking walls with anger . . . not only was I personally offended, but my organization—we had John Adams working for us on this, we had Frances working for us on this, we had Fritz Schwarz working for us on this—and Yolanda and Aureo were saying 'Fuck you' to all of us."

After yet another heated bout of back-and-forth phoning, Hershkowitz noted in his diary that, according to Bruce Pulver, Cardona demanded that he get 50 percent of the financial team's equity-raising fee in exchange for Banana Kelly signing the agreement. He was told, too, that Pulver and Donovan would be offering Cardona 10 percent. Donovan and Pulver went to meet with Cardona in his apartment, and although neither of them would comment on the meeting, Hershkowitz believed that they were negotiating the larger fee arrangement but didn't get anywhere. He didn't participate because, little by little over the last month, Rivera seemed to have ceded her role on the project almost entirely to Cardona, and Cardona and he didn't get along. Cardona had no formal association with the BCPC, but Rivera had made him her surrogate. The meeting with Donovan and Pulver came and went, and by February 22, with only six days to go before their permit-default deadline, Rivera still had not signed. Pulver, clearly upset, called Hershkowitz and said, "You empowered idiots."

Despite the NRDC board's unwavering conviction that NRDC had to get out of the project as soon as possible, his everyday colleagues around the office seemed genuinely thrilled that he had finally nailed the agreement. Frances Beinecke said, "Congratulations, you've got an operator!" and Pattie Sullivan and John Adams, too, seemed sincerely pleased by the latest turn of events.

"John's support and commitment to working this was unwavering. Frances's enthusiasm and commitment to this was unwavering. The program people at NRDC were still behind me and all of them tried to help out with this latest dilemma," he told me. "They called Yolanda and Aureo into the NRDC office to try to talk to them. I was beside myself. At that point I was not talking to Yolanda, I was not talking to Aureo—I felt so betrayed. Meanwhile the deadline is getting closer and closer. She was playing a game of chicken."

The month before the agreement was signed in Montreal, an appointment had been set up for the third week in February for Hershkowitz, Donovan, and Pulver to meet with Hakkarainen's catch, Lord Rothermere, in London. Its purpose was to firm up his offer of a $20 million investment, which remained on the table even after the Stone deal had collapsed and Hakkarainen, after the NAB lawsuit surfaced, had swiftly departed. The publishing magnate said he'd be ready to commit the money as soon as they had a signed agreement from an operator. And now they had it.

Not long after Hershkowitz arrived at his London hotel on February 25, he received a conference call from New York. It was Schwarz, Adams, and Kraiem, who had also spoken with Rivera and Cardona and gotten nowhere, or rather, Rivera had told Adams she'd sign and then reneged on her agreement. Hershkowitz remembers that for the first time words about the grave doubts he had about his community partner were part of the conversation. Another part was that Kraiem, as his legal adviser, told him that he could not go to the Rothermere meeting because he could not say that they had a signed agreement in the absence of Rivera's signature. At one point in the conversation, Hershkowitz recalled, he found himself saying, like a person in a dream, "Okay. Then let the project default!" Although the suggestion was immediately rejected, he'd come to that sorry point because he was mortified that his organization was being pressured for what he considered less than correct reasons. He felt embarrassed that Schwarz, "the man who wrote the ethics law for New York City," and Adams, "the most upstanding guy you'd ever meet in your life," were on the other end of this painful conversation because of someone he'd involved in NRDC matters, someone who he believed was effectively trying to hustle them. "This was not an ethical dilemma about how to get the Kyoto treaty signed or the Montreal Protocol pushed through the United Nations, this was about a thirty-acre plot in the South Bronx, so I said, Let it default. We'll put back the team without Banana Kelly, buy back the permits from the state, and start again." No one thought that was a good idea. In fact, it would have been political suicide, and everyone agreed that he could not go to the meeting.

Hershkowitz put down the phone, then tried without success to reach Rivera. When she finally called him back, he told her what was happening, but she didn't seem to believe him. He recalls looking out the window of his hotel, which was on the corner of Hyde Park, and pleading with her, "Yolanda, I swear to you, I cannot go into the meeting unless it's signed." But again his efforts were unavailing. Pulver and Donovan were unnerved by the news; they were further upset because Hershkowitz, from *their* point of view, was as persuasive an advocate as the project could have. But they went without him, explaining the realities of the situation. Happily, their presentation fell on receptive ears and they flew back home with the publisher's commitment in their pocket. They got back to the city on February 27, 1998, with one day to go before the project defaulted. Rivera signed the agreement that day. Nobody really knew why.

The $3 million of state revolving fund money did not come all at once, but in snippets as the Environmental Facilities Corp. that was channeling the funds received and approved invoices (which still, month after month, continued to need retooling countless times to meet what those involved considered overzealous demands). In March, as everyone was working to reconfigure the project, for financial reasons because of the Kruger agreement, for political reasons because of the latest sortie from Banana Kelly, and for legal ones because of the lawsuit, Meg persuaded her husband that they needed a little break — away from the project, away from the kids, away from everyone. They decided to fly to Barcelona for a long weekend. He had been spending days, weeks, poring over the minutiae of the completed engineering work and relating it to the state revolving fund's program so that the people (especially their nemesis, the indefatigable engineer) at the Environmental Facilities Corp. would release a particular $400,000 check that was desperately needed to pay people who had been owed money for a long time—Gold, Lin, Sears, Pulver, and even NRDC for a small loan they'd made. On March 19, 1998, the Tuesday before the Barcelona weekend, Hershkowitz had lunch with Morse Diesel's Tony Winson at the Greek restaurant across the street from the NRDC office, where he'd had so many project-related lunches that his assistant began calling it "the cafeteria." He'd just secured the BCPC board's approval of the list of payees and of the Morse Diesel loan approval request.

Over lunch Hershkowitz discussed the matter of the extension of Morse Diesel's contract, which had expired in February and which the BCPC team was holding off on signing until they were reassured that the company would make a greater effort than they now seemed to be doing to keep the price closer to the *Times*'s $400 million goal. Several of the financial advisers were worried that Morse Diesel, which hadn't been faring that well financially recently, would try to bloat its profits to prove to its parent company, AMEC, that it was doing better. He also discussed the loan with Winson and said, "Here's who has to get paid," handing Winson a piece of paper. "Winson said, 'Fine.'" Previously Morse Diesel had cut the checks, and Hershkowitz would either pick them up or have them messengered over to NRDC, and then he'd mail them. But because he was leaving the next evening for Barcelona he told Winson that Pulver would pick them up this time. That same day he called everyone to tell them that they were finally going to get paid—for more than three months there hadn't been enough money to pay all the bills—and thanked them for their forbearance; he left with Meg on Wednesday night feeling relieved and, for the first time in months, ready to relax.

Surprise again! At the hotel waiting for him when he arrived was an agitated recorded message from Pulver. "Tony won't pay us. He'll only pay NRDC for the reimbursement, and Phil Sears." Hershkowitz couldn't believe his ears. "He was totally deflated," Meg recalled, "and beyond exhausted." After conferring briefly with a furious and frustrated Pulver, and concluding that this was a crude attempt on Morse Diesel's part to end the negotiating over the contract extension sooner, he called Winson immediately and, because it was still the middle of the night in New York, he got Winson's voice mail. What he basically said, as far as he remembers, was, "Tony, I can't believe that you're doing this. We had an *agreement* on Tuesday. . . . I want to tell you that if you do not release these funds, I'm going to do everything I fucking can to get you out of this project. I swear to you, Tony, I will do everything I can to get you the fuck out of this project."

Never in his life had Hershkowitz left a message like that—for anyone. It was a terrible mistake, a horrible slip. As it happened, that day, as part of his ongoing exploration of the status and complexities of the project, at NRDC's behest Ruben Kraiem was paying a visit to Morse Diesel's office. About five hours after he'd phoned Winson, Hershkowitz called Kraiem from Barcelona because he knew he was heading for Morse Diesel later that day. He told Kraiem what had happened with the checks, mentioning nothing about the message, and said that whatever else was going to transpire when he met with Morse Diesel, he had to try to get those funds released. And Kraiem had succeeded, apparently making their release a condition of any further discussion. While Kraiem was there, however, Winson had said, "Okay, we'll release them, but now you've got to know what *I've* got to deal with," and he played the tape with Hershkowitz's message. If there had been any lingering doubt in the minds of those who were formulating the official NRDC position that Hershkowitz was too close to the project, the message dispelled it. Was this how he conducted business?

After he left the meeting Kraiem called Hershkowitz back. First, he reassured him that the checks were going to be released. "But, Allen, that message. Whatever your disagreements, that message . . ." Hershkowitz, knowing full well that he'd made a huge mistake, said, "Ruben, you have no idea how long I worked to get those funds. I'm sorry. I should never have left that message. I should never have said that thing. I know . . . but I worked so long to get them that money, to get *their* team paid, and we had worked this out, and I've been so burdened with those bills." Silence on the other end of the line. Feeling the ground giving underneath him, knowing that the message had inflicted some kind of mortal blow to his future capacity to negotiate *anything* for this project, he continued, heartsick, trying to convey the reason for his lapse and hoping that Kraiem knew it *was* a lapse. "We had an agreement and I'm just sorry that I lost it . . ." Whatever real sympathy Kraiem might have felt for Hershkowitz or admiration for his advocacy skills (and he had felt plenty), the call did nothing to modify his conviction that Hershkowitz was the wrong person to be fronting this enterprise. From an institutional point of view, Hershkowitz had acted like a hothead.

Later on that day, Hershkowitz also spoke with Adams, who, he painfully recalls, phoned and told him, "'Allen, Ruben tells me you're out of control.' I said, 'John, it was a bad moment. I'm not out of control. It was just a bad moment.'"

All these conversations took place while Hershkowitz was supposed to be sightseeing with Meg and two friends. They ended up visiting the Gaudí Museum without him, and what was supposed to have been a glorious weekend of high art and tapas had turned into yet another tension-filled interlude. Instead of returning to New York feeling refreshed and relieved, now that the agreement had been signed, he stepped off the plane feeling completely off balance and filled with dread.

It's impossible to fully understand, since she never responded to my repeated calls, exactly what had been on Yolanda Rivera's mind during those first few months of 1998. Most of her project colleagues were shocked by what had happened. Jonathan Rose saw the episode a bit differently from anyone else. Rose felt that the seed of the idea of *personal* gain for Rivera from the project had, in fact, been planted years before by Pulver in the period when the paper processer and recycler who preceded Lacavalla, and went bankrupt, was going to be running the sorting plant. Rose vaguely remembered an idea floated early on relating to the sorting plant whereby, for every ton of paper that flowed through it, a dollar would go into some fund and a portion would go to Rivera and a portion would go to Pulver. Rose said to me, "So who brought in the polluting idea that there was going to be some personal gain out of . . . the project? Was it Yolanda first? Or was it Bruce? Who thought up this dollar a ton idea . . . ? Perhaps that was where the idea of personal gain first entered the project." It didn't seem unreasonable to Rose, Banana Kelly's position as a community development group notwithstanding, that Rivera, seeing the project growing and cognizant of the hefty fees that the financial advisers would gain at closing, wanted a bigger share of the pie.

But Rose was mistaken about the "polluting idea," as he put it. In fact, it was a much more ephemeral thing and didn't have anything to do with Pulver. It had originated with a generous gesture made by Lenny Formato, the scrap metal yard owner. Formato, way back when the original recycler was going to be running the sorting plant, was entitled to a brokerage fee for bringing the company in. Because he felt so enthusiastic about the goals of the project, Formato had a conversation with Hershkowitz about the possibility of arranging for some portion of his fee to be turned over to Banana Kelly. Hershkowitz had mentioned Formato's idea to Rivera, but of course when the recycling company fell out of the project, so did that plan, which had never been formalized. Beyond that, however, while Hershkowitz, like Rose, could surely understand Rivera's desire to make more money, and he along with the others might well have found some way to legitimately change their arrangement, the way Rivera and Cardona had gone about their negotiations had seriously undermined the integrity of the team. As it turned out, Rivera had overplayed her hand. No longer did NRDC feel that even with a reconstituted team and NRDC only in the background, could they wholeheartedly put their shoulder to any ongoing effort. With a capricious partner, no longer could they put themselves on the line to ask the governor for support.

And NRDC was scarcely the only team member rudely awakened by recent events. On March 2, a few days after the agreement had been sent to the state, probably the largest meeting ever of the project's participants took place at Morse Diesel's office. The purpose of the meeting was to begin to try to figure out how to structure the project pass-off. The non–Banana Kelly participants were like patients recovering from a recent heart attack—many of them probably wondering how such a complicated, carefully thought out, and professionally coordinated project had briefly been threatened with annihilation because of two people's whims. New to the scene were two lawyers—Hippocrates Kourakis and John Kourakis—a father and son team who were there, they said, to represent Banana Kelly. The elder Kourakis, who has bushy eyebrows and a tough manner, had an announcement to make; he said Banana Kelly would be happy to take part in the next stage of the negotiations, but they would only talk to Morse Diesel—they wanted NRDC out of the room. Everyone, including Rivera, immediately vetoed that (Cardona was silent), but, as the group went about discussing the project's next stages, the aftermath of Kourakis's fire-first-and-then-ask-questions approach, which would turn out to be his general MO, hung over the proceedings. The spirit of collaboration, which was supposed to be an intrinsic part of the vision of the mill, had already been made a mockery of once, and now here was Kourakis undermining it yet again.

Over the next months, a power struggle evolved over who would spearhead the project in lieu of NRDC. Meanwhile, as Hershkowitz, for legal reasons relating to the NAB lawsuit, was prohibited from discussions about financing mechanisms and forbidden to take the lead in any new arrangements, other people had to be found to protect the project's interests for NRDC. Pattie Sullivan was chosen to represent the organization (and eventually would replace Hershkowitz on the BCPC board, and become its secretary and treasurer), and Jonathan Rose agreed to forfeit the development fee he was entitled to so that he could work alongside her as an NRDC consultant. Sullivan suddenly found herself caught in a maelstrom of activity and working overtime to meet an incredibly demanding schedule. She recalled, for example, being in a conference room in Kraiem's office on Good Friday, a day on which she normally did not work, hunched over and phoning her cousin from one desk phone to say she'd be late for services at Saint Ignatius Loyola at the same time that Rose, who had been to Tibet several times and was a serious student of Buddhism, was phoning a rinpoche to make another kind of arrangement, and Gold and Kraiem were discussing the seders they would attend later that evening, since Passover and Good Friday happened that year to fall on the same day.

Sullivan told me that she "adored" Hershkowitz but that one of his strengths also created problems: "He doesn't think that there's anything he can't do. I admire that . . . and it's not unique among my colleagues, this quality—a little brain surgery? He's available." She had not been steeped in the details of the project before the NAB lawsuit came along, Sullivan told me; but she, like others, came to believe that even though the concept of the project was brilliant, and even a watershed model, her organization had been "positioned" wrongly because development is not where its talents lie. "I think we shouldn't be promoting a specific product; I think we should be consultants, I think we should be a catalyst, but we shouldn't be an agent of it." That sentiment, or variations on it, was echoed over and over by everyone I spoke with at NRDC involved in either the lawsuit or withdrawal. Kraiem told me, "On paper, NRDC was of course not the developer," but, Kraiem argued, "because Allen in particular kind of spoke for BCPC, people had some linkage to NRDC through what they could argue was its alter ego, namely BCPC. Now that was legally unfounded, but, because the argument could be made, that was a risk for NRDC." But an issue of even greater substance for Kraiem was that all along, absent a real developer, "at the end of the day, there didn't appear to be anybody playing that role other than a relatively ad hoc, very well intentioned group of very committed people."

Although another member of his firm was handling the NAB lawsuit, Charles Koob provided general counsel to Adams and NRDC staff and regarded himself as more or less their legal duenna—"making certain," as he put it in his lawyerly way, "that NRDC was structurally and financially capable of addressing its worldwide environmental challenges." He became involved with the process of disentanglement because of the issues the NAB lawsuit raised. Koob, a fair-haired, broad-faced man with an easygoing manner, had been associated with NRDC since the early 1970s, when one of its founders asked him to serve as the organization's secretary—a job that has always been held by someone from his firm. Like the others, Koob wondered "whether the role" NRDC was playing "was an appropriate role, given what we were trying to accomplish, and given NRDC's limited charter." Like the others, he concluded that it wasn't. Koob, too, expressed what seemed to be unfeigned strong admiration for Hershkowitz, but said, "The thing that concerned me initially about the litigation was that Allen was wearing several different hats and the problem was it was unclear what hat he was wearing when he was doing what."

It took a while for Hershkowitz to fully absorb the fact that the issues involved in NRDC's changed posture were broader and had wider repercussions, and that they would even cause the organization to question whether it was ever going to be able to back a similar effort. One of the most painful aspects of this new cautious stage in the project, apart from the utter frustration Hershkowitz felt as he saw the train pulling out of the station without him, was his inability to transmit to anyone the enormous store of technical and bureaucratic knowledge he had acquired, because he was expressly forbidden by the lawyers to talk to anyone who might be involved in future dealings with the mill. Although at least one member of the board told me, "Allen was not removed as an adviser, he was removed as a business decision maker," it didn't seem that way to him. In the last week of March he and his family had planned a skiing weekend with Anthony Lacavalla and his family, but because Lacavalla was part of the team contending with Morse Diesel for takeover rights and part of the general BCPC business package, he was told under no circumstance could he talk to Lacavalla—not even to call him to cancel the weekend. This was extremely distressing to him.

By mid-October, hoping that things had eased up, he agreed to a social lunch with Lacavalla and Winson found out and was furious. Winson, Hershkowitz wrote in his diary, "went nuts about it, telling Lacavalla that he couldn't meet with me." Sullivan chided Hershkowitz as well. But Lacavalla had saved the project, he wrote in his diary, when it was about to collapse for lack of funds, and he felt he owed him, at the very least, an explanation of his lack of communication.

Despite Hershkowitz's strong conviction that the people he'd been working with all along ought to be the people who carried the project forward, it soon became clear that that view was not the one that would prevail. NRDC felt that Donovan and Pulver basically brought nothing to the table; Donovan and Pulver were, moreover, part of the team that had brought the project two lawsuits and Banana Kelly. And somehow, the offer from Lacavalla of an additional $2 million to team up with Donovan and Pulver didn't get a serious ear. The NRDC board listened to Morse Diesel, which was eager to take over as developer and contractor with Galesi as a partner and was a *business*. In that situation "you certainly couldn't say, 'We're going to start over without you.' That was inconceivable, right?" Kraiem said, "You had to play with the cards that were dealt and those were the cards that were there. And Morse Diesel said, 'We will commit money to it. We will close it.'"

But the real deal clincher at this juncture was Francesco Galesi, who, as the project's landlord, had the power to declare it in default, since no one had been paying him any rent. This generous arrangement had been made earlier with his blessing, of course, but now, when the project was at a crossroads, he made it clear that from his point of view whatever cards were being dealt were in his hand—if he chose to, all he had to do was tell the state that BCPC was in default on its lease, and they'd lose all their permits.

At a meeting in his apartment, according to Rose, he turned to Pulver and Donovan and told them that he didn't believe they had the capability of closing the deal and even objected to the fees they were charging for their services. Then, turning to the Morse Diesel representatives present, he asked them if they would be willing to take it over and put up whatever money was needed in the next period. When they said they would, he agreed to go forward with them as a co-developer in a joint venture.

Before NRDC finally signed an agreement with Morse Diesel in the spring of 1999, in which the construction company and Galesi formally took over the project and agreed at closing to pay off Donovan and Pulver and the others, the new team tried, not for the last time, to edge Lacavalla out of his sorting-plant deal. Although it was clear to all that Morse Diesel had a very different take on the project from that of any advocate, the agreement would include some protection for NRDC's earlier goals: no modifications to the project's permits, or their arrangements with Maya Lin, or their sewage-water-usage goals, could be made without NRDC's specific approval.

14

The New Order

IN THE FALL OF 1998, the Manhattan District Attorney's office launched what would turn out to be a two-year criminal investigation of the Empire State Development Corp., focusing in particular on the process by which it awarded state grants and contracts and on the activities and possible misuse of the office of its chairman, Charles A. Gargano. In the end, no charges were filed against the ambassador, but his agency underwent an exhaustive and intense going-over: Gargano himself was subpoenaed in October 1998 to testify before a federal grand jury investigating the state's awarding of a $97 million contract to a company owned by one of his friends, and the agency was barraged by subpoenas for documents and requests from investigators for interviews. The cramp all this put in the agency's effectiveness and relatively freer hand that the Pataki camp might now have had to help out the Bronx project might have been a great boon, but it wasn't. The combination of Banana Kelly's recent maneuvers and rumors of its mismanagement problems was beginning to worry various state and city agencies, and the newest round of legal problems had effectively cut off any possibility of their being able to negotiate with the state as far as NRDC was concerned.

When Morse Diesel and Galesi took over the project they were certain that they could get a better deal from another paper company than they were getting from Kruger. They tried to get a better one from him, but failed. Kruger washed his hands of the whole affair, and in the end no other paper company was found.

The evening that Hershkowitz heard that Kruger was no longer in the picture was a bad one for him, because he was certain that no other paper company was going to step in. An e-mail he sent me then was marked, for the first time as far as I know, by an acknowledgment that the project might well fail. He couldn't help feeling angry at his own beloved NRDC for turning the decision making on the project over to conservative corporate lawyers who were not risk-taking activists, who didn't fight for social reform for a living. "I'm bitter toward Banana Kelly for being incredibly greedy," he wrote. "I'm appalled at Morse Diesel. . . . No one believes what they say. Working with them is like living a charade. You pretend to believe what they say, but you have to watch your back each step of the way."

Just before the Morse Diesel takeover, he'd written a memo to the senior NRDC colleagues involved in the organization's withdrawal, pleading with them to reconsider, pointing out that in Morse Diesel's original plan for assuming their new role, their proposal included "no role going forward for Jonathan and no advisory role for either Hershkowitz, Banana Kelly, or Maya Lin." He also wrote that at first they had "indicated that they do not feel bound to compensate Banana Kelly—or anyone else—to the extent we've agreed to in our negotiations. Indeed, they had suggested just the opposite." (After a lot of hard discussion, both the advisory roles and compensations were changed, although few people were paid everything they were owed.) He pointed out that a man named Ian Laird, an investment banker who had several months before joined Pulver and Donovan as a financial adviser, had already succeeded in raising equity and closing on a de-inking pulp project. "Unlike Bruce, Dan, and Ian," he wrote, "neither MDI nor Galesi have ever successfully structured and financed a paper industry deal"; he urged them one last time to change their minds. What he feared most, and judging from his recent conversations he thought he had good reason to, was that the project's advocacy objectives and commitments would soon disappear into the inexorable jaws of the industrial dynamo.

In the first half of 1999, as Morse Diesel began to carry the project forward, Lacavalla's sorting plant at the site became the focus of many heated discussions between the "advisers" and the new team about whether to keep or get rid of it. Neither Morse Diesel nor Galesi was sure the plant was needed, since there were other "waste transfer stations," as they are called, around the city that could sort the paper. On the one hand, using off-site plants would raise the price of the paper because of the cost of baling; on the other, because Galesi was a part owner of U.S.A. Waste, which already ran a number of those stations, the money would be going back, as it were, into his own pocket. And, even if they built a sorting plant, from a business point of view they might well want U.S.A. Waste to build and run it. Lacavalla, who had only been a friend to the project, was perplexed by the way he was being treated, and this time he was threatening to sue. Hershkowitz, now under the strictest of orders not to talk to him, felt that if he were in Lacavalla's shoes, he'd be doing the same thing.

A more alarming problem, related to the fate of the sorting plant, was the issue of jobs. The sorting plant was expected to generate more than half of the permanent jobs the mill was now expected to create. (Estimates of their number varied from 150 to 500.) No sorting plant, many fewer jobs. A lot of words went back and forth between the NRDC advisers and the new team about it, but the matter remained unresolved. By then Banana Kelly had cast its lot entirely with Morse Diesel, and indeed, had even demanded at one meeting that NRDC be kicked off the BCPC board, backing off only when the state told them that if NRDC was not on the board there was no deal.

In the end the sorting plant was saved for a reason no one could have predicted—a lightning bolt from the federal government. In its wisdom, the IRS, in an effort to capture more taxes, issued a Technical Advisory Memorandum (TAM) in which it ruled that recycling facilities were ineligible for the use of tax-exempt bonds because the recycled material was being purchased on the open market. Since the material was sorted and *purchased,* the IRS argument went, it had value and therefore could not be classified as waste. As the executive vice president of the Bond Market Association wrote in a letter to the Treasury Department, "an estimated $2 to $3 billion of outstanding tax-exempt waste bonds could be affected by the conclusion of the TAM." For the mill project, which would so heavily rely on tax-exempt financing, it was a devastating blow—without tax-exempt financing, the project would die. In practical terms, the government was making it impossible for recycling mills—which conserve energy, reduce pollution, and create jobs—to get financed and built, though in theory the government was all for recycling.

The memorandum did not, of course, apply to incinerators and dumps because (although the people who ran them also made money) the waste was as yet unprocessed—*real waste*—when they received it. This Alice in Wonderland state of affairs, which one can only imagine being dreamed up in the remotest cave of some IRS Himalaya, has yet to be resolved, though attempts are in the works in Congress to reverse the ruling. Meanwhile, it has had the effect of penalizing recycling investors—always a worried breed—and encouraging incinerators and landfills. The only way around the new ruling was to accept the paper in its still unprocessed state, and *then* sort it; only then would the project still qualify for the tax-exempt bond financing. And so the sorting plant stayed in, and in the end Lacavalla was the man the new development team picked to run it, because they eventually decided the same thing that the first team had—that he was the best man for the job.

The executives and consultants at Morse Diesel who worked on the mill project, with the exception of Tony Winson and Wallace Turberville (a former Goldman Sachs investment banker now working independently who replaced Bruce Pulver and the other financial advisers), and Charles Ludlow, who became the project's director of development, did not respond to my repeated requests for interviews. Ludlow, who became a central figure in the Morse Diesel effort, agreed to a pre-interview to set up the terms of a real interview, but a year passed before he responded to followup calls. This perplexed me until I discovered that the company possibly had something to hide. Somewhat surprisingly, none of the people on the BCPC team, including Hershkowitz, nor anyone at NRDC, seemed to have been aware that in 1999, even as Morse Diesel was being touted as the rock-solid business that might just cure the project's ills, and even as the company was exerting itself to find a way to make the project succeed, it was also dealing with a serious legal problem in another part of the country.

During the same period that the Bronx mill negotiations were taking place, Morse Diesel was also working in St. Louis as the contractor for a new federal courthouse, and on June 6, 1999, was indicted in St. Louis Federal Court by the U.S. Attorney's office for falsifying an invoice and certification to get payments from the General Services Administration (GSA). According to the GSA's senior procurement executive the company had "front-loaded" contract costs, ignoring clearly spelled-out government procedures in order to get paid earlier. Nine days later, the GSA terminated Morse Diesel's contract on the courthouse and, in December 2000, Morse Diesel entered a guilty plea, thus avoiding the damaging publicity of a criminal trial, and paid a penalty of $500,000. As a result of their activities, at the beginning of 2001 they were proposed for a debarment list by the GSA, and for a while the company's capacity to enter into federal contracts was in question—in fact they were prohibited for a time from doing so. Although difficulties were also arising in other federal projects that Morse Diesel was involved in around the country where there were legal problems that had not yet been resolved (in Sacramento and San Francisco), the GSA senior procurement officer and debarment official who dealt with their case, David Drabkin, reinstated them, he said, after Morse Diesel instituted a company-wide "program on government ethics and training" and replaced their managerial staff. The team that the government insisted had to step down included John Cavanagh, the COO, and the executive vice president and CFO, a man named Norman Fornella. Although Cavanagh also became part of the new team, he had a new title—vice chairman—and he was no longer responsible for day-to-day management. Fornella, whom the Bronx team worked with because he cut the checks, was actually debarred for a year. Members of the old team claimed to have been unaware of the falsely stamped "paid" invoice, but a longtime follower of the company's management style doubted that could have been the case—"they were just playing mickey stupid," he was convinced. The GSA people were favorably impressed by the new team that was brought in by Morse Diesel's British parent company, AMEC, which took the opportunity at the same time to cease allowing Morse Diesel to function as a separate subsidiary and took over as general operations manager. To the GSA people involved with the case, it looked like the company was sincerely trying to right past wrongs. Nonetheless, at least one potential investor in the mill, upon hearing about Morse Diesel's legal problems, decided to withdraw, so what might have been considered a peripheral matter turned out to directly impinge on the project.

Tony Winson, when he talked to me, had recently left his job at Morse Diesel. He made no mention of the company's legal problems. Though he always considered the financing of the Bronx project "a nightmare," he told me—at the time his company had taken over, it was an especially bad nightmare because interest rates had gone up—he nonetheless was convinced it could be done and, moreover, that Morse Diesel was the right company to do it. Their failure to find another paper company to step into Kruger's shoes came as a big surprise to him until he arrived at the same explanation that Mary Cesar, the Jaakko Pöyry recovered-paper expert, had suggested to me—that the paper industry absolutely didn't want the deal to happen and that with their tight control of the market and overcapacity, nobody was going to allow *more* capacity to come into this marketplace.

Nonetheless, he told me, "What we all said was, 'Ah, they don't want to build this plant, but as soon as we put a shovel in the ground, they are going to come knocking our door down.'" (Stephen Golden at the *Times* said something similar: "Every paper company wants that new mill to be theirs if it's going to happen anyway, but no company wants to do anything to help it along.") But what both the new and the old teams missed in their "all-consuming" pursuit of an operator, Winson said, was that they were facing the wrong direction. Even when they finally gave up on finding a paper company and they themselves took over as developers, he said that they hadn't quite grasped the fact, at first, that they should instead have been aggressively pursuing publishers and bringing them into a deal they couldn't resist. Winson didn't seem to have known that Hakkarainen and Hershkowitz had tried hard over a long period to do just that.

From Winson's point of view, the Bronx project didn't get really serious until his company took over. "Allen's intentions were always the highest level in terms of his belief in the project," but, he added, he was a "naturalist, an environmentalist, and a scientist" and those attributes, in the business world, "pissed a lot of people off." Winson thought Hershkowitz deserved a "huge amount of respect" as an environmental advocate. "But stay in that box." While the old team had been in place, Pulver and Donovan had consistently been on Morse Diesel's back to keep their costs down. Unsurprisingly, Winson didn't seem too fond of them. He reminded me that Merrill Lynch had let Donovan go and said that though Pulver was a "nice guy and can do the numbers okay," he thought he was not "a powerhouse guy to do a deal like this. They weren't, in our mind, capable of pulling the deal off."

With no one looking over Morse Diesel's shoulder and battling to keep the construction costs down, however, by the end of 1998 the project cost estimate had climbed to a staggering $630 million, and as time passed it was rumored that the final estimate might come in even higher.

As mere contractors for the BCPC, Winson insisted, Morse Diesel had never really focused on the fact that Banana Kelly had, in the early days of the project, been made the owner of the development project. Since Rivera so rarely seemed to be appearing at meetings and rarely expressed interest in important negotiations, it came as an even greater shock when Morse Diesel came to understand that at the end of the day, it was Banana Kelly that they would have to deal with when they restructured their new deal. (Hershkowitz insists that Winson knew this full well but hadn't taken it seriously enough; he believes he took this stance to cover his back when his superiors had to grapple with it as a problem.) Winson told me that despite mighty battles led by the ever-provocative "Hip" Kourakis, Banana Kelly's new lawyer, the larger sums now demanded by Rivera for the as yet undeveloped plans for the community projects did not go through—Morse Diesel drew on an earlier state document that supported the limits of the entitlements Banana Kelly could expect. (A copy of the new project development agreement that I obtained shows that the originally specified sum for the community projects—$6.2 million—stayed the same; NRDC had successfully protected their environmental objectives and contractual obligations, which were written into the new agreement, though Maya Lin's role, which was one of those contractual obligations, was somewhat ambiguously phrased: they now agreed to "consult and coordinate" with her.)

Should Banana Kelly for any reason not be able to carry forward the project, Winson added, arrangements were being made for the money to go to the community and not into "somebody's back pocket." According to Winson, who chose his words carefully when he talked about this issue, "the actual structure of how that money was going to flow down . . . had to be worked out with the state because it is state funds that are going to do a big piece of this."

One good reason why Winson may have been choosing his words so carefully was that by the time of our conversation, the low hum of rumors about internal mismanagement at Banana Kelly had become a mighty roar. On May 16 and 17, 1999, the *New York Post* had run two stories headed, respectively, CHARITY BIG AXES AIDE WHO CALLED IN FBI and CHARITY CHIEF'S PAL MAY GET $1 MILLION. The first story revealed that Banana Kelly's COO, Claude Gooding (Rivera's second-in-command), had been fired recently for sending a memo to staffers telling them that he planned to contact the FBI about "possible corruption at the agency." Among the more damaging items mentioned was a canceled check suggesting that Banana Kelly funds may have been used for Rivera's personal bills. The article also mentioned that though she was chairperson, Rivera billed the agency for three thousand dollars a week as a consultant offering technical assistance for various projects, including the recycling plant—payments that were not subject to withholding tax; moreover, the agency was in violation of the state nonprofit law because it had not filed tax returns and financial statements with the State Attorney General as required since 1996. In his memo, Gooding had noted, "Many of you have come to me to express your concerns, suspicions and opinions about the day-to-day operations of Banana Kelly" and said that he had formally requested the FBI to conduct "a full and detailed investigation." The other story reported that Aureo Cardona stood to make a $1 million consulting fee for his services for the mill project.

It was perhaps with these reports in mind that Winson pointedly said when I spoke with him that it didn't matter to him whether the money was "administered" by Banana Kelly or the appropriate community board or the borough president's office, "as long as the money gets to where it's supposed to go."

Whatever was happening in the negotiations, Hershkowitz, from 1998 on, was for legal reasons officially out of the loop — except for the many secret calls Charlie Ludlow, the director of development, or others would make to find out about this or that technical or bureaucratic point. However sure Winson and the investment bankers and lawyers on the NRDC board may have been about the greater suitability of a business leader for a business project, the reality was that there were major components of it, economic and technical, that left the new team at sea. Sometimes Hershkowitz would be forwarded a note that made him heartsick. One such note had been written by Winson to Pattie Sullivan — who along with Jonathan Rose was now NRDC's main representative on the project — before he left Morse Diesel. It addressed the matter of the sewage water cleanup and its relation to Bond Act qualification, a complex issue that Hershkowitz had struggled with from 1994 to 1998, and by then knew the ins and outs of as well as he knew his own name. The note was short: "Dear Pattie," it read, "I was aware that some time in 1997 work was done by NRDC on establishing if the project qualified for Bond-Act assistance. I believe this was related to denitrification of the Long Island Sound. I would be greatly appreciated [sic] Pattie if you could advise how our project may qualify under the Bond Act for financial assistance."

Sullivan, a deft administrator who was doing her best to make sure NRDC's concerns were addressed while trying not to stand in the way of the team's business goals, hadn't the faintest idea. She asked Hershkowitz to write a memo; he did his best and wrote a three-page haiku version of the water facts and their history. It didn't help. Then Charlie Ludlow asked him for a little briefing, which he gave him. But when Sullivan found out that he and Ludlow had been talking to each other, she warned him not to do it again. The lawyers absolutely forbade him to speak to anyone at Morse Diesel. In any event, the talk clearly had not done the trick, and ultimately the new team simply gave up — cutting their way through the techno-bureaucratic miasma that surrounded the water cleanup and unraveling the red tape around the Bond Act money acquisition was too daunting. Ludlow told me that with the new plans for a far larger mill, it would also have become too expensive—even with the Bond Act money. They decided it would be easier and cheaper to use fresh water—something NRDC was adamantly opposed to and continued to argue with them about, since they had always looked at the project at least in part as an important large-scale water conservation measure.

All of this Hershkowitz heard through the grapevine because the legal proscription against talking to him continued. The welcome camaraderie that had developed over past years of intense working together was called to an abrupt halt. "It was terrible. I couldn't talk to Marty Gold. I couldn't talk to Phil Sears, Bruce Pulver, Dan Donovan. The walks with Jonathan Rose stopped. No one was allowed to call me and they wouldn't return my calls . . ." Gold, now working as a legal consultant for NRDC on the new development agreement, was struck by the fact that Cardona at the various meetings he attended with him "never mentioned a single program he was interested in. He never mentioned anything in the community to which this money would be committed." A watchful-looking man with a professorial mien and face-transforming smile, Gold told me he'd had a lot of experience with environmental legal work and that he'd been attracted to this project because of its innovativeness and idealism. As far as he could tell, Cardona was uninterested in those aspects of the enterprise—rather he "seemed to be looking and thinking in dollar terms for himself and Yolanda."

From what I gathered, despite Rivera's willingness to ax out former project colleagues—including not joining the effort to ensure their remuneration fees at closing for all the work they'd done—none of the higher fees that she was apparently trying to secure in the new deal materialized. Certainly Winson and others at Morse Diesel wooed her when they were making their play to get the old team out, and she may well have thought that the new, more hardcore business milieu she was moving into would see things more her way. Sullivan remembers her formally asking for more money on several occasions during that period and remarked, too, that whatever sums were "mentioned by Cardona or Rivera tended to be a number that mirrored somebody else's number. Galesi at some point said that he was owed $20 million in back rent or something, so they said they were owed, would you believe, $20 million in back fees." There was always an implied threat in ongoing discussions that at the moment Banana Kelly's signature might be needed, it might be withheld. "Always," Marty Gold told me, "Cardona was there in the middle of the road" as they were trying to establish the balance sheet, and it was always difficult "to drive around him."

One of the few people I spoke to who had a good word for Cardona was, once again, Jonathan Rose, who, as the main person negotiating the new development agreement—a pivotal transitional document—for NRDC, was now often thrown together with him. Perhaps in part because Rose's good will in the negotiating process was important, even necessary, for Banana Kelly at that moment, and Rivera's team had alienated just about everyone else connected with the project, Cardona seems to have exhibited none of the testiness with Rose that he had displayed toward others. "I almost always felt that what Aureo asked for was justified," Rose told me, and added, "he always returned my phone calls. You left a message at his house with his mother, who barely speaks English. He always got it." (This process did not work so well for me—though he may have received my many messages, none was returned.) "If you needed something signed by Yolanda," Rose continued, "he would track her down."

The real "unwinder" of agreements, from his vantage point, was "Hip" Kourakis, who moved into automatic reject mode in every negotiation. "When he entered the picture," Rose said, "he barely seemed to ever read the documents, had no interest in real legal issues, and just seemed to be there to throw bombs and disrupt. He disrupted to see if in the process he could get more for Yolanda or get more for Banana Kelly."

"Did he succeed?" I asked him.

"No, not at all."

But Rose, whose Buddhist interests, combined with his iron-tough business sense, may have predisposed him to a more Olympian view of things than many of his project colleagues had, felt that Kourakis can't have failed to notice that "this project was going to be coming in at $600 million plus and he was probably saying something to Rivera like, 'You are only getting six million, that's one percent; you should be getting ten percent. You should get closer.' Hip has always been the fighter who got money for his community groups."

Rose, like everyone else, believed that it had been a mistake to make Banana Kelly the sole shareholder of BCPC. This gesture, made by Hershkowitz to ensure that the community group did not get cut loose at what businessmen call "cram down"—the moment of closing where a lot of early sureties get thrown out the window—was now causing havoc. "When we got to the point of really trying to consolidate things . . . and hand things over to Morse Diesel as developer, and Hip got in, there was this kind of duel. There was always the threat that a sole shareholder could have voted out their board and taken the project over on their own. Now the bottom line, had they done that, the project would be dead and they realized that, but it was not a wise way to set up the project."

By then no one was more aware of the incautiousness with which Hershkowitz had entered the project than he himself was. "I didn't anticipate evil," he told me. "I didn't anticipate schemes. I thought everyone was on the same page and we all had the same idea—let's do good and let business make money." On the other hand, even the seasoned business types who assumed the leadership role in the new order were stunned by the degree of sheer detail that they had to master to deal with the project.

In the first brief interview that Morse Diesel's Charles Ludlow granted me, he repeatedly stressed the complications of the project and the lack of knowledge all of them had of its incredible multifacetedness: "None of us could clearly see all the moving parts." Describing his own experience with the project, Ludlow, who talks quickly, kept focusing on the surprises they kept encountering and the difficulty of selling the bonds for a project with so beleaguered a history when interest rates were climbing, in a period when most new recycling projects based on a similar financing structure had failed. Ludlow's awareness of the project's environment-improv-

ing, water-saving, job-producing, species- and habitat-preserving
attributes was there, but seemed more or less on the same order
as a butterfly's awareness of a flower's stem or leaves. Like the
enviros, Ludlow relied heavily in his speech on the jargon of his
trade. Discussing the need to provide a steady stream of revenue
to investors when there was always going to be a fluctuation in the
prices of wastepaper and newsprint, the way they figured out to do
this, Ludlow explained, "was, hey, we give up some of the upside
to have them cover the downside, and put a narrow band in with
a hedge." One big surprise to him, he said, was that though when
the project began the city was desperately looking for paper markets, by then the city already had a thriving business marketing its
wastepaper. "Instead of saying, we're fixing your problem by taking
wastepaper off your hands, you dirty messy city, they already had it
all figured out." But they hadn't figured it all out. Of the approxi-
mately 3.6 million tons of paper the city throws out every year, only
15 to 20 percent of it was collected for recycling. The rest—which
was most—of the paper went to landfills and incinerators. While it
was true that there were markets for the amount the city collected
for recycling, the idea was that a broader market would create a
broader demand. In other words the mill would take its share of
the paper and because the export demand would still be there,
there would now be a stronger incentive to recover more paper.
Both Ludlow and Winson felt that they had needed more or less
to start from scratch, since the project had continued to evolve, and
with the more detailed engineering they were now working on, the
old models no longer served. "We used our own resources," Winson
said, "to do a full evaluation of the feasibility of the project." After
running different financial models, they decided that the optimal
output would mean designing a far larger mill—one that could increase sellable output by 50 percent. This entailed doing engineering work on a level of refinement they hadn't before attempted,
largely because the money for it hadn't been available. Reconfig-
uring the project also meant that they would need a far larger machine, that their costs would continue to climb, and that their new
plan would play havoc with Maya Lin's design—the model that,
since the Municipal Art Society show, everyone believed was going

to be *the* design for the mill. In fact, insofar as the public was aware of the project at all, it was generally referred to as Maya Lin's Bronx mill.

Winson tried to put a good face on the fact that Lin's design occupied a place in the company's consciousness about as remote as an anagalactic nebula. "We did it," he said, and "we then ran it by Maya and said, 'This is how it is going to look in its larger format.'"

"When you say, 'This is how it is going to look,' you're talking about the inside, and she would design the outside?"

"No, the box—form follows function."

"But this was a second box that you were designing?"

"This was a second one."

"And what did she do to that box?"

"Very little."

"You mean the design is no longer the Municipal Art Society design?"

"Oh, yeah."

"It is?"

"Conceptually it's very much the same."

"So you took her design and reconfigured it?"

"We worked with her on the original design. Her design, the Municipal Art's, was the product of us telling her what we could live with. And then she decorated that up a bit."

This de facto disregard for the design goals that mattered a great deal to Lin tested her greatly. Though she had been protected from and was largely unaware of the level of down-and-dirty effort to dramatically weaken her input in the new project, she was furious about the modifications being made to her design. She sent an anguished note to Hershkowitz—his newly curtailed role notwithstanding—bitterly complaining of the shambles they were making of her vision. If, on the one hand, she never wanted to stand in the way of the project's viability, she also didn't want to have represented her work one way and receive plaudits for it and have a vastly different building emerge on the site. Like Hershkowitz, Lin was acutely aware of the barely hidden condescension with which her ideas were viewed. Like him, she was committed to the original broad goals of the project, and also like him, she worried that they were now being crushed by the overwhelming force of business as usual.

For all of Hershkowitz's problems with Winson, and disapproval of his attitude toward Lin, he credits him, as he does John Cavanagh, with being one of the most important participants in the project; he feels that it was mainly because of Winson's interest that Morse Diesel committed its resources: "Tony was in charge of it all—his enthusiasm caught the attention of the highest people at Morse Diesel; he was able to corral them and to move things." And for a while the Morse Diesel team seemed finally to have broken the cycle of seeming interest, followed by half commitment by an industry powerhouse, followed by abandonment. There was talk of an imminent closing and groundbreaking in 2000 and, though skepticism remained in the business community, there was a sense of a possible end to what a *Crain's New York Business* article referred to as "the tortured history of the paper plant . . . replete with unwarranted optimism."

Morse Diesel succeeded in getting newsprint-purchasing contracts and equity contracts, but fundamental problems still remained as the project cost eventually ballooned to a whopping $720 million. The most obvious problem was the need for state bond support, which, at the current price and subsequent increased level of need, would have required nearly all of the annual bond allotment the state received from the federal government for all state projects—an impossible requirement to satisfy, since there were many other projects waiting in line for help. Winson seemed not to have understood that Banana Kelly's problems had radically altered the governor's willingness—or for that matter, that of anyone in the state government—to support the project. Winson thought that the perceptible cooling off in the state's attitude that everyone was noticing was somehow NRDC's fault. Presumably, John Adams had a special relationship with the governor. One of the "key anchors" for Winson's company's involvement in the first place, he told me, was that "BCPC told us of the absolute total committed support by the State of New York." At any point, John Adams could "talk to George Pataki . . . and they would embrace each other in love of this project. Quote. Maybe quote."

One hypothesis the new team had come up with to explain the

recent chill was that another competing plant was being contemplated upstate in Republican territory and the developer (the same man who tried to buy the BCPC permits) was a friend of the governor's. Another was that perhaps John Adams and George Pataki had had a falling out, and yet a third, and one that Winson considered the most plausible, was "deal fatigue." The project had simply been around too long. People were saying, "It's never going to happen. We keep hearing the same story. They change the lines, but the script is the same script. Deals do die from deal fatigue. . . . There is actually a publishing line: 'Kill a dead donkey.' " (Some members of grassroots groups I spoke with pointed out that despite the kudos the governor had received as an environmentalist, his record on environmental-justice issues was poor. They were concerned that he didn't care that much about the Bronx.)

Another major problem, according to Ludlow, was the volatility of the paper market. "Wall Street wants to see a steady revenue stream," he said. As everyone connected with the project had known from the start, investors like to be told that there was someone with deep pockets, like Richard Pratt, the developer and owner of the Staten Island mill, who was in with both feet—the equity for the Visy mill was almost bigger than the debt. What Morse Diesel had instead, Ludlow pointed out, was "little equity and huge debt." Like Winson, Ludlow had general words of praise for Hershkowitz but allied himself firmly with the ranks of those who thought that he was the wrong man for the job because he wasn't a businessman. "He likes to slay dragons," Ludlow said, "but the total tonnage of what Allen doesn't know would sink the State of Rhode Island."

Hershkowitz heard this sort of thing said often, so often that he'd begun to consider it useless to repeat to whoever pointed it out to him that he had never intended to represent himself as a business expert; this was meant to be a collaborative effort. The business people were there to tell him how their world worked. Another Emersonian aphorism he'd copied years ago into his diary summed up what he wished everyone understood was his position: "Each man of thought is surrounded by wiser men than he . . . cannot they combine?"

In the winter of 1999, Hershkowitz's ongoing difficult relationship with Vernice Miller had ceased to matter, because Miller had married and moved to Washington, D.C., left the organization, and very soon found a good job at the EPA. But she lost that job before she had a chance to actually begin working, for claiming on her job application that she had a master's degree in environmental policy from Columbia University that a reporter discovered she did not. (She now works for the Ford Foundation.)

Still chafing from the IRS's TAM rule, Morse Diesel hired former senator Alphonse D'Amato, who had chaired the Senate's Banking Committee, to try to use his influence to change it. But he didn't get anywhere. Unbowed, the company marched on with its plan for keeping Lacavalla's sorting plant and thus getting around the ruling. And whatever was happening behind Morse Diesel's closed doors, they had enough confidence in a positive outcome for their labors that at the Millennium celebration at the new Rose Planetarium, John Cavanagh told Rose they now expected to close in the first quarter of 2000. Rose called Hershkowitz to tell him what Cavanagh had said, though it broke the phone embargo.

The always elusive promise of the city paper was something else Morse Diesel had confidence they would, with their broader Republican connections, be able to nail, but that conviction, too, had proved illusory. In the end, the city gave its wastepaper to other bidders, one of whom subcontracted theirs to the politically well-connected Waste Management, and now the one thing the mill couldn't do without, or finesse, was gone. It was the Economic Development Corp.'s Eric Deutsch's thankless task, he told me, to report this to the new project team at Morse Diesel.

Like some of the NRDC board people, Deutsch, at one point, had high hopes for the construction company as a deal clincher, and he knew that they had spent millions of dollars—five, they claimed—on the project and, like their predecessors, had worked like demons to pull it off. Aware of his loyal support for the mill and his reluctance to give up on it, one of his office co-workers presented him at the end of 1999 with the Secret Santa present of a big bottle of gray water and a poem, which celebrated his still unvanquished hope for the project:

Your year-end deal did not go through
But not all's lost there's hope anew
The year 2000 brings one more chance
A brand New Year to take a stance
Where there's a way, there's a will
To create your own Bronx Paper Mill!

As far as anyone can tell, it was the mayor who finally dealt The Beast its death blow, for reasons known only to himself. Giuliani reportedly instructed the Department of Environmental Protection not to continue work on the water issue, and Hershkowitz said he was told by Ludlow that a final communication had come down to Morse Diesel that City Hall had withdrawn all support for the project, including the tax-exempt allocation.

In April 2000, Hershkowitz was in Washington to serve as a judge for the White House recycling awards, when he ran into several staff people he knew from the White House Council on Environmental Quality. They asked him how the project was going. "Down the tubes," he said. They were astonished and asked if it had gotten EPA support. After he said no, the shocked group asked what they could do. He said, "If you think you could do something, get a letter—not from you. Get a letter from Frampton [George Frampton, acting chair of President Clinton's Council on Environmental Quality and since 1998 his chief environmental adviser], get a letter from the vice president or the president. If you think there's something there, write them a letter, but do it now ... it has to be done immediately." Hershkowitz told me that it took about three weeks, and he was disappointed by how long it took, but it was a very high level letter. "The letter was sent to me after everybody else, and Jonathan called me at home. 'This is an amazing letter,'" Hershkowitz recalls Rose saying. Rose went on to say that it was a dream letter, promising real federal cooperation, but that he thought Morse Diesel was not there anymore.

John Cavanagh received the White House letter. It offered to try to figure out some way of creating a federal partnership with the project. The letter was written by George Frampton; he wrote that he understood the project faced "heightened financial burdens due to interest rate increases and other factors." Frampton suggested a meeting as soon as possible at the White House Conference Center to try to find options that might rescue the project. He also stated, "As you know, the Council on Environmental Quality (CEQ) has the responsibility to coordinate environmental policy issues among the various federal agencies. Based on previous communications with the Natural Resources Defense Council, we understand that the Bronx Community Paper Company will provide a showcase example of this administration's interest in creating jobs while slowing global climate change, saving energy, redeveloping urban brownfield sites, and significantly reducing water pollution. Accordingly, I view the BCPC as an ideal model for sustainable community development and industrial ecology."

The White House offer was refused. Morse Diesel basically replied: We need $600 million in credit guarantees for the bonds and $20 million in grants, and then we'll come and see you.

"Unfortunately," Cavanagh wrote to Frampton, "we cannot construct a financial plan around grants we may or may not receive." According to the team's new financial adviser, Wallace Turberville—who'd also told me that the price of the mill had climbed as high as it had because of all the guarantees needed, absent a deep-pocketed owner—Morse Diesel felt that they had already met once with some people in Washington and gotten nowhere, and what they were being invited to do was to meet with a bunch of different people at different agencies and fill out masses of applications and then maybe, just maybe, they'd get a few grants that would be the equivalent of Band-Aids on a severed artery. The only member of the new team who argued for responding positively to the letter was Anthony Lacavalla, who wrote to Cavanagh and Galesi that if they weren't interested in pursuing the inquiry, he was. But no one picked up on Lacavalla's offer. No one even answered his letter.

Hershkowitz was watching all this from afar, hearing about it mostly through Rose, and was helpless to intervene. From where he sat, it looked as if Cavanagh's lack of knowledge of Washington's *modus operandi* was preventing him from understanding what every lobbyist knew: "You have to work these things," he told me sev-

eral days after a copy of the letter was sent to him. "You go in . . .
you give the confidence in your project's environmental attributes
. . . its social benefits. You give the confidence in the development
team. You reiterate your commitment to developing it. You explain to them how it complies with the White House agenda. And
then," he went on to say, his voice accelerating as his exasperation
mounted, "you strategize on how to build the political support
that's necessary. . . . Writing a letter saying, 'Look, we'll come down
if you tell us we are going to get all this' is ridiculous. . . . Their letter back should have said, 'Thank you for your letter. We are coming down on Thursday. What would you like us to prepare?' And
gradually you build a team . . . that encompasses people from the
White House, from the various agencies, even the legislature . . .
but they can't just write back a letter and say, 'Okay. You've got a
$600 million credit guarantee.'" What wasn't being factored into
the equation by Hershkowitz and everyone else in the dark about
Morse Diesel's legal problems, of course, was that their ability to
enter into new federal contracts was seriously in question.

Hershkowitz's sense even at that late date was that some federal
CPR could still pull the project through. Similarly, a highly placed
Washington official who'd seen Cavanagh's letter and used the
same word to characterize it that Hershkowitz had, "ridiculous,"
told me that the deal might well have been saved with federal cooperation, in fact, particularly if NRDC had been willing to pull out
all stops and use its considerable legislative sophistication to try to
get a rider for the mill placed on a bill. But, he said, they seemed
unwilling to jump into the trenches and do that. "All kinds of projects get done that way," he said, "but the organization had more or
less vetoed that possibility." Several days after it had become apparent that nothing could induce the current development cadre
to make the journey down to Washington, Hershkowitz sent Pattie
Sullivan a short note. It read: "Does this qualify as seizing defeat
from the jaws of opportunity?"

On July 21, 2000, the demise of the mill project was announced
in the *Times*. By then Hershkowitz had raised, all told, about $5.7
million in non-NRDC funding and about $2 million in NRDC
funding—for staff salaries, travel, consultants, supplies, and so

forth. Over the past months, he had begun to wear his old advocacy mantle more frequently and was working along with his colleague Jacob Scherr (director of NRDC's International Program) in Belize, trying to prevent a badly designed landfill from being placed where it threatened a river that was a source of drinking water for many villages and also had a bad impact on the Belize Zoo. He had traveled down the river in a canoe under a wide blue sky and seen emerald hummingbirds, bare-throated tiger herons, and the tracks of a tapir, and had been smarmily attacked by the pro-land-fill forces in the local paper. It was all very familiar. His colleagues were happy to see him back at his old advocacy tasks and he was pleased when their efforts with the river in Belize eventually succeeded. But he was far from convinced that the failure of the mill meant that the model was not a good one; he'd learned a lot of lessons from the mistakes he'd made, he told me, and expressions of interest he'd received from city officials and businessmen in other parts of the country and other parts of the world had only whetted his appetite to try to replicate the model under better circumstances.

Nearly a month before the announcement in the paper that the mill project was dead, a front page article in the *New York Times* by Amy Waldman about Yolanda Rivera and Banana Kelly appeared under the headline A DREAM FORECLOSED . . . BUILDINGS' SAVIOR NOW A TROUBLED LANDLORD. The article confirmed many of the worst suspicions and fears of those connected with the project and mirrored much of what I'd found talking to people connected with the agency. A long list of grievances of tenants of many of Banana Kelly's houses was given — including inadequate heat and hot water, water-cracked walls, rats, sinking floors and leaking ceilings, and long-time negligence in doing major repairs — along with allegations about Rivera's poor management record. The concern raised by her consolidation of control at the agency, the suspicion that Banana Kelly funds had been used to pay nearly $33,000 of her personal taxes, and serious questions about the agency's bookkeeping methods, as well as about her remuneration, which had leapt from $76,440 in 1995 to more than $170,000 in 1997, were all mentioned. Even as many of her building superintendents were apparently having to reach into their own pockets to pay for building needs, and staff members had been scrounging to find enough money to carry out their work, as many of them reported to me, Rivera and some associates were traveling as part of an international venture the group had established several years before. The article said the FBI was reportedly looking into whether federal program money was used to pay for a trip to Kenya and whether Rivera's relatives had gone along on that trip. Among those who had gone along on the trip was Aureo Cardona, whose company, Crescendo, Inc., according to Waldman, had been paid $15,000 a month to manage Banana Kelly properties. During that period Cardona had also been given access to a $50,000 expense fund, the *Times* reported, "to be replenished as needed—to do 'national and international engagements.'" At that point Cardona and Rivera had parted company, and he was reportedly suing Banana Kelly for breach of contract.

Eight months later, the Attorney General's office subpoenaed Banana Kelly's records to determine whether there were grounds for a criminal or civil case against the agency. And many other grassroots groups let out a collective groan. In the community development world, and even beyond it—because over the years its reputation as a group that had done so much to help the Bronx had spread widely—people were saddened to learn that the agency had lost most of the programs established by Rivera's predecessors. Not long afterward Father Gigante, Rivera's old mentor, announced that his own nonprofit group was taking control of the management of twenty-five of Banana Kelly's buildings, and another organization took over fourteen more. While two buildings, one abandoned and another in a state of advanced deterioration, still remained in Banana Kelly's portfolio, that change effectively ended Banana Kelly's long and formerly glorious history as a housing group and model for neighborhood revitalization. Though it was still functioning, it was burdened by legal troubles, heavy debts, and ongoing management problems. I tried five or six times to reach Rivera by phone to question her about these allegations. I also presented myself at her headquarters. But the calls were unavailing and though she came out of her office when I showed up, she said she was too busy to talk and would get back to me, but she never did. In the late spring of 2002, the investigation was being handled by the Charities Fraud Bureau of the Attorney General's office. (Some months later, Rivera announced that her organization was taking back its management role. This came after she apparently learned that the city was planning to spend $8 million to fix the buildings Banana Kelly formerly managed and still owned—though the influx of city capital was to depend on the organization's relinquishment of its ownership. Rivera's action caused near apoplexy among various concerned groups, including the city, and several parties were moving to block the takeover and suing for breach of contract.) Then, in early November 2002, New York's attorney general, Eliot Spitzer, announced that Rivera's old nemesis, Fernando Ferrer (who by then had left his job as borough president to run for mayor and was heading a public policy organization), had been chosen to be the chairperson of Banana Kelly and that Harry DeRienzo, one of the organization's founders, would serve as its interim president. Rivera and her board of directors, as part of an out-of-court settlement, had agreed to step aside. The state, in turn, would end its investigation of Rivera, though Spitzer pointed out that other investigations "by other prosecutors and jurisdictions," including a federal one, would be unaffected by the agreement. It was further stipulated, the attorney general's office disclosed, that neither Rivera nor the members of the Banana Kelly board would be permitted to serve as officers, directors, or key employees of any charitable trust, not-for-profit corporation, or other charitable institution for ten years.

In the days and months after Morse Diesel's announcement that the project was dead, nearly all the people who had worked on it settled on varying interpretations of why it had failed. To Hershkowitz's sympathetic colleagues, it was a death from a thousand cuts. Most of the business people felt convinced that the main reason was that the market didn't want it. Tony Riccio, Galesi's right-hand man at the Harlem River yard, said, "The stars just weren't aligned right." He stressed the antagonism of the powerful Canadian paper industry. In fact, Morse Diesel's parent company, the British-based AMEC, merged with a Canadian construction, engineering, and building-services company, AGRA, in 2000. AGRA had recently completed a conceptual design for what was purportedly going to be the largest greenfield mill in Brazil, and among its largest clients were virgin paper producers. Why, after all, would AMEC be interested in giving its blessing to a new, competing American recycling mill designed to supply the large New York publishing market?

Ruben Kraiem thought the project failed because there was no "real" developer involved. "That was the fundamental problem, and you can't get around it," he told me. "In a project of that magnitude," he said, "there needed to be more trade-offs. There needed to have been a developer who would say, 'I have many different goals here — fuel efficiency, energy efficiency, materials efficiency, esthetic value, community development. . . . Now maybe one or more of those things have to go in order for the economics . . . to be viable — and there was no one willing to do that, there was no one in that role." As a result, he suggested, "What we ended up designing and promoting was an ideal project because it had all the benefits, but none of the trade-offs, and the only negative was that it wasn't viable in the industry." Kraiem remained convinced that NRDC had been in the wrong role in the project.

The quandary was that if someone like Hershkowitz didn't do it, who would? I posed that question to Kraiem. His answer was, "Somebody in the business." But what chance would there be that people "in the business" would want to similarly focus on the project's environmental or social goals? The business community, like the legal profession, is practically and culturally constituted to avoid risk.

Eric Goldstein disagreed with the idea that the mill failed mainly because of business reluctance. He thought that a more serious problem was that the project didn't have a political champion, and in particular he faulted Mayor Giuliani. A mayor who recognized and supported its long-term civic and environmental benefits might well have made a crucial difference by seeking additional state support, or finding special federal funding, which, as he pointed out, is always available if you look in every nook and cranny, or by putting the city on the line and really pushing to make paper available.

Phil Sears, who struggled alongside Hershkowitz for nearly the full eight years of trying to make the project happen, said that he thought one of its more resistant problems was the volatility of the paper markets. Sears also believed that a daunting problem had been the absence from the beginning of "an overall financial plan." He explained, "They were cobbling together grants here, loans there, instead of having the whatever it was—twenty million dollars—that was really needed to get it going." Sears agreed that institutionally NRDC as it is presently structured had the wrong mindset and skills to build a project and in fact is "institutionally *incapable* of building a project," but he thought that they missed a great opportunity to try to figure out how, as an institution, they might learn how one was done.

The *Times*'s Stephen Golden, while acknowledging Hershkowitz's limitations as a non-businessman, stressed the fact that the project wouldn't have existed at all "without his direct involvement—not the NRDC's involvement, not an environmental scientist's: Allen's . . . There were times along the way when the project needed a rabbit, and Allen went and found a hat and pulled a rabbit out of it. And he did it over and over again."

Hershkowitz still hopes that at some point NRDC might support another venture with the same goals without putting themselves in a similar position of vulnerability. Over the year following the project's demise he made intermittent inquiries in the financial community to see if he might find support. Interest in replicating the Bronx model also kept surfacing from business people, politicians, and bureaucrats in other cities and countries. But John Adams says he continued to worry about the appropriateness of NRDC being in that role, even without legal liability, though he, more than most people, was and is deeply sympathetic to the vision that underlay the mill project.

Frances Beinecke repeatedly stressed the rapid growth of NRDC over the years of the project's struggle. Nowadays, they have a far larger staff and far greater resources. If NRDC had to do it all over again, she told me, they'd get the same board team, or one like it, that became involved toward the end of the project working on it at the start. "But we didn't bring them in in the beginning. We didn't sit them down and say, Okay, it's NRDC's institutional priority to get a model plant built in the Bronx to recycle paper on a brownfield site with social services. That's the institution's priority. Let's get these five board members to work on them. Let's get an MBA in here to do the financial side. We didn't do it that way, but that's the way we'd do it now."

Because of all the lessons they'd learned about the real-world obstacles the project faced, Beinecke put forth the idea that the project might well be considered "as great a model not having been built as it would have been being built . . . for the people who are thinking about issues of sustainability, it had terrific resonance. They know all about it even though it's not sitting up on the Harlem River Railyard, it's alive."

Whatever doubts Adams and Beinecke might have had about putting NRDC's institutional toe in the same waters again, they seemed genuinely awed by the magnitude of Hershkowitz's effort. "He put his heart and soul into something he really believed in," Adams said. "And I think he came very close to succeeding." And it might have succeeded, he thought, "had the financial times not shifted on him and had we had an early push, like with Scott Paper." But both were equally convinced that their colleague didn't have the kind of independent business advice he needed—whatever his advisers were telling him—right from the start. Had he had it "from day one," Adams was convinced, ". . . we might have closed the process down earlier, or we might have won. I think Allen *could* have won had he broken out the right way from the start, because it was such a good idea." To venture forth again with any similar project, Beinecke said, "We would have to have the right partner. We would have to have partners who wanted a business to succeed and wanted us to provide input on how to make it sustainable. I really believe that."

For a long time after the project finally crashed, Hershkowitz felt seriously depressed. At the Harlem River yard, a backup power station and warehouse were being discussed as possible tenants; the *New York Post,* whom the team had considered a potential purchaser, was building a plant next door and a waste-transfer station was already operating. His colleagues' public support and expressions of commiseration notwithstanding, he felt sure that his stock at NRDC had edged subtly downward and that symbolically it was as if he was walking around with a big T for troublemaker emblazoned on his shirt—even though the NAB lawsuit had been dropped. While he had been focused day and night on a relatively small tract of land in the city, he kept reminding himself, in an effort to regain some sense of proportion, NRDC had saved North America's largest untouched wilderness by helping the Cree defeat the James Bay hydroelectric project in Quebec; it had helped win commitment from more than three hundred companies, including Home Depot, Kinko's, 3-M, and Starbucks, to help save temperate rain forests; and NRDC's intense worldwide campaign to force the Mitsubishi Corporation to withdraw its plan to build a giant salt factory next to the last unspoiled breeding ground of the gray whale in Laguna San Ignacio, in Baja California, had succeeded.

Hershkowitz still felt enormous pride being associated with an organization that could do all that. But struggling to regain his footing, he also felt tremendous impatience when he thought about the ongoing burdens placed on the world's eco-systems by virgin paper production and by the landfills and incinerators that continued to be the major destinations for wastepaper. He longed to find a way to successfully make his model work. Europeans like Per Batelson, whose countries have already made great strides in that direction, find it nearly incomprehensible that U.S. policies seem stuck in some nineteenth-century fantasy of infinite plenitude.

Phil Sears thought that in the long term, the world would be *forced* to embrace models similar to the one Hershkowitz proposed. But he doubted he'd see it in his lifetime. Besides Batelson, who had quit the BCPC board in protest when Hershkowitz was forced off it, probably the only participant in the project's eight-year rollercoaster ride who to some degree didn't think that Hershkowitz was the wrong man for the job was Maya Lin. "I firmly believe," she told me, "that its goal, its success, wasn't necessarily measured by whether it got built, but by whether you could create a strong argument that it should get built."

By the fall of 2000, five months after the mill project's demise, a paper broker told Hershkowitz that the newsprint market had finally turned tight. "Everybody," he wrote him in an e-mail, "is looking for newsprint." It was a gray day and the message gleamed brightly on Hershkowitz's computer screen; he left it just sitting there for a while but felt as if the message were bouncing off his desk, the windows, and every wall: "Looking for newsprint. Looking for newsprint." He'd obviously been caught at the wrong point in a classic business inventory cycle; coming home on the plane from Belize the month before, he'd been thinking about the mill, and underneath a terrible sense of defeat he realized there was a lurking feeling of cautious optimism. The night after he'd arrived home from the airport, he wrote in his journal that he realized that all in all, it had been "the most enjoyable experience I ever had in my life." Before he knew it, with the broker's message still glimmering on the screen, he told me, he began mentally crunching some new figures for another theoretical mill. What if you found a smaller site and halved Morse Diesel's minimal output per year, you could do 110 thousand tons a year. What if you made it a $200 million project? A small mill—a 98-thousand-tons-a-year machine? Make it a 150-thousand-ton project. How much bond help would you need then? A lot less . . .

Since the collapse of the plans for the Bronx mill, there hadn't been even the slightest wink of interest from his colleagues whenever Hershkowitz mentioned possible future projects. Someone showed him the famous Theodore Roosevelt quotation in praise of those who take on difficult worldly enterprises: "Credit belongs to the man who is actually in the arena, whose face is marred by dust and sweat and blood, who strives valiantly; who errs and comes short again and again, because there is no effort without error and shortcoming; but who does actually strive to do the deeds, who knows the great enthusiasms, the great devotions, and spends himself in a worthy cause; who at the best knows in the end the triumph of high achievement and who at the worst, if he fails, at least fails while daring greatly"—but it didn't make him feel that great.

He was being encouraged to speak in public about the need for greater collaboration between business and enviros, and NRDC had even formed a group for green businessmen called Environmental Entrepreneurs. Many of the group's initiatives in environmentally sound design and investments were laudable, but these efforts fell drastically short of making major impacts on the large-scale industries that continue to adversely affect climate change and biodiversity.

Hershkowitz read recently that the virgin pulp and paper industry, which had been trained in his sights for the entire eight years of the project, and which is already the most rapidly growing of the world's wood-based industries, is expected, according to the Organization of Economic Cooperation and Development, to raise its global production by 77 percent from 1995 to 2020. Since that growth is also expected to require 71 percent more water and 53 percent more energy, the environmental impacts of the industry that have troubled enviros for so long—deforestation, water contamination, soil and air pollution, and loss of biodiversity—are also expected to grow alarmingly; worldwide carbon dioxide and sulfur emissions from the paper industries of the industrialized nations alone are expected to roughly double. With what he knew about the paper industry, with its nineteenth-century methods of production and deep-seated suspicion of innovation and outside meddling, he could only read the OECD's far-sighted recommendations for the pulp and paper industry, he told me, with appreciative wonder: *"The most important policy options,"* some obviously European-based member of the OECD technical staff had concluded, *"are the diffusion of the best available technology, integrated regulatory approaches, the use of taxes, and voluntary agreements."*

When he read the statistics published by the OECD, they'd had the same effect on him that the e-mail about the newsprint-market upturn had: he wanted to pick up the phone and start all over again. The trouble was, he didn't know who to call.

Appendix: Dramatis Personae

John H. Adams, a founder of NRDC; executive director, 1970–98, president, 1998– .

Carmen E. Arroyo, assemblywoman, Bronx County, 74th Assembly District, 1994– .

James L. Austin, pulp and paper sales representative, MoDo North America, 1992–94.

Per Batelson, director of corporate development, MoDo, 1989–94.

Frances G. Beinecke, deputy executive director for programs, NRDC, 1990–95; associate director, 1995–98; executive director, 1998– .

James Black, chief representative for S.D. Warren for mill project, 1993–95; a vice president in charge of paper production for S.D. Warren.

Henry R. Breck, treasurer, NRDC, 1991– ; chairman, Ark Asset Management Co., Inc.

Richard L. Campbell, investment banker and financial adviser; attorney specializing in companies focused on recycling and environmental matters; BCPC board member, 1994–98.

Aureo Cardona, vice president, National Center for Housing Management, 1990–92; consultant, Banana Kelly, 1997–99; president, Crescendo, Inc.

Margaret Carey, wife of Allen Hershkowitz; president, MCEnergy, Inc.

John A. Cavanagh, executive vice president, 1992–98, chief operating officer, 1993–98, and president, 1998, Morse Diesel International, Inc.; vice chairman of AMEC Construction Management, Inc. of New York (successor to Morse Diesel International, Inc.).

Mary Cesar, consultant specializing in recovered paper, Jaakko Pöyry Consulting, 1988–98.

Randy A. Daniels, senior vice president and deputy commissioner of economic revitalization, Empire State Development Corp., 1995–99; secretary of state, New York, 2001– .

Robert E. Denham, chairman and CEO, Salomon Brothers, 1991–98; board member, NRDC; lawyer, partner, Munger, Tolles & Olson, LLP.

Harold DeRienzo, founder and director, Banana Kelly, 1977–81; president, Parodneck Foundation, 1981– .

Eric Deutsch, senior vice president, 1996–98, 1999– ; vice president, 1995–96, New York City Economic Development Corp.; EDC project manager, 1994–95.

John Doherty, commissioner, NYC Sanitation Department, 1994–98, 2002– ; deputy commissioner, 1989–94.

Daniel J. Donovan, director, Municipal Capital Markets Group, Merrill Lynch, until 1997; mill project financial adviser, 1997–99; managing member, Prospero, LLC.

James Doughan, president and CEO, Stone Consolidated Corp., 1993–97; president and CEO, Abitibi-Consolidated, Inc., 1997–99 (following Stone Consolidated Corp. 1997 merger with Abitibi-Price to create Abitibi-Consolidated, Inc.).

Ben Esner, chief of staff, NYC Department of Environmental Protection, 1994–96.

Fernando Ferrer, borough president, Bronx County, 1987–2001.

William M. Ferretti, director, New York State Office of Recycling Market Development, 1988–98; executive director, National Recycling Coalition, 1998–2001.

Michael C. Finnegan, chief counsel, New York State Governor George Pataki, 1995–97; managing director in charge of environmental finance activities, JP Morgan Securities, 1997– .

Leonard A. Formato, owner, Boulder Resources, Limited, 1979– ; owner, Central Iron and Metal Co., Inc., 1975– .

Francesco Galesi, developer; leased Harlem River yard from Department of Transportation, 1991; mill project's landlord, 1994–98; mill co-developer, 1998–2000.

Charles A. Gargano, chairman, Empire State Development Corp., 1995– ; ambassador to Trinidad and Tobago, 1988–91.

Marilyn Gelber, commissioner, NYC Department of Environmental Protection, 1994–96.

Michael B. Gerrard, lawyer, partner, Arnold & Porter; environmental counsel to BCPC; worked on permitting, 1993–2000.

Martin E. Gold, lawyer, partner, Sidley Austin Brown & Wood; expert in real estate law and project finance; BCPC attorney, 1993–98; legal consultant to NRDC, 1999–2000.

Stephen Golden, corporate vice president of forest products, health, safety, and environmental affairs, 1990–99, president, Forest Products Group, the New York Times Company, 1994–99.

Eric A. Goldstein, lawyer, NRDC, 1976– ; senior attorney, 1981– , and co-director, urban program, 1998– .

Niilo Hakkarainen, managing director, United Paper Mills, 1974–95; co-developer of mill project, 1995–96; adviser, 1996–97.

Allen Hershkowitz, senior scientist, NRDC, 1989– .

Charles Koob, lawyer, partner, Simpson Thacher & Bartlett; board member, NRDC, 1987– .

Ruben Kraiem, lawyer, partner, Paul, Weiss, Rifkind, Wharton & Garrison; board member, NRDC, 1994– ; chair, NRDC Legal Committee, 1996– .

Joseph Kruger II, chairman and chief executive officer, Kruger Paper, Inc., 1989– .

Anthony Lacavalla, paper broker, recycler, and sorter; co-owner of Crystal Paper Co.; had contract to operate BCPC mill sorting plant, 1996–99.

Robert Lange, director of NYC Department of Sanitation, Bureau of Waste Prevention, Reuse and Recycling, 1994– .

Maya Lin, artist, architect, designer of the paper mill and the National Vietnam Veterans Memorial.

Philip E. Lippincott, chairman, 1983–94, and chief executive officer, 1982–94, Scott Paper.

Emily Lloyd, NYC commissioner of sanitation, 1992–94.

Charles Ludlow, project director, 1997–99, and director of development, 1999–2000, mill project, Morse Diesel International, Inc., 1997–2000.

Madeleine Marquez, director of economic development and environmental initiatives, Banana Kelly, 1992–97; director, Bronx Initiative Corp., 1999– .

Tim Martin, Greenpeace activist, 1987–92; paper consultant, NRDC, 1993; resource associate, NRDC, 1993–97.

Roland Martin-Lof, president and CEO, MoDo, 1991–94; executive vice president, paper division of Kvaerner Pulp and Paper, Inc., 1995–2000, deputy managing director, 2001– .

Anita Miller, program director, Comprehensive Community Revitalization Program, 1991–98; chairman and CEO, AmeriFederal Savings Bank, 1984–89; member and acting chairman, Federal Home Loan Bank Board, Washington, D.C., 1978–79; program director, Lisc Foundation, 1978; senior program officer, Ford Foundation, 1971–78.

Vernice Miller, director of environmental justice, NRDC, 1993–99; member, community and resource development unit, Ford Foundation, 2000– ; co-founder of West Harlem Environmental Action Group (WE ACT), 1988.

Getz Obstfeld, president and CEO, Banana Kelly, 1982–91.

George Pataki, governor, State of New York, 1994– .

Angelo Ponte, owner, V. Ponte & Sons, Inc. (formerly the largest commercial carter in NYC; sold to National Waste Services, Inc., July 1996); indicted on racketeering charges, 1995; pleaded guilty, 1997.

Bruce F. Pulver, financial adviser, BCPC, 1995–99; investment banker, Hambros Development, Inc., U.S. subsidiary of Hambros Bank, PLC, 1993–94.

Anthony M. Riccio, Jr., vice president, Harlem River Yard Ventures; NYC commissioner of ports and trade, 1989–90.

Yolanda Rivera, chair, Banana Kelly Community Improvement Association Board, 1985– ; executive director, 1992–93, 1995, 1997–98, and president and CEO, 1994, 1996, Banana Kelly.

Jonathan F. P. Rose, planner and developer; development adviser, BCPC, 1994–2000; president, Affordable Housing Development Corp., 1989– ; president, Jonathan Rose & Cos., 2000– .

Richard Schrader, NYC commissioner of consumer affairs, 1993–94; deputy commissioner, 1990–93; BCPC project adviser, 1994–97.

Frederick A. O. Schwarz, Jr., lawyer, partner, Cravath, Swaine & Moore; chair, board member, NRDC, 1992– .

Philip C. Sears, environmental planner; vice president, Allee King Rosen & Fleming, Inc. (an environmental planning firm).

Gary L. Simpson, owner and president, NAB Construction Company, 1993– .

Ricardo Soto-Lopez, urban planner, Comprehensive Community Revitalization Program, 1992; legal intern, NRDC, 1992; board member, Banana Kelly, 1993–95.

Roger W. Stone, president and CEO, Stone Container Corp., 1979–99; major shareholder, Stone Consolidated Corp., 1989–99.

Patricia F. Sullivan, deputy executive director for administration, NRDC, 1973–98; deputy director, 1998– .

Kenneth L. Wallach, president, 1997, CEO, 1998, and chairman, 2001, Central National Gottesman, major paper marketers.

Carl Weisbrod, president, New York City Economic Development Corp., 1990–94; president, Alliance for Downtown New York, Inc., 1994– .

Lennart Westberg, chief financial officer, MoDo, 1991–94.

Tony Winson, vice president, New York operations for Morse Diesel International, Inc. until March 2000; project executive.

John Wissman, paper cost analyst and principal, Jaakko Pöyry Consulting.